Empire for Liberty

Empire

for

Liberty

···

A HISTORY OF AMERICAN IMPERIALISM
from
BENJAMIN FRANKLIN
to
PAUL WOLFOWITZ

Richard H. Immerman

PRINCETON UNIVERSITY PRESS

PRINCETON AND OXFORD

Library of Congress Cataloging-in-Publication Data

Immerman, Richard H.
Empire for liberty : a history of American imperialism from
Benjamin Franklin to Paul Wolfowitz / Richard H. Immerman.
p. cm.
Includes bibliographical references and index.
ISBN 978-0-691-12762-0 (hardcover : acid-free paper)
1. United States—Foreign relations. 2. United States—
Territorial expansion—History. 3. Imperialism—History.
4. Liberty—Political aspects—United States—History. I. Title.
E183.7.I46 2010
973—dc22
2009040885

British Library Cataloging-in-Publication Data is available

This book has been composed in Centennial LT STD

Printed on acid-free paper. ∞

press.princeton.edu

Printed in the United States of America

1 3 5 7 9 10 8 6 4 2

To those who educate and those who learn

CONTENTS

....

Acknowledgments ix

INTRODUCTION
Contending with the American Empire 1

CHAPTER 1
*Benjamin Franklin and
America's Imperial Vision* 20

CHAPTER 2
*John Quincy Adams and
America's Tortured Empire* 59

CHAPTER 3
*William Henry Seward
Reimagines the American Empire* 98

CHAPTER 4
*Henry Cabot Lodge and
the New American Empire* 128

CHAPTER 5
*John Foster Dulles and the
Conflicted Empire* 163

CHAPTER 6
Paul Wolfowitz and the Lonely Empire 196

POSTSCRIPT
The Dark Side 232

Notes 239

Index 257

ACKNOWLEDGMENTS

....

IN FUNDAMENTAL WAYS I have been writing this book since I began to study the history of U.S. foreign relations as an undergraduate at Cornell University in the late 1960s. There, in an environment defined by the Vietnam War, I along with hundreds of my fellow students gathered in Bailey Hall on Tuesday, Thursday, and Saturday mornings to listen spellbound to lectures by Walter LaFeber. It was during this time that I started to think about an American empire, and more precisely, the relationship between that empire and America's "mission" of expanding the sphere of liberty. For this I owe my first thanks to Walt; to those to whom he introduced me either directly or indirectly, William Appleman Williams, Lloyd Gardner, Tom McCormick, and their colleagues; and to my peers at Cornell who were so responsible for encouraging me to think differently than I had thought before.

Over the subsequent decades, as I developed my own courses, taught my own students, and wrote my own books, the seeds of this book continued to germinate. I won't even try to acknowledge all of those who contributed to its growth. They know who they are. But I must single out two. No one has influenced how I think and write about history as much as a political scientist—Fred Greenstein. Not only did Fred reassure me that, notwithstanding the historiographic trajectory that accompanied that of my career, individuals do matter, but he also instructed and inspired me in ways that transformed my disposition to write about people into a scholarly undertaking. The second person I must thank specifically is at the other end of my professional spectrum: Jeffrey Engel. I did not know Jeff until he came to Temple some half-dozen years ago as a visiting fellow at the Center for the Study of Force and Diplomacy (recommended, as is only appropriate, by Walt LaFeber and Tom McCormick). But since then, particularly as I struggled with a variety of administrative responsibilities and other "diversions," Jeff's energy, commitment, and relentless good cheer helped me keep my eye on the ball. Indeed, he may not remember, but it was over lunch one day with Jeff that the format of this book took shape.

Then there are my Temple students and colleagues. Few people can understand what could possibly have motivated me in 1992 to move from Hawaii to Philadelphia. For me, however, the decision was an easy one. I was coming to Temple University, where the students are not only bright but also ravenous about learning and unafraid to speak their minds. Moreover, at Temple I could collaborate with special historians like Russell Weigley and David Rosenberg to build something special—the Center for the Study of Force and Diplomacy. I spent countless hours discussing with both the ideas that found their way into this book. When Jay Lockenour, Regina Gramer, and Vlad Zubok joined us, I immediately started to bend their ears. Then in 2004 our department went on a hiring spree that brought to Temple a remarkable group of brilliant, vibrant, and innovative young historians. For advising me, challenging me, and making me feel young again, I thank Petra Goedde, Will Hitchcock, Drew Isenberg, Todd Shepard, Bryant Simon, and Liz Varon.

I reserve two others from that group to the end. Beth Bailey and David Farber arrived at Temple in 2004 as well, but they have been my close colleagues and closer friends for decades. For that reason alone this is a better book; there are no two better historians anywhere. Further, no two scholars better appreciate the joy of writing history, and their joy is infectious.

Because of the subject matter I did a lot of the reading, writing, and thinking about this book in England. I cannot thank enough my dear friend Saki Dockrill for arranging my visiting fellowship at King's College's Department of War Studies. High tea with Saki was always a true education as well an unadulterated pleasure. I must likewise thank Helen Fisher for making my stay at King's so delightful.

At Princeton University Press I am grateful to Brigitta van Rheinberg for her invitation to turn my ideas into a book and selecting such outstanding referees (to whom, anonymous as they are, I am also grateful), to Clara Platter for her attention and management, and to both of them for their patience. Not long after my return from England, just as I began to see the light at the end of the draft's tunnel, I received an offer from Tom Fingar, the Deputy Director of National

Intelligence for Analysis, to come to Washington. As Assistant Deputy Director for Analytic Integrity and Standards, my mission would be to evaluate and improve the quality of analysis across the Intelligence Community. I knew that my accepting would delay completion of the book, but I accepted nevertheless. Brigitta and Clara were wonderfully understanding. And while I won't claim that my experience in the intelligence community directly affected this book, I certainly learned a great deal about thinking more rigorously as well as critically. For that I thank Tom, my colleagues in the DDNI/A, and especially my staff in the Office of Analytic Integrity and Standards. (I'm obliged to write the obvious: The views expressed in this publication are my own and do not imply endorsement of the Office of the Director of National Intelligence or any other U.S. government agency.) Richard Isomaki's copyediting helped me avoid multiple hiccups in expressing my thinking.

Finally I acknowledge my wife, Marion, and daughters, Tyler and Morgan. While I've been writing this book my entire career, none of them ever had a "vote" in that choice of career. That choice has led to workdays that were much longer than they bargained for, absences from home much lengthier than they liked, and from their points of view, multiple other less-than-ideal circumstances (such as denying them their Hawaiian lifestyle). Over the years I've taken my lumps from each of them for my priorities. Yet at the same time each of them always pushed me to revise that sentence one more time, to visit one more archive, to read one more book. But at the end of the day, it's simple: I thank them—and love them—because they are who they are.

Empire for Liberty

....

Contending with the American Empire

IN 1783, the year the United States formally gained its independence from Great Britain, George Washington described the newborn republic as a "rising empire." He elaborated a few years later, as the fledgling nation struggled for viability under the restraints imposed by the Articles of Confederation and the constraints imposed by the European powers. America was but an "infant empire," Washington conceded to his former comrade-in-arms, the Marquis de Lafayette. "However unimportant America may be considered at present," he nevertheless predicted, "there will assuredly come a day, when this country will have some weight in the scale of Empires."[1]

Washington could not have been more prescient. Yet it remained for the young Alexander Hamilton to capture the complexity of what would become the American experience. For the purpose of generating support for the new Constitution, Hamilton characterized the United States in the lead *Federalist Paper* as "an impire [*sic*] in many ways the most interesting in the world." That it was, and that it still is.[2]

Little about the history of the United States is more contested than the question of whether it warrants the label *empire*. It took eight years of bitter war to liberate America from the shackles of the British Empire. To classify the United States with its imperial ancestor, let alone more recent exemplars and wannabes—the Germans and Soviets, for example—seems perverse, an affront to America's self-identity as well as history. Former president George W. Bush is but one among many to scoff at the suggestion that the United States should be tarred with the imperial brush. "America has never been an empire," he proclaimed indignantly when campaigning for the presidency in 1999. This denial was not enough. Bush added, "We may be the only great power in history that had the chance, and refused—preferring greatness to power, and justice to glory."[3]

Allowing for political hyperbole, Bush expressed American orthodoxy at the dawn of the twenty-first century. A small minority did dissent, even at the height of the Cold War. One of the first books I read as an undergraduate was Richard Van Alstyne's *The Rising American Empire*, the title of which he took from Washington's words. Bracketing the Vietnam War era, William Appleman Williams spearheaded an interpretive school of the history of U.S. foreign policy developing the premise that in the United States empire was "a Way of Life" and a tragedy of American diplomacy. Three of his celebrated students collaborated on a textbook entitled *The Creation of the American Empire*.[4]

Yet the farthest most (although not all) historians and other commentators would go was to admit that the United States joined the "new imperialism" of the late nineteenth and early twentieth centuries. During this era the world's great powers claimed some one-quarter of the world's landmass as colonies; Queen Victoria added *Empress* to her list of titles. For the United States to be perceived as a great power by the British, the Germans, even the Russians and Austro-Hungarians, it had to behave like one of "them." So it did, by annexing Hawaii, conquering Spain's colony of the Philippines, establishing a protectorate in Cuba, acquiring sovereignty over the Panama Canal Zone "in perpetuity," and more.

But this burst of American empire-building was the exception that proved the rule—the "Great Aberration," as Samuel Flagg Bemis characterized it. After the clash of empires ignited World War I, the United States returned to normalcy. Every subsequent U.S. president proclaimed America was the enemy of empire. If the United States was denounced as an "imperialist," the fault lay with the denouncer. "We have no interest in conquering territories," explains former Speaker of the House Newt Gingrich, who holds a Ph.D. in history. "We have every interest in getting people to believe in their freedom and getting people to govern themselves. And those are inherently threatening." Niall Ferguson, who wishes that the United States wore the mantle of empire proudly, captures the national delusion best: "The great thing about the American empire is that so many Americans disbelieve in its existence . . . . They think they're so different that when they have bases in foreign territories, it's not an empire. When they invade sovereign territories, it's not an empire."[5]

Following on the heels of all the post–Cold War talk about, and protests against, "globalization," however, the Bush administration's military response to the tragic attacks on the United States of September 11, 2001, a response that included the invasion and occupation of Iraq as well as assaults against Al Qaeda bases in Afghanistan and the ouster of its Taliban government, created a sea-change in perspective—and scholarship. Suddenly, an avalanche of writers rejected the mind-set that "America was the empire that dared not speak its name."[6] "The American Empire (Get Used to It)" was the title of a lead article in the *New York Times Magazine.* Similar coverage appeared in *Time, Newsweek, Atlantic Monthly, National Journal, U.S. News & World Report, Foreign Affairs*, and other diverse publications.[7] An article in *Foreign Policy* quoted an anonymous "senior advisor" to Bush as confiding, "We're an empire now," and pointed out that Vice President Dick Cheney's 2003 Christmas card featured the question, "And if a sparrow cannot fall to the ground without His notice, is it probable that an empire can rise without His aid?"[8] Soon lining bookstores' shelves were such titles as *American Empire, Irresistible Empire, The New Imperialism, The Sorrows of Empire, The Folly of Empire, Incoherent Empire, The Sands of Empire, America's Inadvertent Empire, Among Empires*, and *Habits of Empire.* According to Ivo Daalder and James Lindsay, the term *American empire*, which had virtually disappeared from common parlance, appeared more than 1,000 times in news stories during the six months prior to May 2003.[9]

The majority of these books, whether written by liberals or conservatives, blame the ascendancy of a small number of disproportionately influential "neoconservatives," an amorphous group or cabal, for what the authors perceive as a misguided, counterproductive departure from, and violation of, America's traditions and values.[10] Others, again liberals as well as conservatives, support or supported Bush administration initiatives because they maintain that "many parts of the world would benefit from a period of American rule," but they lament that America's traditions and values deter it from acting as the empire that it is. "Nobody likes empires," writes one respected journalist who covered crises in Bosnia, Kosovo, and Afghanistan. "But there are some problems for which there are only imperial solutions." As an "Empire Lite," he complains, America cannot, or will not, provide them."[11] Niall Ferguson, perhaps the most prolific writer about and advocate of an American empire, ardently concurs. "Most Americans will probably always reject the proposition that the United States is (or operates) a de facto empire," he writes. "Such squeamishness may be an integral part of the U.S. empire's problem. To be an empire in denial means resenting the costs of intervening in the affairs of foreign peoples and underestimating the benefits of doing so."[12] Most who consider modern American imperialism the lesser of the contemporary world's evils nevertheless suggest that with a bit of fine-tuning, the United States should be able to manage an empire that's just, and just about right.[13]

Despite this explosion of literature, the debate continues over whether the United States is an empire, is not an empire, or is, in the words of one of America's most thoughtful political scientists, "something very much like an empire." One historian is so ambivalent that even while arguing that the United States is an empire he insists on enclosing the word in quotes each times he modifies it with *American*. Another prefers the label *hegemon* because "empire does not suffice. It evokes a picture of colonies and spheres of influence that falls well short of describing the U.S. position." Current president Barrack Obama is purposefully obtuse. In an address specifically targeting the Muslim world, Bush's successor would go only so far as to describe America as "not the crude stereotype of a self-interested empire" and remind his listeners that "we were born out of revolution against an empire."[14]

Whatever America is now, has it always been that, or has it changed over time? This book addresses these two most fundamental of questions. Its primary purpose is not to judge the American empire in terms of good or bad, up or down (although I do make such an assessment). Rather, it seeks to persuade the reader that America is and always has been an empire. Further, as I will explain, by historicizing six exemplary individuals who influenced U.S. behavior in a variety of ways, the book will not only chronicle the trajectory of the "rising American empire" from its inception to the present, but will also analyze what that phrase means and how that meaning has evolved. The definition of empire is no less dynamic than the history of American expansion. Appreciating the dynamism of both is essential in order to weigh the varying motives that drove American empire-building: greed and racism, for example, versus progress and protection. That appreciation is likewise essential in determining whether the American empire is and has been an "exceptional" antidote to truly "evil" empires.

Indeed, there has been one constant in the evolution of the United States, and it is suggested by this book's title. The American empire, regardless of what the term denoted and connoted at any given time, has always been inextricably tied to establishing and promoting "liberty" in the contemporary context. Further, the extension of America's territory and influence has always been inextricably tied to extending the sphere of liberty. The "core ideas that had led Americans to nationhood were the same ones that commanded them to seize the vastness of America and transform it in their images," recently wrote one non-American expert on American history. "First among these core ideas was the American concept of liberty. . . . It is what gave meaning to the existence of a separate American state."[15]

Perceived through the lens of America's ideology, empire and liberty are mutually reinforcing. Here again, though, the historian's perspective allows for a more complex and nuanced understanding. Prior to the ratification of the Constitution, when the viability of the new nation was highly precarious, Thomas Jefferson famously labeled the United States the "Empire of Liberty." More than a quarter-century later, however, after Jefferson had abandoned his initial optimism regarding the potential for the peoples native to America to embrace liberty as defined by immigrants to America, and having played an instrumental role in America's enactment of the Northwest Ordinance and purchase of the Louisiana Territory, the Declaration of Independence's lead author relabeled America the "Empire for Liberty." This book argues that Jefferson's revision signaled a commitment to a more aggressive, proactive extension of that sphere of liberty—and hence a greater American empire.[16]

Further, for Americans *liberty* is even more difficult to define than *empire*. Americans believe in liberty and they support the advancement of liberty, but they interpret the word so broadly, and in so many different contexts, that it all but loses its meaning. Were not both sides during America's Civil War committed to defending liberty? Do contemporary Americans on the political left or political right "stand" for liberty? In Hawaii I used to shop in the Liberty House department store. The branding was popular, yet meaningless. Near where I live in Philadelphia is a district called Northern Liberties. What does that name signify? When it comes to liberty, about the only thing Americans agree on is that it is good. Long before Paul Revere's ride from Boston to Lexington, explains a recent book, "'liberty' became a battle cry, a placebo, a panacea." So it has remained.[17]

Having disclaimed the purpose of evaluating empire, I am not agnostic. Nor do I seek to conceal my views. They are as follows: I appreciate the arguments that America has been a force of good in the world, that its ideals and values, especially those concerned with liberty, do have universal applicability, that its missionary zeal to modernize less developed areas can be beneficial, and that the pursuit of foreign policies and strategies designed to promote the security of domestic and international constituents is legitimate and necessary for any state. That said, my judgment is that by building an empire through either direct conquest or informal control the United States has frequently done evil in the name of good. I do not accept the proposition that some problems require imperial solutions, a proposition that leads to what a British historian, referring to recent American behavior, calls "the imperialism of human rights."[18]

In addition, I identify what I consider the greatest contradiction—and irony—in the history of the American empire. Through much of the nineteenth century Americans considered the word *empire* benign, not the term of opprobrium it became once the United States began to behave more like a traditional empire in the decades following the Civil War, the touchstone for Bemis's "aberration" and Williams's "tragedy." The means by which the United States expanded across the continent may at times have appeared unsavory to observers within and beyond Washington. The prevalent opinion was, nevertheless, that Americans goals and motives were consistently benevolent or defensive, not imperialistic. (The concept of imperialism, initially associated with France's Napoleon III and Benjamin Disraeli in England, did not come into vogue until the late nineteenth century.) Yet it was precisely during the earlier years—the century preceding America's annexation of Hawaii and conquest of the Philippines, that the United States was most ruthless in creating its empire and least respectful of non-Americans' (even if they were Native Americans) liberty. Those who criticize America's current empire-builders for violating U.S. history have it wrong.

What complicates the history of the American empire, and adds further irony to that history, is, like *liberty*, the ambiguous meaning of the word. In fact, Americans became increasingly defensive about their "status" as an empire after, combining force (primarily) and diplomacy (secondarily), they acquired uncontested political control— sovereignty—across the North American continent from the Atlantic to the Pacific oceans. Washington, Hamilton, and Jefferson proudly juxtaposed America with empire. That was the norm until after the Civil War. But then the ethos, or at least the rhetoric, began to change. William McKinley, Teddy Roosevelt, and Woodrow Wilson recognized the baggage that accompanied the term. By their time Americans had divided between anti-imperialists and imperialists. And only very recently did George Bush vehemently deny that the United States ever was an empire. Scholars have had to grapple with this dynamic even as they seek to distinguish "empire" from "hegemon," "great power," and other terms that frequently serve as euphemisms for empire and generate less emotion and controversy.

Empire, as a noun, was value-free at the time the United States gained its independence. While its precise definition is elusive because of the problem of translation, it derived from the Latin *imperium*, which in English approximates the words *rule* and *sovereignty*. Hence its definition was functional or instrumental. Greeks used it to describe the relationship between the city-states that united to oppose the Persians (who also comprised an entity called an empire). But Athens exercised leadership over its fellow city-states; it did not really rule them. Consequently, empire gained greater currency during the Roman era. Indeed, the first century AD, following Augustus's defeat of Marc Anthony at Actium, constitutes a watershed in the evolution of the concept of empire. To borrow Michael Doyle's phrase, this period was the "Augustan Threshold." Augustus implemented a range of administrative reforms that centralized the imperial state. Cities, provinces, the army, government appointees, economic decision-making, and other functions all came under the control of the emperor. So did citizenship—in the second century AD, Augustus's successor Caracalla proclaimed all "free men" within the empire to be Roman citizens. Transcending the limited concepts of sovereignty and rule, the Roman Empire incorporated administrative centralization and political integration.[19]

Centralization and integration are distinct from equalization— equality. Class and regional (ethnic/national) differences remained.

This fundamental feature of empire is of critical significance to the history of empires. It was likewise of critical significance to Rome, especially after "empire" in the later Roman era came to envelope another dimension—size. This addition produced a combustible amalgam of centralized control, class and regional inequality, and an expansiveness that created the conditions for the Roman Empire's fragmentation and collapse. Its fate notwithstanding, the Roman Empire's experience explains the definition of empire inherited by the British, especially following their defeat of the French in the eighteenth century. Americans, "classically educated and self-consciously looking backward," as well as contributors to the growth of the British Empire, embraced this definition at the time of their War of Independence. When George Washington used the word *empire*, he meant a polity that exercised sovereignty over and was responsible for the security of a large expanse of territory that, composed of previously separate units now subordinate to the metropolis (thus distinguishing an empire from, for example, a commonwealth or even an alliance), included many peoples of diverse "races" (as broadly defined at that time) and nationalities. As would be expected because of violence's historic role in the establishment of empires, not all the people within the heterogeneous population could qualify as citizens, not all were equal, not all could or would assimilate, and not all consented to the rule of the sovereign.[20]

There is thus merit to Arthur Schlesinger's argument that Washington and his fellow Founding Fathers used *empire* interchangeably with *state*.[21] But their use of *empire* was not due simply to their desire for a synonym. They had ambitions that went beyond consolidation and were signaled by the word *empire*. They had in mind a particular "genre" of state that would grow in size, strength, and prosperity, exercise control over populations that either considered themselves autonomous or resided beyond America's political boundaries (a consensus had not yet been reached on how this control would be achieved and exercised), and possess a centralized government (again, how centralized was hotly debated). Further, theorists of empires and political leaders normatively thought of empires as land-based entities that acquired additional territory through the formal annexation of conquered territories administered as colonies. The Founding Fathers conceived of the United States even in its infancy as expanding prodigiously—certainly across the North American continent, perhaps southward to Cuba and beyond. Under the Articles of Confederation Congress enacted the Northwest Ordinance in 1787 to prepare for this eventuality. Americans did not consider war-making against the Indians conquest, however, and to them the establishment of colonies was anathema. Hence from its birth America would indeed be a "most interesting" empire.

The meaning of empire changed over the course of the nineteenth century, especially by its latter half. Until then its definition remained primarily functional, with the emphasis on the exercise of governance. In this anodyne sense there was little reason to associate empire with anything pejorative. Americans did not, even as they annihilated or forcibly relocated Native Americans, executed foreign nationals, and conquered territories. This was because *empire* and *state* were still largely synonymous, and U.S. behavior was acceptable for a state with its capabilities; because U.S. expansion remained continental and restricted to contiguous territory (in the view of many, as a consequence, "natural") with the purpose of bringing civilization to what was perceived as wilderness; because empires were commonplace features of the international system (what nation did not aspire to be an empire?); and because there were few audible voices of opposition or protest. That the U.S. Constitution required the incorporation of added territory as states, and the populations of these states were invariably eager to apply for membership, reinforced the consensus that Americans should be proud of their empire.

The Civil War and the occupation of the Southern states during Reconstruction served as a catalyst for changing views about empire. Contesting the meaning of liberty, white Americans as well as black, Native Americans, Mexican Americans, and others challenged the central government's authority to deny them self-rule. The implications transcended traditional disputes over federalism, republicanism, and states' rights. Further, the extension of the British Empire through the exploitation of its commercial dominance to acquire political jurisdiction without establishing colonies, for example in Asia and Latin America, indicated that a metropolis could exercise rule informally. It was not until the mid-twentieth century that scholars, following John A. Gallagher and Ronald E. Robinson, began to use the phrase *imperialism of free trade.* In the late nineteenth century, nevertheless, imperialism as a stand-alone concept dramatically entered the political vocabulary.[22]

In contrast to empire, imperialism refers to a process by which one state employs instruments of power to acquire control over peripheral peoples and territory. This process may result in the extension of liberty for some (for example, the liberty to attain more wealth and power), but the loss of others' liberty is unavoidable. As such, from the beginning *imperialism* was a much more value-laden term than *empire*, freighted with negative weight. There is no euphemistic substitute. What is more, no sooner did the concept of imperialism originate than it spawned competing theories to explain its origins. The dominant ones tied the word to militarism, the selfishness and greed of special interests, or the requisites of rapacious monopoly capitalism. Advocates of American expansion in the late nineteenth century consequently were not "merely" empire-builders. They were imperialists. And they generated opposition not only among subject peoples, but also from Americans themselves. The key debate, as one historian frames it, was whether American imperialism resulted from "the conscious choices of statesmen ... or [was] the inevitable result of the industrial capitalist political economy and social structure."[23]

That the American empire was imperialistic in the nineteenth century was not disputed then or now. No one doubts that the acquisition of such far-flung noncontiguous territories as Hawaii, the Philippines, Puerto Rico, and Panama, none of which at the time was considered by virtually any American as qualified for statehood, fit the definition of imperial behavior. The two questions are whether the United States "practiced" imperialism during its more formative decades and whether it continued to behave imperialistically as the twentieth century wore on and *imperialist* became such a widely applied adjective that it lost much of its meaning.

Because the connotation of *empire* underwent change that can be correlated to the origins of *imperialism*, the answer to both questions is yes. The United States fit even the most restricted definition of empire by the outbreak of the Civil War. It exercised sovereignty over a large expanse of territory that enveloped previously autonomous units and included peoples of disparate races and national origins whose residence within that empire was not voluntary. Further, at least its continental expansion was the product of violence. Antebellum Americans used the word *empire* to describe the United States as a sovereign state. But that sovereign state grew by wresting away the sovereignty of non-American, indigenous populations, just as had the more traditional "Old World" empires of that day. This was not an Empire for Liberty.[24]

More open to debate is whether subsequent to World War I (the United States acquired formal control of the Virgin Islands in 1917), America continued to rank as an empire. While George W. Bush probably is unaware that the literal definition of empire derived from *imperium*, he surely recalls the orthodoxy he learned in grade school: empire-building requires the conquest and colonization of alien territory. America, in contrast, fought two wars in the twentieth century to defeat empires bent on conquest. Indeed, whether represented by Woodrow Wilson's Fourteen Points, Franklin Roosevelt's Atlantic Charter, or the body of Cold War rhetoric, the United States has stood for anticolonialism.

Yet twentieth-century scholarship such as Gallagher and Robinson's on the "imperialism of free trade" demands a more expansive definition of empire. Focusing on the British experience, they and others afterward argued that the latter part of the nineteenth century did not constitute an era of "new imperialism." It was imperialism by other means. The concept of new imperialism suggested that the colonization of Africa, the most notorious example, represented a return to the imperialism characteristic of the European empires from the Age of Exploration through the Napoleonic Wars. This periodization, however, required defining imperialism and the resultant empire as the acquisition of formal control of one people over another. This is the limited definition identified with William Langer—and it characterizes the antebellum American experience. The more expansive definition popularized by Gallagher and Robinson posits that the acquisition of informal control—through trade arrangements, political mechanisms, and the like—is no less "imperialistic" (even if indigenous collaborators facilitate the acquisition). By this definition, "The U.S.A. had something that should rank as an empire long before it became fashionable to talk about one."[25]

Likewise, by this definition the United States remained an empire following World War I. The operative principle is the exercise of effective control. Effective control can result from assuming various functions of government, such as the collection of customs and taxes; participating in treaty systems that deny sovereignty to a nation; orchestrating trade agreements that create the dependency of one nation on the other; deploying military forces directly or taking on the responsibility for the training and supplying of indigenous armed sources of control; and dominating cultural institutions (which is more difficult to achieve than many have suggested). The form is less important than its power. The barometer is whether the external influence can shape the lives of the native population in such a way that it molds the population's politics. Throughout the twentieth century the United States effectively exercised control of national politics in the states of the Caribbean and Latin America, the Pacific and Asia, the Middle and Near East, Africa, and to some extent even Europe. In certain cases one can argue that the nation America controlled benefited, and that America has not always profited. Yet these were all imperial relationships that impinged on people's liberties.

The empire that America constructed in the twentieth century is the most powerful empire in world history. Its rival Soviet empire, and its antecedent British Empire, pale in comparison. Its global leadership, when measured in terms of technological innovation, manufacturing, gross domestic product, or any other frame of reference, far eclipses all competitors. Its military superiority is breathtaking, and it continues to grow. It has assembled institutions—the North Atlantic Treaty Organization, the International Monetary Fund and World Bank, the Organization of American States, the World Trade Organization, and more—that provide potent mechanisms for global management. Arthur Schlesinger, for decades a vigorous critic of William Appleman Williams and likeminded theorists of America's empire, asks, "Who can doubt that there is an American empire?—an 'informal' empire, not colonial in polity, but still richly equipped with imperial paraphernalia: troops, ships, planes, bases, procounsuls, local collaborators, all spread wide around the luckless planet?" Who can doubt indeed?[26]

As Schlesinger implies, when it comes to empires one size does not fit all. Empires reflect a mix of formal and informal, direct and indirect rule, and that mix differs. Whether the empire is essentially land-based or commercial and transoceanic affects this mix. An equally robust variable is the structure of the empire, whether its basis is primarily iron-fisted hard power (military, sometimes economic) or less coercive soft power (ideology, culture, expertise, even language).[27] Related to this structure, but again to differing degrees, empires can be either "multicultural" or "homogenizing." In the former, the governing elite of the dominating metropole makes little effort to change the languages, religions, rituals, and other "habits of the heart" of the diverse national and ethnic constituents that comprise the empire. The British Empire is a modern example. Homogenizing empires, conversely, seek to establish an all-inclusive national identity. The U.S. metaphor of the melting pot, or Frederick Jackson Turner's famous "crucible of the frontier," illustrates this type.[28]

No two empires in history are identical, and the American empire is like none other. The reasons include but transcend America's refusal to consider itself an empire, and for that matter, its power and reach. One of its peculiarities is that because so rarely in U.S. history has it been willing to pay the price of empire as measured in human lives, administrative costs, and ideological "contamination," once Americans acquired control over the territories of North America, they preferred indirect rule. For example, even as the United States agreed to serve as the temporary "trustee" for former Japanese or Germany territories after World War II, it "liberated" the Philippines. Moreover, with a small percentage of U.S. citizens choosing to live abroad (and of these three-fourths live in Mexico, Canada, or Europe), America is an "empire without settlers."[29]

It follows, therefore, that not only is the United States an imperialist with a history of opposing imperialism, but it has also experienced an unprecedented amount of trouble imposing its will on its dependents. In part this difficulty inheres in the informal nature of its domination; in part it is a function of its lack of international population and institutions; and in part it evolves from America's reluctance to look like an empire. At least as salient, however, is Americans' self-image as the bastion of liberty and their identification with the Constitution and historic struggle to strike the proper balance between central government and states' rights. To borrow from David Hendrickson, America projected its domestic system onto the international arena.[30]

As a consequence, despite having built its empire on a foundation of military might and a combination of trade, loans, and investment,

America has rarely flexed its military and economic muscle fully. In many instances, moreover, it has sought to present at least the appearance of encouraging consultation and dissent. That Americans do genuinely value liberty as an ideal deters them from imposing, or exercising, the degree of political control that they could have. Until the dawn of the twenty-first century, the United States preferred the status of being but the first among equals. Ironically, although former president George Bush may prove to be the most vigorous denier of an American empire among all U.S. presidents, he was forced to issue so many denials because among all U.S. presidencies he acted the most imperially in the classical sense.

Bush illustrates that the American empire developed into what it is today because individuals make—or made—choices. This is not to play down the power of broad political, economic, social, and cultural forces at the national and international levels. But when one sifts through the multiple influences that are the stuff of history, one ends up with individuals who choose to do one thing and not another. That is a crucial ingredient of contingency. Blessed with abundant natural resources and exceptional geopolitical assets, the likelihood that American would grow in size and power was great from the start. Because certain individuals made certain choices, nevertheless, it grew in a certain manner and with certain consequences. From this perspective the story this book tells is an American story. The American system provides its leadership with the political space not only to make choices but to act on the choices leaders make.

The following chapters will historicize and contextualize six American leaders whose choices affected the growth of the American empire and whose lifetimes span America's history. Readers will doubtless quarrel with the selection. Not all were primary decision-makers. None were presidents, with the exception of one, whose single term in the White House was of marginal significance compared to his prior and subsequent careers. The priorities and programs of presidents will figure prominently in the narrative. Still, too often America's chief executive receives undue credit—and blame—for initiatives undertaken during his administration. The individuals on whom this book focuses were (or are) exceptional in who they were and what they achieved. But they were not unique. They represent attitudes toward, and visions of, the American empire that were grounded in a specific time and environment. Further, they debated other representative Americans whose attitudes and visions differed.

At the core of these debates were questions about how the United States should behave within the constellation of domestic and global actors to promote its national interests (which often included the pursuit of a contested sense of American "mission") while at the same time preserving and frequently expanding a particular definition of individual and collective liberty. These debates expose the fissures in the respective contemporary political cultures even as they illuminate those political cultures. Neither the formulation nor implementation of U.S. foreign policy is democratic. Only an elite few get a "vote." But neither are they conspiratorial. Without broad public support, policies are unlikely to succeed. By their rhetoric and by their actions, these individuals gave voice to the values and aspirations of the many who remained silent, thereby shaping both politics and policies. As a consequence, they played pivotal roles in shaping the course of the American empire.

I did not hesitate to choose Benjamin Franklin as the individual with whom to begin. He was the "foremost believer in an expanding American empire," writes one scholar. According to another, Franklin articulated the "first conscious and comprehensive formulation of 'Manifest Destiny.'" At the same time, yet for intellectually consistent reasons, he was counterintuitively reluctant to break free from Britain's imperial shackles. Franklin personified the link between the two empires and expressed elegantly and explicitly the principles of reciprocity vital for an empire to function effectively—and virtuously.[31]

Franklin thought longer and deeper about the relations between individuals and governments, and governments and governments, and security and liberty, than any principal player at the time that America achieved its independence. An avid proponent of landed expansion, he forcefully argued the "American" case for the British acquiring Canada, not Guadeloupe, after the Great War for Empire. Yet born in Boston and escaping to Philadelphia, Franklin is inextricably linked to these commercial and later industrial centers. His sympathy for Jefferson's agrarian ideal and Hamilton's promotion of a strong central government reflects American's continuing effort to resolve the difficulty of democratic management of an ever-growing empire. This issue bedeviled each of the individuals in this book as they sought to reconcile liberty, stability, and security.

It certainly bedeviled John Quincy Adams, by most accounts the outstanding secretary of state in American history and peerless exponent of America's mission to expand the sphere of liberty. Schooled in international relations at his father's knee during the War of Independence, Adams matured politically and intellectually during the initial years of the American Republic. He observed America's vulnerability as it struggled against the British Empire after gaining independence, he won election to the U.S. Senate the year before Thomas Jefferson orchestrated the Louisiana Purchase, and he was a member of the negotiating team that reached an accord at Ghent to end the War of 1812. As secretary of state in 1819, Adams exploited Andrew Jackson's misbehavior in Florida to conclude the Transcontinental Treaty with Spain. Among the greatest triumphs of any U.S. diplomat, it gave the United States title to East and West Florida, established a western boundary of the Louisiana Purchase, and provided the United States with a claim to the Northwest Territory equal to that of the British. In 1823 Adams authored the Monroe Doctrine, described by Williams as "the manifesto for the American empire."[32]

Yet no one was more ardent in insisting that America's had to be an empire of, albeit not an empire for, liberty. Not only did Adams turn his back on what he judged an empire of slavery, but he also came to oppose the very expansion he had so strenuously advocated. Further, it was Adams who pronounced that Americans must not go abroad in search of monsters to destroy, regardless of their sympathies for "freedom fighters." Literally up until the time of his death, Adams personified the paradoxical America's relationship with both empire and liberty.

While William Seward has received less scholarly attention than Adams, he is almost his equal in his contribution to the design of the American empire and—at least initially—his devotion to liberty. Seward also detested slavery, and he joined with Adams in the 1840s in opposing expansion unless uncontaminated with chattel labor. His consolation prize for failing to realize his ambition to be president was his appointment as secretary of state under Abraham Lincoln, a post he retained under Andrew Johnson. During the Civil War Seward distinguished himself as a resolute opponent of France's effort to extend its empire to Mexico. He distinguished himself more in the post–Civil War years by envisioning a transoceanic empire, earning from Walter LaFeber the title "prince of players" in the creation of America's "New Empire"—"new" in that it exchanged territory for trade that would serve as an outlet for production, not population.[33]

Seward was convinced that the United States could exercise political control of foreign territories without bearing the costs of establishing colonies. He was likewise convinced, or convinced himself, that such an "informal empire" did not violate the fundamental principles of liberty. Seward therefore conceptualized a systematic program of insular expansion. He proposed that the United States negotiate reciprocal trade treaties, acquire scattered strategic outposts across the Pacific, and purchase the Alaskan "drawbridge" in order to facilitate access to the fabled China Market. Moreover, the intrinsic appeal of America's ideals and values, what Seward referred to as the "process of political gravitation," would ultimately lead to U.S. predominance throughout the nineteenth-century version of the Third World, thereby endowing its peoples with liberties they had not previously experienced. Domestic concerns—the politics, racialism, and constitutionalism that infected the Reconstruction Era—frustrated Seward. But he left a vibrant legacy for his successors.[34]

No one embraced that legacy more ardently than did Henry Cabot Lodge, perhaps the most controversial choice for inclusion in this study. A teenager during the Civil War and Reconstruction as well as a scion of one of America's leading families in one of its leading commercial states, Lodge accepted Daniel Webster's words "Liberty and Union now and forever" as articles of faith.[35] As an adult he bestowed upon the American empire the same sanctity. During his lengthy public career Lodge played a defining role in the successes and failures of the ambitious international agendas pursued by Presidents William McKinley, Theodore Roosevelt, and Woodrow Wilson. Yet Lodge charted a course independent of each of them. He exercised his power from Congress.

Lodge was as complex as he was powerful, as intellectual as he was political. He represents the conventional "realist" perspective on

America's empire and its relationship to the global constellation of great powers. His reasons for supporting the aggressive policies of McKinley and Roosevelt in the 1890s and first decade of the twentieth century and then fiercely opposing the Versailles Treaty provide an insightful perspective on the yin and the yang of America's global ascendancy even as they illuminate the conflicting points of view on the use of force as an instrument to spread "the American Dream." In the end Lodge's defeat of Wilson resulted in the antithesis of his prescriptions. America's interwar "Empire without Tears" arose from a foundation of trade, loans, missionaries, and movie moguls. This "Awkward Dominion" did not last.[36]

John Foster Dulles, caricatured as the Cold War zealot who combined Wilson's crusading moralism with Lodge's faith in force, was personally and politically affected by the battle over Versailles. Born in 1888, Dulles grew up under the watchful eye of his grandfather, John Watson Foster, Benjamin Harrison's secretary of state. His other grandfather was a missionary in Asia, and his father was a Presbyterian minister and intellectual. This ancestry had consequences. Although a Republican, Dulles was attracted to Wilsonianism, and in the run-up to World War II he wrote a damning indictment of the traditional European empires. *War, Peace, and Change* is one of the most eloquent and thoughtful expressions of American anticolonialism and global progressivism written in the first half of the twentieth century.[37]

After the onset of the Cold War, however, Dulles became identified with the very empires from which he distanced America. No less critical of the British and the French, and fearing their follies would cost the "Free World" hearts, minds, territories, and resources, he advocated that the United States wrest from its allies their stewardship of former and even current possessions. Some historians argue that Cold War America accepted an "Empire by Invitation." Dulles did not wait to be invited. According to his weltanschauung, as the defender of the Free World America was and had to be an Empire for Liberty.[38]

The final chapter focuses on Paul Wolfowitz. A college and then graduate student during the turbulent era of the Vietnam War, from an intellectual standpoint Wolfowitz personifies the most salient factors driving America's contemporary global posture. He began his Ph.D. program at the University of Chicago intending to study political theory with Leo Strauss. He ended up studying strategic theory with Albert Wohlstetter.

The two scholars contributed to an idiosyncratic worldview that reflects and influences America's present idiosyncratic empire. Strauss, whose "disciples" have been labeled the "key ideologists of empire," aroused Wolfowitz's impulse to export liberty and democracy; Wohlstetter impressed upon him that the dangers inherent in the anarchic international environment require the willingness to use force to ensure security, without which there can be neither liberty nor democracy. These absolutist convictions propelled Wolfowitz's rise through the ranks of America's national security establishment. While still in his thirties he served as the director of the State Department's Policy Planning Staff for Ronald Reagan. As undersecretary of defense for policy during the administration George H. W. Bush, he became the trusted lieutenant of then-secretary of defense Dick Cheney. For George W. Bush he was the deputy secretary of defense and a chief architect of the 2003 Iraq War. During these years Wolfowitz, in his dual capacity as government official and public intellectual, progressively extended the concept of an Empire for Liberty to its logical conclusion. By doing so, he exposed America and the world to the flaws in that logic.[39]

CHAPTER I

Benjamin Franklin and America's Imperial Vision

B Y THE TIME that Benjamin Franklin left for Paris in 1776 to represent the cause of liberty and independence, he was "the greatest man whom the new world yet produced, and he was, with the possible exception of Voltaire, the best-known person in the world." He was also the New World's foremost expert on and advocate for empire—first for that of the British, then for that of the Americans. While Franklin's boundless ambitions for territorial expansion may not have been predictable, his preoccupation with empire and liberty was.[1]

Franklin's life spanned a century during which the frequency and intensity of imperial conflict produced the modern global system. He was born in the first month of 1706, in the midst of the War of the Spanish Succession, which colonists in America knew as Queen Anne's War. The initial stage of this global struggle among empires, the War of the League of Augsburg or King William's War, had ended less than a decade before. Like its predecessor, Queen Anne's War pitted the British and lesser, declining, or aspiring empires in Europe against France and Spain for the purpose of preventing a union of the French and Spanish thrones following the death of Spain's King Charles II. In the North American theater, French and British forces, each with Indian allies, launched a series of attacks against the other's border settlements. The Treaty of Utrecht in 1713 restored peace to the continent. Britain received Nova Scotia, Newfoundland, and a series of fur-trading posts in the Hudson Bay area; France retained control of Cape Breton and the islands along the St. Lawrence River. The British also wrested control of the *asiento*, thereby undermining the Spanish monopoly on the slave and additional trade with the West Indies. While the treaty recognized Louis XIV's Bourbon grandson as the King of Spain, it divided much of the Spanish Empire between the Holy Roman Empire, the Duchy of Savoy, and various Italian kingdoms. The British came away with Gibraltar and Minorca. Reflective of the settlement and suggestive of geopolitical developments a century later, the Treaty of Utrecht for the first time explicitly referred to the concept of a "balance of power."[2]

As a child Franklin lived in Boston throughout the conflict, and much of the fiercest fighting took place in his home state of Massachusetts. As a grown man he followed attentively the next phase in this collision of empires, the inconclusive War of the Austrian Succession

(King George's War) that extended to North America in 1744 and lasted until 1748. Not until several years later did Franklin become personally involved in promoting British expansion at the expense of the French. Long before that, nevertheless, he had traveled sufficiently north, south, east, and west to understand the stakes. What is more, no one with the intellectual curiosity of Benjamin Franklin could ignore the contemporary seismic shifts among empires. In the aftermath of Utrecht the rapid decline of the Spanish and Holy Roman empires was manifest; the Portuguese Empire was a vestige of its past, and the Dutch Empire was reduced almost to insignificance. To the East, the Ottoman Empire stagnated, and the Russian Empire, suffering from a series of short-lived and ineffectual czars and czarinas, continued to slumber. The future would belong to the British or the French. America would be pivotal in determining which.

In this atmosphere Franklin made a name for himself. Like the colonies, although Franklin's beginnings were modest, he was endowed with exceptional assets. His father immigrated to Boston from Banbury, England. Josiah Franklin probably arrived in 1683 at the age of twenty-five, along with his wife, a son, and two daughters. He had made a comfortable living in England as a dyer, but his nonconformist views on religion were seriously at odds with Charles II's Catholic-leaning leadership of the Church of England. In Boston he joined the Congregationalist Old South (Third) Church. The religious aspect of his migration thus met his expectations. Unable to earn a sufficient income manufacturing dye, however, he turned to soap and candles. His hard work paid off. In short order Josiah was more than able to provide for his family. But he had little time for them. Anne died in 1689, while giving birth to her seventh child. Less than a year later, Josiah married Abiah Folger. Born on January 6, 1706, Benjamin was the eighth of ten children born to Josiah and Abiah, the fifteenth of Josiah's total of seventeen.

Franklin could never remember a time when he could not read. Josiah sent him to school on the premise that he could better serve the church if he were literate. Yet because he could not afford to educate Benjamin to the extent necessary for him to enter the clergy, he decided two years of schooling was adequate. At age ten Benjamin went to work for his father.

Two years later Josiah apprenticed Benjamin to his older brother, James. A printer with ambitions of his own, James could use Benjamin's assistance more than Josiah needed it. The younger brother helped with typesetting pamphlets, and even with some of the composition; he also became James's primary street vendor. After three years James launched the *New England Courant*, Boston's first newspaper. The two extant "papers" simply reprinted news from abroad. James intended the *Courant* to publish articles of opinion as well as local "features." He expected Ben's contributions to this venture to be the same as previously. But Ben had bigger plans: to write a "column" himself. He came up with a strategy. Using the pseudonym "Silence Dogood," a middle-aged widow, during the evenings for six months beginning in 1722, the sixteen-year-old Franklin wrote more than a dozen letters offering advice on subjects ranging from the public drunkenness to higher education to the treatment of women. They would mysteriously appear under the door of the print shop, and James, recognizing their potential for boosting sales, did not let their anonymity deter him from publishing them. They became so popular that Ben decided to admit his authorship. James's resentment for having to share credit with Benjamin was palpable.[3]

Yet even as the relationship between the two brothers deteriorated, circumstances forced them together. Ben used sarcasm in many of his Dogood letters to criticize Boston's Puritan leaders, Increase Mather and his son Cotton most of all. The two legendary Puritan clergymen were at the center of a controversy over smallpox. The Mathers, especially Cotton (Increase died in 1723), supported inoculation. Much of Boston's medical profession opposed it; in their view, Cotton Mather's faith in inoculation was analogous to his belief in witchcraft. Whether James agreed or not is ambiguous, but he appreciated that doing battle with the Mathers would sell papers. By 1722 the *Courant's* scathing criticism of them, and by extension the Puritan canon, landed James in prison. Ben kept the presses rolling. The next year the *Courant* resumed its attack on Cotton Mather. The Massachusetts General Council barred James from publishing the *Courant* without its approval.

James circumvented his sentence by assigning authority to publish the paper to Benjamin. For this purpose he released his brother from his contract as an apprentice. He insisted, however, that in secret they conclude another. Ben's tenure as publisher started in February; the paper's circulation increased almost immediately. James's resentment grew with the *Courant's* sales, as did Ben's over his continued subservience. With three years remaining on his new contract and reckoning that its secrecy and probable illegality would deter James from enforcing it, Ben broke his indenture and fled from Boston. Chafing under what he considered his condition of servitude, he resolved that greater space afforded greater liberty. This act would prove emblematic of his life story, and that of America.[4]

The French and British had settled into an uneasy truce in the colonies when Franklin ran away to gain his freedom. This peace worked to his benefit, and he took full advantage. Journeying south to Philadelphia, he found employment and a connection with Pennsylvania's governor, Sir William Keith. For the first but not the last time, a provincial governor disappointed Franklin. Keith promised to provide the credit and introductions necessary for Franklin to purchase in London the equipment he needed to establish his own print shop. He reneged on both counts. The skilled and self-reliant Franklin, nevertheless, earned the seed money required to return to the United States to set up his own shop. By the end of 1730 he had purchased the *Philadelphia Gazette*; but he dreamed bigger. He organized the Junto, a collection of young intellects who gathered regularly to discuss matters from ranging from politics to science to art, and he became the husband of Deborah Read Franklin and father of William (who was illegitimate; later Deborah gave birth to Franklin's second son, Francis, who died in 1736).

Franklin's accomplishments over the next two decades are the stuff of legends. In his case the legends are true. Within a few years he had turned the *Gazette* into one of the colony's leading newspapers, under the pseudonym Richard Saunders begun to publish his celebrated *Poor Richard's Almanack*, and won the concession for printing Pennsylvania's paper currency. Before the decade was out he was wealthy as well as wise. He was also Philadelphia's most public-spirited citizen. Franklin was either responsible for or instrumental in founding Philadelphia's fire department and police force; its public library and hospital; and the American Philosophical Society, the Library Company of Philadelphia, and the Academy of Philadelphia, which grew into the

University of Pennsylvania. And then there were his scientific experiments, most dramatically those with electricity. To contemporaries on either side of the Atlantic, Franklin became "the very incarnation . . . of a new and enlightened spirit."[5]

Franklin's ambitions; his civic-mindedness; and his intellect, belief system, and insatiable curiosity explain his emergence in the 1750s as the colony's "most articulate and vigorous lobbyist for aggressive imperial action against France." His business expanded so that Franklin's printing "empire" eventually enveloped branches of the *Gazette*, interests in other papers, agreements to sell *Poor Richard's Almanack*, and the concession to print currency in Pennsylvania, New Jersey, New York, Connecticut, South Carolina, Rhode Island, Delaware, Antigua, Dominica, and Jamaica. He probably had financial connections to Georgia and North Carolina as well. By his fiftieth birthday no "other man in America had seen so much of it as Franklin had first hand or had so wide an acquaintance among its influential men."[6]

Franklin may have been the least provincial of America's leading colonials. What is more, even as Franklin's personal network grew from colony to colony, he became engaged in promoting increased intercourse among all the colonies. Beginning with his 1737 appointment as postmaster of Philadelphia, Franklin rose over the subsequent decades to the position of joint postmaster general of the colonies (and, by decree of the Continental Congress in 1775, the United States' first postmaster general). In this regard the "Father of the American Postal Service" was from the beginning "intercolonial" in his vision. Franklin "made the postmasters and riders from Maine to South Carolina aware of the unity and vitality of the postal service. . . . No one man before him had ever done so much to draw the scattered colonies together." The lesson Franklin drew from his multiple undertakings was that unity was an "indispensable prerequisite for power and efficiency." Over the following decades he would add liberty to the list.[7]

Franklin believed that he owed his successes to Britain's empire in America, and he eagerly sought to pay back that debt by serving it. Having in 1748 sold his printing business to pursue his scientific and other endeavors, he ran for election to the Pennsylvania Assembly. His initial year as Philadelphia's representative was 1751, the first of almost forty years in public service. It was also when he turned his considerable mind and energy to the problem of empire that would engage him for the rest of his life.

Franklin sold his printing business the same year that the Peace of Aix-la-Chappelle brought to an end the third phase of the struggle for global supremacy, King George's War. On the North American continent the primary consequence of the short-lived truce between the French and the British was to accelerate the collision of their two empires even as it eviscerated the Indian buffer between them. The cessation of hostilities allowed for increased colonial migration westward across the Appalachian Mountains, spurred on by land speculators whose home colony frequently claimed title to what was disputed land. This expansion, then, was as disorganized as it was competitive. It also increasingly alienated and antagonized the Indians by following "a path that led more toward apartheid than cultural engagement with the native peoples."[8]

French colonials had the support of their state, which sought to cement the foothold of Louis XV's empire between the St. Lawrence and Mississippi Rivers by thwarting British migration through its influence over Indian tribes and the network of forts that it constructed. The British colonials came to fear French "encirclement." Franklin was directly involved in the intensifying crisis. On the one hand, although not as avid a speculator as, for example, George Washington or his own son William (by then the governor of New Jersey), Franklin was not "a playful or disinterested student" of what was taking place. He had speculative land interests of his own, particularly in the Ohio River Valley. On the other hand, he had the official responsibility of looking out for the interests of Pennsylvania. Because it did not possess formal claims to the western lands, Pennsylvania was at a disadvantage relative to those colonies that did—notably, Virginia. The synergy among these considerations produced in 1751 the "first systematic expression of Franklin's expansionism."[9]

This expression, and the plan for western empire that evolved from it, reveal that Franklin's project was "less personal than imperial."[10] Notwithstanding his well-deserved reputation as an Enlightenment thinker, Franklin's perspective on the problems confronting the British and his fellow Pennsylvanians evolved more from his "realistic" assessment of geopolitics than his faith in human reason and progress.

His multifaceted life experience taught him that "few in public affairs act from a mere view of the good of their country." In other words, polities as well as people behaved according to "their present general interest, or what they take to be such." Further, although religion was an important facet of Franklin's worldview, he rejected the rigid Puritanism of his Boston childhood. "Some of the Dogmas of that [Presbyterian] Persuasion, such as the Eternal Decrees of God, Election, Reprobation, &c.," he confessed in his *Autobiography*, "appeared to me unintelligible." As a consequence of this Deist outlook, secularism inspired his prescriptions for empire more than the missionary zeal often associated with American expansionists. Still, there were providential dimensions to Franklin's counsel that were rooted in his Puritan background. The French and their Indian allies had to step aside or be banished "in order to make room for the [divinely anointed] cultivators of the earth." Franklin's definition of liberty, at least as applied to those who deserved liberty, now enveloped the right to expand.[11]

Characteristically, Franklin committed to paper his ideas about future imperial developments once the French threat was eliminated. Drawing on such past theorists as Machiavelli and inspiring future ones like Thomas Malthus, Franklin's *Observations Concerning the Increase of Mankind, Peopling of Countries, etc.* synthesized politics, economics, sociology, and demography. The "earliest clear statement of the function of the American frontier," this pamphlet articulated "a large, new conception of the whole of American life." It thus served as the foundation for much of Franklin's subsequent commentary on and prognoses for empire, and inspired generations of Americans to come. *Observations Concerning the Increase of Mankind, People of Countries, etc.* is a seminal document in the history of American imperialism.[12]

Franklin predicted that only the French, and more ambiguously the Indians, would suffer from the inexorable expansion of British Americans across and up and down the continent. For both British and Americans, which Franklin saw as pieces cut from the same cloth, the benefits of this migration would be as majestic as the alternative (restrictions on settlements) would be costly. He derived his argument from three interlocking premises. First, because in contrast to Europeans Americans marry early and produce on average eight offspring per marriage, the colonial population in North America would double every twenty years. Second, notwithstanding this impressive population growth, territorial expansion would guarantee for the indefinite future that the supply of labor would not outstrip the demand for it; labor in America would remain too expensive to support manufacturing (he computed that American slaves cost more than British workers). As a product of these first two premises Franklin postulated a third: the British should recognize the peculiarities of the colonial project—American exceptionalism—by promoting continental expansion and revising the mercantilist principles that guided London's imperial policies. Doing so was a win-win proposition for colonizers and colonists.

Franklin drew on formative social science theory to support his conclusions. According to data he collected from his "observations," the abundance of land that had been available to the early colonial settlers had produced a need for cheap labor to work it. This dynamic explained the early marriages of Americans and their large families. It also explained the cyclical demographic pattern that evolved, because the children of one family could readily afford to purchase their own land and, by producing an adequate number of offspring, remained optimistic that they could sustain their economic independence by farming it. It served the best interests of the British Empire that both the Crown and Parliament take all measures possible to assure continuation of this pattern by not only encouraging this population growth and expansion but also preventing any developments detrimental to it. Franklin identified six "Things" in particular certain to "diminish a Nation": "being conquered," "Loss of Territory," "Loss of Trade," "Loss of Food," "Bad Government and insecure Property," and the "Introduction of Slaves." Conversely, the goal for London should be to satiate the colonists' appetite for more and more land in order to provide sufficient "living space" for their agrarian paradise. Franklin could not have been clearer about the rewards. The "Prince that acquires new Territory, if he finds it vacant, or removes the Natives to give his own People Room; the Legislator that makes effectual Laws for promoting of Trade, increasing Employment, improving Land by more or better Tillage; providing more Food by Fisheries; securing Property, etc. and the Man that invents new Trades, Arts or Manufactures, or new Improvements in Husbandry, may be properly called *Fathers* of their Nation, as they are the Cause of the Generation of Multitudes."[13]

Franklin's argument challenged the mercantilist framework that structured the very conception of empire at this time. According to the era's received wisdom, an empire's periphery served the core. The purpose of colonies was to serve the metropolis by providing it with money or, in the case of Britain, the raw materials required to bring in the most money (by selling manufacturers at a cost much higher than that of production). With this zero-sum configuration, wealth and power flowed in but one direction. Any diversion produced a net loss. Consequently, conventional-thinking Londoners perceived colonies in North America from Maryland to Nova Scotia, and even more so the western territories, as all but worthless. Worse, they could turn into competitors, most dangerously in the area of manufacturers.

Franklin reversed the equation and redefined the variables. Rather than serve the British as a supplier of materials for manufacturers, America would "serve" Britain as a market for those manufacturers. Because the colonies' population would grow, that market would grow to the extent that it became "a glorious Market wholly in the Power of *Britain*, in which Foreigners cannot interfere, which will increase in a short Time even beyond her Power of supplying, tho' her whole Trade should be to her Colonies." Moreover, London need not worry about the colonists turning to manufacturing and vying with the British—so long as there remained a surplus of land as opposed to surplus of labor. "So vast is the Territory of North-America, that it will require many Ages to settle fully," wrote Franklin confidently."[14]

Franklin's analysis was revolutionary. In contrast to the orthodox subservience of periphery, the relationship between the American colonies and British metropole would be symbiotic, based on liberty, equality, and harmony. The empire would grow stronger as both its critical components prospered. Franklin was too sensitive to the politics of power not to acknowledge the potential for a strategic imbalance. Even if the colonial population doubled only every twenty-five years, by the next century "the greatest Number of Englishmen will be on this Side the Water." Nonetheless, because he had faith in London's enlightened imperial management, Franklin could hardly contain his excitement over this prospect: "What an Accession of Power to the *British* Empire by Sea as well as Land! What Increase of Trade and Navigation! What Numbers of Ships and Seamen!"[15]

Franklin conceded that not everyone would share in the bounty, or for that matter in the blessings of liberty that underpinned his imperial construct. Although intrigued by Indians as a subject to study, he was "partial to the Complexion of my Country" and imagined it colored "lovely White." Hence he wrote that Indians had to be pushed aside to make room for the British. Franklin was equally adamant about limiting the "Importation of Foreigners" to the continent, whether they be "black" Africans, "tawney" Asians, or "swarthy" Europeans (he referred to Germans as "Palatine Boors"). Franklin was anything but a typical American. Yet his vision of empire reflected the racial overtones that dominated American thinking. Anglo-Saxons, he concluded, comprise "the principal Body of White People on the Face of the Earth." The British had the power to make "this Side of our Globe reflect a brighter Light to the Eyes of Inhabitants in Mars or Venus."[16]

Even as Franklin set down to write his first treatise on empire, tension between the British and French intensified, as did the British colonials' designs on the western territories and their anxieties over French efforts to preserve their empire. Crucial to France's strategy was its alliance with equally anxious Indian tribes. The behavior of Pennsylvanians contributed significantly to heightening those fears. Less interested in William Penn's commitment to brotherly love than in maximizing the profits from his proprietorship, Penn's descendents antagonized the Delawares and other Pennsylvania tribes by extending the parameters of the royal grant. The Indians responded with greater violence and closer partnership with the French. In 1753 Pennsylvania governor Richard Hamilton appointed Franklin to a delegation instructed to meet in Carlisle, Pennsylvania, with the Delawares and their allies—the Shawnees, Owandaets, and the most recent addition, the Twightwees (later called the Miamis)—and those tribes that remained sympathetic to the Crown, the six-tribe confederacy that comprised the Iroquois Nation. The goal was to establish a peaceful accord among all the parties that would isolate the French.

The four-day meeting and subsequent Treaty of Carlisle produced little of consequence. But the experience left an indelible impression on Franklin. In 1751, the same year that he drafted *Observations*, Franklin wrote several letters outlining his preliminary thoughts on an association among the colonies. The primary justification was to allow the colonies more effectively to deal with the Indians by concerting in the regulation of trade and otherwise projecting greater strength by demonstrating a unity of purpose equal to that of the French. At the time Franklin did not consider the implications of his expressing his preference that this "Union of the Colonies" (his phrase) result from the voluntary agreement of the colonial assemblies rather than the Crown or Parliament. His objective was to facilitate the agreement, not promote autonomy, let alone independence. He took as his inspiration the Iroquois Confederation. "It would be a very strange Thing," Franklin mused, "if *Six Nations* of ignorant Savages should be capable of forming a Scheme for such an union, . . . and yet a like Union should be impracticable for ten or a Dozen *English* Colonies, to whom it is more necessary, and must be more advantageous; and who cannot be supposed to want an equal Understanding of the Interests." His meeting at Carlisle reinforced in his mind this paradox even as it provided impetus for him to resolve it.[17]

Franklin did not follow up on these early ruminations, and nothing materialized from them. Nor did the Treaty of Carlisle alleviate conflict on the western frontier or undermine French influence with their Indian allies. And from the British and American perspective, in 1754 the situation deteriorated precipitously. In the aftermath of Carlisle the governor of Virginia dispatched the colonial militia to the Ohio Valley to protest France's construction of a series of forts on what the British—and Virginia—considered their territory. With the death of Colonel Joshua Fry, in May 1754 command fell to newly commissioned Lieutenant Colonel George Washington. Although just twenty-one, Washington, already immersed in land speculation, "fully embraced the expansionist values, attitudes, and behaviors of the Virginia gentry." His rank and promotion, moreover, demonstrated his leadership and military skill. He thus took it personally when in July the French forced him to surrender and then burned Fort Necessity, which Washington had just finished hastily building. Because of whom Washington represented and the potential consequences of his expulsion, Virginians and Pennsylvanians took the rout personally as well.[18]

In part because of their Quaker pacifism, but in larger part because of the miserliness of the Penn proprietors, Pennsylvanians had passed the buck for western security to Virginia. In June Pennsylvania accepted Virginia's invitation to meet with it, the other colonies, and the Iroquois Nation in Albany, New York, to develop a strategy for the common defense. Better prepared this time, Franklin targeted the problem that would bedevil British on both sides of the Atlantic for the remainder of his life—and beyond: how to govern effectively and securely an expansive empire while protecting the liberties of its inhabitants. On route he drafted a plan for colonial union, "Short Hints towards a Scheme for Uniting the Northern Colonies." To drum up support for united resistance to the French threat, moreover, he published a woodcut in his *Philadelphia Gazette* with the pointed caption, "Join, or Die." Considered the first American political cartoon, it portrayed a snake cut up into multiple segments, each labeled with the initial of a colony stretching from New England to the Carolinas.[19]

The conferees quickly agreed to propose a plan for a loosely structured union. Franklin headed the drafting committee, which used his "Short Hints" as its basis. Each colonial assembly would in proportion to its contribution to a common treasury elect representatives to a "Grand Council." They would empower this council, subject to a veto by a Crown-appointed president-general, to conduct trade and other relations with the Indians, which included the purchase of their lands, to coordinate military operations in the name of all the colonies, and, when necessary, to impose taxes for these purposes. It would likewise establish policies for establishing new colonies in the future.

This last prerogative foreshadowed a proposal Franklin soon circulated to establish two colonies in the Ohio River Valley in order to accelerate colonial expansion ("A single old colony does not seem strong enough to extend itself otherwise than inch by inch"), and prevent Virginia from exploiting its advantage to claim the territory as its own. This proposal completed Franklin's vision. The Albany Plan conceived of union as a means to defend against the encroachment of the French Empire at the expense of the British even as it provided for the expansion of the British Empire at the expense of France's. Franklin's thinking had evolved to the point where "the mere concern for security, without losing its sincerity or its urgency, [had become] blurred by and scarcely distinguishable from the dream of a powerful realm, offering millions of people of future generations safety and prosperity." From the perspective of this bigger and better British Empire, moreover,

Franklin perceived the colonial union established by the Albany Plan as a "a stepping-stone to a larger union in which Britain and the colonies would somehow be joined on equal terms."[20]

The Albany conferees authorized the submission of the Plan for Union to the Colonial Assemblies and to Britain's Parliament. Each retained too much concern for safeguarding its existing authority to accept it. As Franklin wrote retrospectively, "The Assemblies did not adopt it, as they all thought there was too much *Prerogative* in it; and in England, it was judged to have too much of the *Democratic*."[21] The fault line was liberty. Variations on this theme would divide Americans for decades and ultimately produce a civil war. The establishment of union proved necessary but not sufficient for establishing unity. Further, with the expulsion of Washington from the area where the confluence of the Allegheny and Monongahela Rivers form the Ohio, the deterioration of relations between the British and French empires passed the point of no return.

In 1755 Washington joined with Major General Edward Braddock, the new commander-in-chief of Britain's American forces whose mission was to dislodge French control of the region west of the Alleghenies. Setting out from Maryland in May with cannon in tow, the imperious general planned to capture Fort Duquesne and then move on to France's other forts. Franklin exploited his connections and political skill to provide Braddock with the requisite wagons, supplies, and equipment. His assistance enabled Braddock to reach Fort Duquesne—almost. Rather than wait for the British to set up their cannon, the French, with Indian allies drawn from sundry tribes, ambushed the force as it crossed the Monongahela in July. The British regulars, as Washington wrote, "were struck with such a panic that they behaved with more cowardice than it is possible to conceive," exposing "all others, that were inclined to do their duty, to almost certain death." Of the three companies of Virginia troops; all but "scarcely thirty" died. So did Braddock. Washington (and an even younger Daniel Boone), despite having two horses shot out from under him and discovering four bullet holes in his coat, lived to fight another day. It came soon. The next year the Great War for Empire (or misnamed French and Indian War) officially began.[22]

The Great War for Empire marked a watershed in world and, of course, American history. It also marked a watershed in Franklin's biography. The Pennsylvania Assembly "commissioned" Franklin as the commander of the Philadelphia militia. If anyone could organize independent-minded Quakers into a coherent military structure, it was he. Moreover, even as Braddock's defeat forced the Assembly to prepare to do battle with the French and Indians, it had to do battle with the Penn family and its political agent, the Pennsylvania governor. All agreed on the need to pay for defense. At issue was how. Following the Penns' instructions, the governor refused to approve legislation to tax the proprietors' lands. A desperate Assembly resolved to send a delegation to London to present its case against the Penns directly. Franklin comprised that delegation. He left Philadelphia in April 1757 and reached London in July. There he would remain until 1762.

Boston and Philadelphia were small towns compared to London in 1757. It was the seat of the British Empire, and Franklin loved it. Leaving his wife Deborah at home but bringing with him his twenty-six-year-old son William, both of their slaves (Franklin called them servants), and Joseph Galloway, who had read law with William and just entered the Pennsylvania Assembly, he found a home with the widowed Margaret Stevenson and her daughter Polly at 36 Craven Street, just down from the Strand near what is now Trafalgar Square. Developing an expansive social network among Britain's intellectual and political leadership, Franklin came to identify himself as much with the colonizers as the colonized. Initially, nevertheless, he focused on his responsibilities to the latter. Franklin used all his intelligence, cunning, and charm to persuade London to change the terms of the Penns' proprietorship. Frustrated, he even proposed that the British rescind the Penn grant and restore direct ownership of Pennsylvania's lands to the Crown. Although the proposal went nowhere, it contributed to a compromise. The Privy Council ruled that the Assembly could collect taxes on developed land. But with regard to the relationship between the governor and the Assembly, the governor, and hence the proprietor, retained decisive power.

Not until 1760 did the Privy Council deliver its verdict. By this time the urgency of the issue that brought Franklin to London had lessened. Especially with the ascendancy of William Pitt (Lord Chatham) to the post of prime minister, the tide of the war turned irreversibly in favor of the British. Between 1757 and 1759 the French surrendered their forts at Pittsburgh, Niagara, Louisbourg, and Quebec City. Franklin shifted his concern from the defense and solvency of Pennsylvania to the future of what he conceived of as the British Empire's Atlantic world. By now a mature statesman (Franklin was fifty-one when he arrived in London; to put his age in perspective, Jefferson was fourteen; Madison, six; Hamilton, six months), he was confident that he represented all things British as much as did those who lived in London. Despite the "accident of an American birth," his perspective was "not merely as I am a colonist, but as I am a Briton." The colonies' "most articulate and vigorous lobbyist for aggressive imperial action against France," Franklin zealously intervened in the debates over what was best for "the greatest empire since Rome."[23]

The catalyst for Franklin's intervention was the British victory on the Plains of Abraham. Reflecting orthodox mercantilist thought, a vocal contingent of Britons advised that London restore Canada to France in return for retaining control over the Guadaloupe archipelago in the eastern Caribbean. The "home-grown" supply of sugar would mitigate the need for the British to purchase it from outside the empire, thereby draining money from the home economy. Supporters of acquiring Guadaloupe buttressed this economic argument by playing the geopolitical card. Acquiring Canada would saddle the Crown with a vast territorial expanse of little value while requiring it to pay the cost for its defense and governance. In addition, the very size of this North American appendage, combined with its distance from the metropole, would generate momentum for greater autonomy and eventual independence. The population would come to rely on its proximate resources and exploit them to develop their own shipping and manufacturing industries. Their need for and hence loyalty to Britain would decrease commensurately.

Franklin responded in the spring of 1760 by publishing *The Interest of Great Britain Considered with Regard to her Colonies and the Acquisitions of Canada and Guadeloupe*. Identifying himself only as a "concerned citizen," he dismissed the mercantilists' arguments as hogwash. In doing so, he presented his most fulsome expression of his imperial, or what one historian characterized as "his most grandiose," vision. Rejecting the core/periphery dichotomy, Franklin insisted that the North American continent was not an appendage but the western frontier of the British Empire. Its security and prosperity were therefore integral the empire's, regardless of which side of the Atlantic the population lived.[24]

Because the conflict between the French and Indians and the British over the northwestern territories had ignited the war, Franklin stressed that a peace treaty that left Canada in French hands would lay the foundation for renewed hostilities, just as Aix-la-Chappelle had. The Canadian French would still scheme with the Indians to regain the territory west of the Alleghenies and extending south to the Mississippi River. Acquiring Canada would not immediately transform the French Canadians into loyal British Canadians. But denied the support of the French state, their capabilities to make trouble for the current and future colonies would become negligible. Further, by defanging the French Canadians, the colonies, and therefore the British, would avoid the prospect of a two-front war. An attack could only come from France itself, and that threat was easily manageable. Once in possession of Canada, Franklin explained, "We shall then, as it were, have our backs against a wall in America, [and] the seacoast will be easily protected by our superior naval power." Franklin's strategic argument for acquiring Canada heralded a vital justification for American policy as it constructed its empire over the next century. The best guarantor of security was the removal of alien powers from the continent; the ocean barriers would do the rest.[25]

Countering the arguments of the orthodox mercantilists was more complicated. But it was also more fruitful. Denigrating the economic potential of Guadeloupe even as he underscored the risks of taking possession of an island inhabited by people "of different language, manners and religions," Franklin again implored the British to recognize that the value of the colonies lay in their role as a market, not a supplier. Franklin had already established the multiplication table for the population increase: it would double every twenty years. The scarcity of land was the sole deterrent to this demographic explosion. Acquiring Canada would eliminate that possibility. What is more, the acquisition of Canada would affirm that land remained sufficiently cheap—and labor sufficiently costly—to compel Americans to pursue their livelihood in the way that Franklin thought best for them: farming. The British could be assured of a complement to their home economy, not a competitor. "No man who can have a piece of land of his own, sufficient by his labor to subsist his family in plenty, is poor enough to be a manufacturer, and work for a master. Hence while there is land enough in America for our people, there can never be manufactures to any amount or value."[26]

This dynamic should likewise allay concern in London about a colonial march toward independence. The more intertwined and mutually beneficial was the colonists' relationship with Britain, the less their incentive for wishing to separate from it. What is more, challenging the contemporary orthodoxy and anticipating the arguments James Madison used in Federalist No. 10 three decades later to support ratifying the Constitution, Franklin suggested that the larger the expanse of the empire's territory, the more diffuse the settlements, the more numerous the disparate priorities, and the more remote the chance of colonial cohesion. Franklin was an avid proponent of unity among the colonies. Yet disappointed by the rejection of the Albany Plan, he turned this disappointment to his advantage. The colonists' refusal to unify when faced before with the threat of having their villages burned and families murdered should calm London's anxieties. "Their jealousy of each other is so great," Franklin wrote, "that . . . they have never been able to effect such an union among themselves, nor even to agree in requesting the mother country to establish it for them. . . . If they could not agree to unite for their defence against the French and Indians . . . can it reasonably be supposed there is any danger of their uniting against their own nation . . . which 'tis well known they all love much more than they love one another?"[27]

Franklin added a caveat. Perhaps recalling his motives for breaking free from his brother in Boston, he counseled that London must extend to the colonists the liberties and opportunities for self-reliance expected by all Britons. "When I say such a union is impossible, I mean without the most grievous tyranny and oppression. . . . The waves do not rise but when the winds blow." A quarter-century later the significance of this caveat would become monumental. In 1760, however, Franklin was describing what he considered an inconceivable scenario. He expected the treaty with France to produce the "the greatest Political Structure Human wisdom ever yet erected." With the acquisition of Canada, he wrote his Scottish friend Lord Henry Home Kames,

"all the country from the St. Lawrence to the Mississippi will in another century be filled with British people. Britain itself will become
vastly more populous, by the immense increase of its commerce; the
Atlantic sea will be covered with your trading ships, and our naval
power, thence continually increasing, will extend your influence round
the whole globe, and awe the world!" Doubtless in his mind Franklin
substituted the pronoun "our" for "your." But the language he used to
make his fundamental point was forthright: The "foundations of the
future grandeur and stability of the British Empire lie in America."[28]

Franklin's influence on the Peace of Paris signed in 1763 was minimal at most. Still, he could hardly have been more satisfied if he had
written the terms himself. The treaty changed the political face of
North America in a way that, in Franklin's words, "awe[d] the world."
The British did acquire Canada, and in addition the French ceded all
their territory east of the Mississippi save for Louisiana with its capital, the port of New Orleans. From France's ally Spain the British
obtained Florida (in compensation for which France transferred to
Madrid the Louisiana territory). The French retained two islands off
the coast of Newfoundland as unfortified bases to facilitate fishing,
but the treaty assured British domination of the St. Lawrence River
and hence the Northwest Territory. The British allowed France to keep
Guadeloupe, Martinique, and the western part of Santo Domingo in
the Caribbean, and Spain to keep Cuba; it took for itself political control of the Floridas. Franklin proclaimed the settlement "glorious"—
"the most advantageous to Great Britain, in my opinion, of any our
history has recorded."[29]

Franklin had little time to bask in the glory. Although he seriously
considered making his residency in London permanent, he fulfilled his
responsibilities to the Pennsylvania Assembly when the Privy Council
decided on the Penns' tax liability in 1760. He remained afterward
in part to wage his battle for Canada, in part to observe firsthand
the transition from King George II (who died in 1760) to King George
III (Franklin attended the coronation), but mostly because he wanted
to. He enjoyed London thoroughly. Yet he had never lost his affection for the colonies, and appreciated that he still had responsibilities
across the Atlantic—to his wife Deborah, to Philadelphia and Pennsylvania, to the other colonies. He returned in 1762, eager to pursue

speculative ventures in the Ohio River Valley, in many cases in partnership with his son William and other associates.

London interfered with Franklin's plans. As prime minister, William Pitt had guided British policy during the war. Viewing North American expansion much as did Franklin, he pursued it aggressively. The "Great Commoner" ran afoul of the young King George III, however, who fell under the influence of Pitt's political enemies. He resigned the same year Franklin departed London. As a result, just as Franklin reimmersed himself in colonial affairs, Parliament came under the control of those who had never enthusiastically supported a war that in their view colonists had instigated for their own benefit. They also worried that the acquisition of the Canadian territory would precipitate incessant hostilities with the Indians as the colonists' insatiable appetite for land drove them to extend the frontier ever farther to the west. The outbreak of Pontiac's War in May 1763, but a month after the signing of the Treaty of Paris, seemed to confirm their worst fears.

The solution was simple, or so it seemed to Parliament and King George. In October 1763 the king issued a royal proclamation restricting the establishment of colonial settlements west of the Appalachian Mountains. The ostensible reason was to protect the Indians by putting an end to the colonists' practice of claiming the land as their own or purchasing it unfairly. The real reason was to minimize the opportunities for the colonists' interactions with the Indians to erupt into warfare. As the colonists saw it, though, London was denying them the liberty to live and to prosper. Adding insult to the Pennsylvanians' injury, moreover, even as they suffered from the Crown's policies, with the war over, the Penn family refused all requests to assist in the colony's recovery from the expense of the war and security requirements for the future. The Assembly voted to petition the Crown to revoke the Penns' charter and govern the province as a royal colony. In December 1764 Benjamin Franklin again boarded a ship for London.

Franklin was as outraged as his fellow Pennsylvanians and other colonists over the king's proclamation. It violated Franklin's most profound beliefs about the imperial union. Nevertheless, he had no idea that virtually from the day he moved back into his house on Craven Street until his return to Philadelphia the year of the battles of Lexington and Concord, he would fight an increasingly desperate and ultimately futile battle to preserve that union. His unsuccessful effort to strip the Penns of their proprietorship mattered relatively little. Although he was disappointed, Franklin's priorities shifted dramatically. Acting at the behest of Prime Minister George Grenville in May 1764, Charles Townshend, the Board of Trade's president, enacted the Sugar Act, a tax on molasses and similar luxury products imported by the colonists. Franklin was not unduly concerned. The tax was moderate, and he understood London's need for revenue. But he fretted over the establishment of a precedent by which the colonies would lack a voice in such decisions. Further, he feared that if the tax burden on the colonies became too onerous, it would undermine the symbiotic economic relationship he considered fundamental to the empire's strength and vitality. You should "take care for our own sakes not to lay greater burdens on us than we can bear; for you cannot hurt us without hurting your selves," Franklin wrote a British friend about the Sugar Act. "All our profits center with you, and the more you take for us, the less we can layout with you."[30]

Franklin had barely unpacked in London when in March 1765 Grenville and Townsend put through Parliament the Stamp Act, taxing all legal documents, almanacs, newspapers, even playing cards. With the tax scheduled to take effect in November, riots broke out in several cities, including Franklin's Philadelphia. At the urging of Massachusetts's James Otis and other colonial leaders, in October a Stamp Act Congress convened in New York City to formulate a collective response. It was the first such gathering since the Albany Conference. The resultant Declaration of Rights and Grievances was drafted largely by John Dickinson, who had squared off against Franklin and his allies in the Pennsylvania Assembly by defending the Penn family. A restrained document, the Declaration distinguished between the Crown's legitimate authority to place duties on colonial trade and its illegitimate effort to tax the colony's internal affairs.

Franklin's response was muted. He was long retired from printing and publishing, and he appreciated Parliament's position. In addition, he had been involved with the controversy over the cost of Pennsylvania's defense since prior to the Great War for Empire, and he was now in London to advance the colony's crusade against the Penns. His empathy for the British buttressed his sympathy for their empire.

Yet however temperate his opposition, Franklin was unequivocally opposed to the legislation. He had taken "every step in my power to prevent the passing of the Stamp Act."[31]

For the first time Franklin now considered the possibility of fissure within the empire. He did not predict a break to occur soon. Still, his notions about the dynamics of empire and the competition among empires drove him to identify a most disturbing trend. Franklin agreed that the colonies should pay their fair share for the war and their continued security. But he vigorously objected to the sentiment in Parliament that they were freeloading, and more fundamentally, that they felt "safe" in opposing the British because they no longer needed to share the continent with the French. In short, whereas Parliament accused the colonists of asserting their independence because they took for granted Britain's protection and trade, Franklin believed that the reverse was true. It was the British who had become emboldened, and the implications for the colonists' liberties as imperial partners were ominous. Had "the French Power continued, to which the Americans might have had Recourse in case of Oppression from Parliament," railed Franklin, "Parliament would not have dared to oppress them."[32]

Topping Franklin's agenda for the next year, then, was the repeal of the Stamp Act and the erosion of the thinking on both sides of the Atlantic that had produced it and the violent response. At stake for him was not only the freedom and rights of the colonists, their salience notwithstanding, but also the nature and evolution of the British Empire, the future of which depended on a symbiotic metropole and periphery predicated on liberty and opportunity. He did not concur with the Virginia Resolves, which Patrick Henry submitted to the House of Burgesses and which claimed the colony autonomous and not subject to Parliament. He did, however, blame Parliament for driving the colonists toward Henry's radicalism. Hence, from the summer of 1765 to early 1766, he spent most of his days and nights lobbying for repeal of the Stamp Act. He spoke to whoever would listen, and he wrote letters, usually anonymous, to the press. Franklin suggested less onerous ways by which Parliament could tax the colonists. He recommended currency reform. He proposed that London allow for the representation of each colony in Parliament. Most important, Franklin offered advice on imperial unity. "We know we cannot in any form support a contest with you," he wrote when drafting an outline of what he would say if ever invited to address Parliament. "Not only in arms, etc., our superiors infinitely, but in abilities of mind, knowledge, cultivated reason, etc. We cannot subsist without your friendship and protection, etc. But the greater you are, and the more we are in your power, the more careful you should be to do nothing but what is right."[33]

In February 1766 Franklin appeared before the House of Commons. He was not invited to address it; he was asked to respond to questions, some 170 of them. Although not a polished or elegant speaker, he did so very productively. Franklin's basic points were that the Stamp Act was unfair, that it could be enforced only at great cost and, even then, ineffectively, and that its passage had severely damaged ("very much altered") the colonists' respect for Parliament and affection for the Crown. What influence Franklin's commentary had on the British is impossible to calibrate. More significant was the replacement of Grenville's ministry by one headed by the Marquis of Rockingham, (Charles Watson-Wentworth), whose policies were much more in line with those of William Pitt. More significant still were the legions of British manufacturers and traders who subscribed to Franklin's analysis of the colonies as an essential and bountiful market for British goods, an analysis reinforced when colonial shopkeepers acted in concert to prohibit the sale of British manufactures (the nonimportation agreements). Within a month of Franklin's appearance before the House of Commons, King George approved a bill passed in both chambers of Parliament to repeal the Stamp Act. Franklin's relief was palpable, but he was not confident that the empire was out of danger. "I will let you know what an escape we had in the beginning of the affair, "he wrote, "and how much we were obliged to what the profane would call luck and the pious, Providence."[34]

Less than a year later Franklin had all but reached the conclusion that his, and the empire's, luck had run out. If anything, he had become even more certain that while imperial unity was the empire's greatest asset, the colonies were its greatest source of strength. With its "immense Territory, favour'd by Nature and all Advantages of Climate, Soil, great navigable Rivers and Lakes, &c. [America] must become a great country, populous and mighty," Franklin wrote to Lord Kames. Despite the pernicious effect of the Stamp Act, he was sure that there "remains among that People so much Respect, Veneration and Affection for Britain, that, if cultivated prudently . . . they might be easily govern'd still for Ages, Without Force of any considerable Expence." That was Franklin's ideal. But his doubts about whether it could still be realized surfaced in the form of a warning: America "will in a less time than is generally conceiv'd be able to shake off any Shackles that may be impos'd on her."[35]

London continued to impose shackles. As if to signal that it did not repeal the Stamp Act because it recognized the legitimacy of the colonist's grievances, Parliament passed the Declaratory Act, reasserting its supremacy over the colonies by confirming that they were bound by any legislation enacted. Soon followed the Townshend Acts, targeting lucrative American smuggling even as it imposed new taxes on glass, lead, paint, paper, and tea. The colonists renewed their protests, reinstating nonimportation, proclaiming greater colonial autonomy, and in ever greater numbers taking their demonstrations to the streets.

This time Franklin was more zealous in his support for the colonial cause. He still held out hope that Parliament would come to its senses before it was too late. He worked assiduously with members of Parliament to affect reconciliation and stem the tide of imperial dissolution. But no longer did he attempt to moderate between the two sides. Franklin wanted passionately to preserve imperial unity, but it had to be on the colonies' terms. Indeed, over the next several years the British came to perceive Franklin more than any single other colonist as the advocate for "American" claims of liberty and justice. In this capacity he truly did represent the colonies. Not only did Franklin remain the Pennsylvania Assembly's representative in London, but he also added Massachusetts, New Jersey, and Georgia to his portfolio. Moreover, he exercised immense influence over the political leadership of the colonists. Many had visited England and had "formed the circle of Benjamin Franklin, to whom, as the one American with a great reputation in Europe, Americans turned for introduction into English society." He alone possessed an "intimate knowledge of the English discussion of foreign policy." Consequently, the British came to view and in many cases vilify Benjamin Franklin, North America's most ardent champion of the British Empire, as the leading exponent of American independence.[36]

Franklin by circumstance and inclination was uninvolved in the escalating violence that characterized the late 1760s and early 1770s. He was in London trying to replicate the previous success and win repeal of the Townshend Acts during the riots that erupted when in 1766 New Yorkers resisted quartering British troops. He was likewise in London for the 1770 "Boston Massacre." Yet he could not escape the fallout. What is more, his problems, which drove his tortured decision to support the establishment of an empire in North America distinct from his beloved Britain's, originated and escalated because of an unlikely source.

One casualty of the intense colonial protest of the Stamp Act was Massachusetts's lieutenant governor, Thomas Hutchinson. Hutchinson had been Franklin's closest ally in promoting the Albany Plan for union. He also sympathized with colonial opposition to the Stamp Act a decade later. Nevertheless, on August 26, 1865, rioting Bostonians first ransacked and then burned his home in Milton. Albeit sensitive to the forces that inflamed the protestors, Hutchinson blamed the incident on the collapse of Britain's control over its subjects, or put another way, the colonists' abuse of their liberty. Reacting to the "unparalleled outrage," he wrote of the "infinite hazard there is of the most terrible consequences from such daemons when they are let loose in a government where there is not constant authority at hand sufficient to suppress them."[37]

As conditions deteriorated over the subsequent years, Hutchinson demanded progressively more draconian measures against these "loose daemons." He was acting governor in March 1770 when the Boston Massacre caused the death of three (eventually five) colonists and forced British troops to evacuate to islands in Boston's harbor. As governor in December 1773, Hutchinson engaged in brinkmanship that precipitated the Boston Tea Party. Following the Boston Massacre, Parliament had repealed the Townshend Acts, but it had retained the tax on tea. The colonists responded by preventing the offloading of tea on American soil. In some cases the ships turned around, while in others the tea was offloaded but stored in warehouses. Hutchinson insisted that the three ships remain in Boston's harbor until the tea merchants paid the tax on their cargo. Crying, "If Hutchinson will not send tea back to England, perhaps we can brew a pot of it especially for him!" Samuel Adams and other radicals dressed up as Indians and dumped the tea into the harbor.[38]

Franklin's pessimism deepened as the chain of events unfolded. He remained convinced that most colonists preferred unity with London. Few had experienced the intimate relations with the British that Franklin had, and fewer felt as much at one with the empire. But almost all recognized the benefits they derived from the imperial relationship. Accordingly, Franklin could only fault the British, and held accountable a minority of influential Britons. In this context he not only blamed those in London like the Earl of Hillsborough, who following the resignation of William Pitt in 1868 became the initial occupant of the post of secretary of state for the colonies, but also the British agents in the colonies. In Franklin's opinion, few of Britain's "best and brightest" wanted to live in the colonies. Thus, those representing the Crown in America were "needy men," whose "offices make them proud and insolent, their insolence and rapacity make them odious, and, being conscious that they are hated, they become malicious." Their malice exacerbated Parliament's resistance to correcting its errors and provoked the colonists to take the actions that Parliament felt compelled to punish, thereby arousing greater resentment and protest. "History shows that by these steps great empires have crumbled," wrote Franklin in 1771 to Boston's newly established Committee of Correspondence. The "late transactions we have so much cause to complain of show that we are on the same train, and that without a greater share of prudence and wisdom . . . we shall probably come to the same conclusion."[39]

Franklin would never characterize Hutchinson as among the "needy men" who owed their office in the colonies to the refusal of more qualified Britons to accept one. Yet he identified the Massachusetts governor as an exemplar of the causes of this vicious cycle. The burning of his house in 1765 changed Hutchinson into someone Franklin no longer knew. He grew obstinate, hostile, and vindictive toward the colonists. He became as much a liability to the Crown as a catalyst for outrage among the colonists, Franklin wrote, because "it can never be for its interest to employ servants who are under such universal odium." Adding fuel to the fire, Hutchinson's perception of Franklin became the mirror image. When the Massachusetts Assembly protested the governor's behavior, Hutchinson attributed the impudence to its agent in London, Franklin, whom he labeled "the great director of Massachusetts radicals." Especially after Pitt's retirement in 1768 and the establishment of the ministry of Lord (Frederick) North in 1770, Hutchinson's charge received a sympathetic hearing. Franklin irritated many in Parliament. He never missed an opportunity to champion the colonial cause, or to admonish the British for their misconduct. Though still respected by many, he made enemies of no fewer. At the same time, by continuing to cherish his ideal imperial unity, Franklin alienated the radicals in the colonies.[40]

Because of some combination of his frustration with the North ministry, his conviction that his effectiveness as a colonial representative required greater confidence in him from his constituents, and the animosity that developed between himself and Hutchinson, Franklin took the fateful step that led him to abandon his advocacy for the British Empire and champion an American one. Franklin acquired a series of letters written by British authorities from 1767 to 1769. Particularly revealing was the correspondence between Governor Hutchinson and his brother-in-law, the lieutenant governor. In reading Hutchinson's recommendations about the measures necessary to restore his authority in Massachusetts, Franklin located evidence to support his bleakest analyses. "There must be an abridgment of what are called English liberties," wrote Hutchinson. "I doubt whether it is possible to project a system of government in which a colony 3000 miles distant from the parent state shall enjoy all the liberty of the parent state." Hutchinson concluded, "I wish the good of the colony when I wish to see some further restraint of liberty rather than the connexion with the parent state should be broken; for I am sure such a breach must prove the ruin of the colony."[41]

Hutchinson's transgression went beyond the behavior and attitude that Franklin found so destructive to the empire. His assessment violated the precepts that Franklin considered made the British Empire great and destined to become greater. Chief among these precepts were equality, reciprocity, and mutuality. When Franklin spoke of liberty, it was not an abstract principle. He was not a Sam Adams or Patrick Henry. Hutchinson's advice about abridging liberties meant denying the colonists the right to enjoy the benefits that the British

Empire could produce, benefits that inhered in the symbiotic relationship that stretched across the Atlantic. Geographical separation should not undermine this relationship so long as the autonomy of the colonial economy correlated with autonomous institutions of government. Hutchinson compounded his sin by failing to recognize that the colonies were the greatest source of British wealth and power.

Franklin's motives for bringing the letters to the attention of Sam Adams and others on Boston's Committee of Correspondence were complicated and surely conflicted. Furious with Hutchinson, he wanted to expose him. He may also have wanted to present Sam Adams and his allies with evidence why they should focus their wrath on Parliament's representative in Boston even as he allayed their concerns about his personal devotion to America's liberty. Nevertheless, Franklin's primary purpose was probably to bring the growing crisis to a head in a last-ditch effort to force all sides to reconsider the paths they were taking and embark on a course "towards a reconciliation." Franklin cautioned against making the letters public; yet he was too politically sophisticated to think that they would be kept private. They were not. Sam Adams read them to the General Court in June 1773. Soon copies were circulating throughout Massachusetts.[42]

The disclosure of the letters ignited an explosion. Rather than dampen it, Franklin escalated his attack on those who were destroying his dream. Heading the list was Lord Hillsborough. Reverting to the satire and sarcasm that had served him so well from his days as Silence Dogood, in September 1773 Franklin published in London "Rules for Reducing a Great Empire to a Small One." Dedicating it to Hillsborough, Franklin wrote that "a great empire, like a great cake, is most easily diminished at the edges." All that a statesman had to do to shrink an empire was to follow some simple "rules." Chief among these were taking "special care the provinces are never incorporated with the mother country; that they do not enjoy the same common rights, the same privileges in commerce; and that they are governed by severer laws, all of your enacting, without allowing them any share in the choice of the legislators."[43]

Franklin's enemies were not amused. In light of the distribution of Hutchinson's letter (for which Franklin publicly took responsibility), the Massachusetts General Court's petition to remove Hutchinson from office on the basis of those letters, the publication of "Rules for Reducing a Great Empire to a Small One," and the Boston Tea Party, to these enemies Franklin had a lot to answer for. In January 1774 he was summoned before the Privy Council's "Cockpit" to do just that. Alexander Wedderburn, the British solicitor general, did the examining. Wedderburn lived up to his reputation for razor-like personal attacks. For close to an hour he excoriated the colonial representative for all but causing by himself the rift with the colonies. Franklin, Wedderburn argued, was the "first mover and prime conductor," the "actor and secret spring," and the "inventor and first planner" of the current unrest. Because of Franklin's lust for power, he was "the true incendiary, the great abettor of that factor at Boston which . . . [has] been inflaming the whole province against his majesty's government." Franklin listened silently throughout. The Privy Council could not punish Franklin for making public Hutchinson's correspondence. But it did dismiss him as the colony's joint postmaster.[44]

Franklin was crushed. "When I see that all petitions and complaints of grievances are so odious to government that even the mere pipe which conveys them becomes obnoxious, I am at a loss to know how peace and union are to be maintained or restored between the different parts of the Empire," he wrote a week later.[45] Concluding that he was no longer of use to either the Americans or the British, he prepared to leave London. Still, he could not pass up one final opportunity to save the imperial relationship. Responding to the initiative of Admiral Richard Howe, who soon reluctantly took up arms against the colonies, Franklin threw himself into a plot to reconcile core and periphery. The principal conspirator was none other that William Pitt, now Lord Chatham, who virtually rose from his deathbed to prevent the implosion of the empire he had worked so hard to build. The plot's premise was that Chatham's prestige would be sufficient to overcome Parliament's resistance to conciliatory measures. Surprising the House of Lords, accompanied by Franklin on January 19, 1775, Chatham after a long absence appeared in person to introduce a bill calling for the evacuation of the British troops that had occupied Boston since the Boston Tea Party. When this small step failed, Chatham went for broke. Two weeks later he traveled to the House again to propose a comprehensive plan to limit Parliament's prerogative to regulate trade, ban its unilateral imposition of taxes, recognize the Continental Congress (which held its initial session the previous September), and repeal all the legislation enacted between 1764 and 1774 that the colonists detested. Franklin thought the proposal too little too late. He was certainly right about the latter. Parliament dismissed it out of hand. Shortly thereafter, Franklin returned to Philadelphia.

At age sixty-nine Franklin began the most momentous chapter in his momentous life. In many respects it was also the most painful. Franklin disembarked at Philadelphia on May 5. Greeting him was the news that the month before Massachusetts Minutemen had exchanged deadly fire with British Redcoats at Lexington and Concord. A day later Pennsylvania's Assembly selected Franklin as a delegate to the Second Continental Congress. That it would resolve to declare its independence from the Crown was a foregone conclusion. Franklin's decision to serve as a delegate signaled his resolve to support that declaration and contribute to its realization. His choice of an American empire over Britain's was his most difficult, agonizing decision. For more than a quarter-century he had, in his words, "with unfeigned and unwearied zeal" pursued first the promotion and then the preservation of the "fine and noble China Vase," his metaphor for the British Empire. Now he would pursue its fracture.[46]

Exacerbating his anguish, Franklin knew that for the most personal of reasons this fracture would be a compound one. Franklin's son William had by then served as the governor of New Jersey for a dozen years. Father and son remained close throughout this period, frequently collaborating in speculating for land and supporting the empire. But particularly after the Boston Tea Party and contretemps over Hutchinson's letters, their politics diverged. Each sought reconciliation. Unlike Benjamin's, however, William's allegiance to the Crown remained unshakable. "So long as the King remained loyal to him . . . like any other royal governor, [he] would remain loyal to the King." In a last-ditch effort to prevent an irrevocable split, Franklin met with his son halfway between Philadelphia and Trenton: at the Bucks County, Pennsylvania, home of Joseph Galloway. It was a poor choice of venue, but a natural one. Galloway and William were like brothers—and sons to Ben. They had accompanied him to London in 1757 to challenge the Penn proprietorship. Whereas William had gone on to be New Jersey's governor, Galloway had become speaker of the Pennsylvania Assembly. His opposition to independence was even more intense because it was personal as well as political. As a delegate to the First Continental Congress, Galloway had proposed a Plan for Union that closely resembled Franklin's Albany Plan a decade earlier. The delegates received it with jeers and catcalls. Galloway interpreted the reception as evidence that the trappings of the Continental Congress "cloaked the ambition and self-interests of a small group of demagogic leaders trying to bring the colonists into sedition and rebellion." Franklin arrived at Galloway's home as one of those demagogic leaders. The reunion went as one would expect—badly. Like the British Empire, Franklin's family divided between patriot and loyalist.[47]

In 1776 William Franklin became a prisoner of war. In 1778 Joseph Galloway moved to England, where he served as the chief advocate for the loyalist community and drafted plan after plan to return the colonies to the imperial fold. Benjamin Franklin put his life at the service of the American empire. In July 1775 the Continental Congress elected him postmaster general, and the Pennsylvania's Committee of Safety elected him president. In September the Congress appointed him to the committee for the importation of gunpowder, the committee on American trade, and the next month, to the Committee of Secret Correspondence. America's first committee on foreign affairs, this committee was the grandfather of the United States Department of State.

Albeit to no avail, along with Samuel Chase and Charles Carroll (and unofficially Charles's brother, the Jesuit John Carroll), Franklin traveled to Montreal to persuade Canada to throw its lot in with the rebels. Then in June, when his failure to entice the Canadians led Congress to approve their conquest (which likewise failed), Franklin joined with Thomas Jefferson, John Adams, Roger Sherman, and Robert R. Livingston to form the committee to draft the Declaration of Independence. Probably his most significant contribution to it was his support and signature. His most significant contribution to the birth and form of America's empire, however, began at the end of the 1776. When the British gained control of New York City in mid-September, the rebels realized their need to intensify their quest for help. By the end of the month Congress had appointed Franklin, Jefferson (almost immediately replaced by Arthur Lee), and Silas Deane, who was already in

Paris, as representatives to the court of France. Franklin left for Paris on October 27. He had been back on American soil for less than two years. He would not return for another nine.

Robert Livingston was America's first secretary of foreign affairs. But Benjamin Franklin was its first diplomat. And because Franklin was who he was, had done what he had done, and had written what he had written, his diplomacy was pivotal not only to the birth of the American empire but also to its expanse and character. In the words of one venerable historian, to the French Franklin was the "American virtuoso" who "personified the American cause." Franklin fully exploited this image and the negotiating skill he had honed over the decades. His ally but at times his adversary was Charles Gravier, the Count de Vergennes, who became France's foreign minister in 1774 when Louis XVI inherited the crown. Vergennes was well schooled in European realpolitik. For this reason he instinctively sympathized with the Americans' rebellion, but not with their cause. Liberty was not in his vocabulary, but empire was. Vergennes's motive for assisting the colonies was to punish the British for the defeat they had inflicted in 1763. By doing so he intended to revive the reach, fortunes, and grandeur of the French Empire at the expense of Britain's. Vergennes had no interest in promoting the American empire, except to the extent that it could damage London. Because Franklin was under no illusion that he and Vergennes were natural "friends," he and the French foreign minister got along exceptionally well.[48]

There were serious obstacles for Franklin to surmount, however. The first and most urgent was the negotiation of a treaty to provide for French (and Spanish) assistance to America's independence without impinging on that independence. Another committee that Franklin had sat on was the one Congress established, also in June 1776, to draft a "model treaty" to be offered to France and serve as a template for other European nations. John Adams was the chief drafter, and also its chief architect. Inspired by Thomas Paine's *Common Sense*, which extended Franklin's own arguments by proclaiming that America would always have legions of suitors "while eating is the custom of Europe," he crafted a document that granted America's unrestricted trade but required no political commitments or territorial concessions. The pragmatic Franklin presented Adams with "a printed volume of treaties" that he could use as source material for his draft. Adams borrowed some of their provisions, but his emphasis on reciprocity and free trade without a single string attached was unprecedented. Franklin had qualms. His lengthy experience in international affairs combined with the British rejection of his analysis of imperial union had taught him that "the interests of power politics [took precedence] over those of economics." He did not press the issue, however, and in September Congress approved the treaty almost wholly as Adams wrote it. Franklin took it with him to Paris as the starting point for negotiations with Vergennes.[49]

It was not the end point. Vergennes was too seasoned a European-style diplomat to accept the Americans' initial offer. He intended to ally with the enemies of the British Empire. But the longer he waited and the more desperate the Americans became, the more concessions he could win. Time was on his side—until the close of 1777. By this time Franklin had so endeared himself to the "French public" that the pressure on Vergennes to come to America's aid had become irresistible. More concretely, the surrender of General John Burgoyne's army at Saratoga in October 1777 dashed British hopes for bringing the insurgents to their knees. Vergennes learned that North was prepared to offer home rule in return for an end to the insurrection, a deal that only a couple years before Franklin among many others would have gleefully accepted. Vergennes, especially with Washington's army suffering through the winter at Valley Forge, could not be sure that they would not accept it now.

Franklin played the diplomatic game as adroitly as Vergennes. Both gave some ground, and in February 1778 they agreed to two treaties. The Treaty of Amity and Commerce adhered to Adams's template of 1776: free ships make free goods, the right of neutrals to trade in noncontraband goods with all belligerents, a restricted definition of contraband, and most-favored-nation status. The second treaty, however, was a Treaty of Alliance that stipulated that France and America, should their relationship precipitate a war between France and Britain, would fight together until a mutually agreed-upon peace. It also included territorial guarantees. For Franklin, America's entitlement to all conquered British territory in North America was nonnegotiable. That was fine with Vergennes. But in return, France received the authority to do what it wanted with the British West Indies. Franklin had no objection. Each satisfied, they specified that the treaty would remain in force "from the present time and forever." Congress ratified both treaties by unanimous votes.[50]

The treaties were necessary but not sufficient. By the end of 1778 the French fleet had been badly damaged, and the British had embarked on a campaign to subdue America's South. In Spain John Jay was unable to replicate Franklin's triumph in France. John Adams later suffered the same fate in the Netherlands. Franklin stayed in France; after September 1778 he was America's lone diplomatic representative there. No matter that he was the toast of French society; it was a frustrating time. The war was not going well, as American forces lost two battles for every victory. Congress buttressed its efforts to reach an accord with Britain by appointing a commission to assist John Adams. Predictably it named Franklin to that commission. But the British opposition to recognizing independence had not changed. The negotiations occurred in Paris, moreover, and Congress insisted that the commission adhere to the French alliance and inform France of every detail. Progress was impossible.

The October 1781 surrender at Yorktown of General Charles Cornwallis and his British forces changed everything. The surrender left Britain's southern strategy in shambles. It also enabled the opposition in Parliament, those who had supported Franklin when attacked in the "Cockpit" in 1774 and supported Franklin's plot with General Howe and Lord Chatham in 1775, finally to overthrow the North government. Returning as prime minister, Lord Rockingham appointed Charles James Fox his secretary for foreign affairs. Fox advocated recognizing American independence as a means to a quick peace. But Lord Shelburne, the secretary for home affairs, hoped to use recognition as a bargaining chip. Shelburne's influence increased dramatically when he succeeded to the prime ministry after Rockingham's death in July 1782. The Treaty of Alliance's prohibition on America's reaching a peace with Britain without Vergennes's approval likewise thwarted progress.

Franklin's imperial vision made negotiations even more difficult. His ambitions for the American empire had not diminished during the long and costly war. Nor had his concept of that empire, and ironically, its synergy with Britain. No sooner had Congress ratified the Franklin-negotiated alliance with France that provided essential assistance to break free of London than Franklin began formulating a strategy for patching up America's differences with London and breaking free of France. He proposed that England could win back America's hearts and minds by ceding to the new nation "all that remains in North America, and thus conciliate and strengthen a young power which she [Britain] wished to have a future and serviceable friend." Franklin predicted that London would not "be a loser by such a cession." To the contrary, foreshadowing the arguments of American anti-imperialists a century later, he counseled that Britain could avoid the "vast expense" it would incur trying to secure and administer these noncontiguous possessions, even as it undermined America's dependency on France, by resuming mutually beneficial economic intercourse and promoting a "solid lasting peace." Besides, postponing the inevitable was pointless. After all, the United States, continually growing stronger, "will have them [Britain's North American colonies] at last."[51]

What drove Franklin's prescriptions were his devotion to reconciliation with Britain and certainty about America's manifest destiny, which he regarded as intertwined. His recommendations fell on deaf ears in 1778. They all but became his mantra in 1782, however, when Franklin began to negotiate a peace accord in Paris with his acquaintance from pre-Revolutionary days, the former slave trader and current Shelburne envoy, Richard Oswald. Franklin followed his own counsel more than Congress's instructions or Vergennes's guidelines. In confidence he proposed to Oswald terms that he called necessary, and others that he deemed desirable. None of the former was surprising: British recognition of U.S. independence, the evacuation of British forces from American soil, a border with Canada that restored the boundary to where it was prior to the Quebec Act (which the British enacted in 1774 to institutionalize the 1763 Proclamation Act), and the rights of Americans to fish off the Newfoundland coast. All were required for peace; reconciliation demanded more. Thus Franklin itemized his desirable terms: indemnification along with an apology for the American damage the war caused, London's agreement to extend to American shipping and trade a status equal to any Briton, and Britain's ceding Canada to the United States. For good measure

Franklin raised the prospect of acquiring the Floridas, Bermuda, and the Bahamas. But Canada was his "diplomatic hobby horse," a fixed "quest in Franklin's subtle mind."[52]

Franklin believed British recognition of independence inevitable. But joining him in Paris for the negotiations was John Jay, who considered it an insult to treat with the British on any terms that were not equal. Further, he suspected Vergennes of subordinating America's priority of independence to France's relations with other empires, especially Spain's, which had its own agenda. Jay was also less sanguine than Franklin that Vergennes was willing to countenance America's gaining control of territory west of the Allegheny Mountains, let alone Canada. After all, by extending the Canadian boundary to the Ohio River in the south and the Mississippi River in the west, the Quebec Act had expanded the orbit of the French Canadians' Roman Catholicism. Jay was convinced that Franklin's focus on wringing Canada from the British was blinding him to France's intrigues.

Jay was more right than wrong. In the end it made little difference. Franklin fell ill, and Shelburne seized on Jay's suspicions of the French as a means to drive a wedge between America and France. He dropped his resistance to recognition. Negotiations then progressed rapidly between Oswald and Jay. Jay took Canada off the table and, disregarding Congress's instructions, substituted a provision granting both the United States and Britain the right freely to navigate the Mississippi. By the time Franklin recovered sufficiently to rejoin the negotiations, that deal had been done. Though disappointed, Franklin threw himself wholeheartedly into negotiating the other items.

In the end the Americans received as much as they (save for Franklin) could hope for. The British recognized American independence and boundaries north and west of the original thirteen colonies that closely resembled Franklin's vision, agreed that Americans were at liberty (but did not possess the right) to fish off on the Newfoundland banks, and pledged to evacuate their forces. Both countries would have unencumbered access to the Mississippi River, and each acknowledged the obligation to repay legally contracted debts. The American Congress would "earnestly recommend" that states compensate loyalists for their lost property and guarantee against further confiscations. In violation of their instructions from Congress and the spirit if not the letter of the Treaty of Alliance, Franklin, Jay, Adams—who joined them at the latter stages—and Henry Laurens, who had spent much of the war in a British jail, signed a preliminary accord with Oswald in November 1782. The following September, after a series of treaties among the continental powers, according to which Spain regained the Floridas and retained the Louisiana Territory, Franklin, Jay, and Adams signed the Treaty of Paris. On January 14, 1784, Congress ratified it.[53]

The United States was established as an independent empire. Franklin wanted more, but he was satisfied. Certain of America's manifest destiny, he had no doubt that Canada would ultimately join the union. Further, the same reasons that motivated Franklin to champion imperial union for decades drove him to champion reconciliation decades afterward. He fervently believed that both Britain and America would grow stronger through harmony more than conflict. Many in Britain agreed. But those who counted most bent to the pressure of public opinion and Britain's shipping and commercial interests. British orders of council allowed American ships to carry raw materials Britain considered essential to its national interest. But they prohibited the importation of American manufacturers, banned American ships from trading with any British possessions in the Western Hemisphere, and tried to strangle America's commerce—and hence its economy.

Other sources of Anglo-American discord, such as the refusal of the British to evacuate forts in the Ohio River Valley, their intrigues with American Indians, the problems inherent in both collecting debts and compensating loyalists, and American claims against the British for liberating their slaves, lingered. Suffering Americans, whose loyalties remained principally with their states, developed doubts about the capacity and efficacy of the national government. Unable to find relief, in 1786 farmers in western Massachusetts followed the lead of Daniel Shays and took up arms against the state lest they face foreclosure. The local militia thwarted the rebellion, but the discordant perspectives on liberty were manifest. Spain, meanwhile, sought to use its control of New Orleans to lure western settlers to embrace the Louisiana appendage to their empire. Even as George Washington described America as a "rising American empire," he conceded that a "rope of sand" was an equally apt description for the thirteen discontented states strung along the continent's Atlantic coast.[54]

Franklin was in Europe through the early turmoil, negotiating other treaties to mitigate America's distress. He was all but tilting at windmills. In 1785 Franklin returned to the United States for the last time. Although now a year shy of eighty, he hoped finally to relax. But he became enmeshed in the dispute over what form of government would both promote and protect Jefferson's Empire of Liberty.[55] This issue had long preoccupied the Founding Fathers. In their view, liberty and the definition of a citizen was the fundamental cause of America's War of Independence. By denying citizenship to Americans, Britain had forfeited the title Empire of Liberty. America had to claim it. Yet a consensus on the question of how to strengthen the union in order to withstand assaults (by the British or another foreign power or by domestic malcontents) was elusive. The goal for the American Revolution was "to create the institutions under which *ordered* liberty could thrive, to transmit the benefits of this condition to posterity, and [at least to some degree and at a future date] to extend it elsewhere in the world through the power of example."[56]

Notwithstanding his intellectual curiosity and predisposition for philosophy, Franklin only tangentially engaged such issues. He often spoke of liberty, or the costs of its absence, yet he was more concerned with power and relationships among the powerful. He did envision a North America populated with independent, self-reliant farmers. Still, his complaints against the British revolved around the rights of colonies more than the rights of colonists. Even after concluding that Parliament became corrupt and arbitrary, he avoided the passionate rhetoric about liberty associated with James Otis or Patrick Henry. For him, liberty was a means to an end, not an end in itself. More than many of his contemporaries, Franklin respected much about Indian culture. But it never occurred to him to grant Indians the liberty to remain on the land required to accommodate America's population growth. Indians "have never shewn any inclination to change their manner of life for ours, or to learn any of our arts," he explained. For that matter, it never really occurred to him that Canadians were at liberty to resist envelopment by the American empire. As for slavery, not until the end of his life did Franklin support liberties for slaves. When he went to England to fight against the Penns' subjugation of Pennsylvania's liberty, he brought his slave with him.[57]

In the last years of his life, nevertheless, the need to reconcile the requirements of sustaining the American empire and preserving American liberties preoccupied Franklin as it did Washington, Jefferson, Hamilton, Madison, and their colleagues. Despite his age, Franklin served as a delegate to the Constitutional Convention. Franklin played a prominent role neither in drafting the new Constitution nor in encouraging its ratification. He did not write a *Federalist Paper*. But, predictably adopting a moderate position between the advocates of a strong federal government and states' rights, he fully supported its federalist principles that, he hoped, would allow America's "diverse, geographically immense political community [i.e., empire] [to] be held together without creating a sovereign power that would threaten the liberties and rights the Revolutionary War had been fought to preserve." He likewise fully supported the enactment of the Ordinance of 1787, which provided a mechanism for achieving his vision of "indefinite expansion" by the orderly acceptance of new states into the republic as "self-governing republics, immune to the possibility of despotic rule from the center." Madison was mimicking Franklin when he wrote about "extending the sphere" as a means of preventing tyranny, thereby "evoking the image of an 'extended republic' as 'one great, respectable, and flourishing empire.'"[58] Nevertheless, when at the age of eighty-four Benjamin Franklin died in Philadelphia on April 17, 1790, he could not have been sure whether either empire or liberty would survive.

CHAPTER 2

John Quincy Adams and America's Tortured Empire

DURING THE LAST MONTHS of his life Benjamin Franklin, like most Americans, cheered the onset of the French Revolution. Also like most Americans, the name Napoleon Bonaparte meant nothing to him. Within the next decade, however, the twists and turns of the French Revolution and Napoleon's ascendancy gravely upset the balance of empires, precipitating another face-off between Britain and France. As the new empire on the global block, albeit a struggling one, the United States became a pawn caught in game played by two grand masters. With the unity and even survival of America increasingly at risk, by 1800 this dynamic brought an end to its Federalist era and led to the political ruin of its second president, John Adams.

Yet this same dynamic provided means, motive, and opportunity for Adams's son, John Quincy Adams, to emerge as the premier diplomat of the early American Republic and the greatest secretary of state in U.S. history. The result was some of the most glorious days of the American empire—the "Golden Age" of U.S. foreign policy, as one historian called the era. Nevertheless, even as these were the days when America secured the expansive territory that both Adams and Franklin believed was its destiny to possess, they were the days that sparked a debate over the very meaning of "Empire for Liberty" so intense as to trigger the bloody ordeal that tore the empire apart. In seeking to ensure that the American empire embodied his holy trinity—"Religion, Morality, and Liberty"—Adams "attempted to reach the pinnacle of statesmanship." That he had more success conquering international than domestic forces makes him, in the apt words of Walter LaFeber, "a heroic and tragic figure whose failures are as instructive as his triumphs."[1]

The story of John Quincy Adams is the story of the birth of America. He was both exceptional and representative. America's first first family, the Adams's roots ran deep in Braintree (now Quincy), Massachusetts, Henry Adams having emigrated from Bristol, England, less than two decades after the arrival of the Pilgrims. Henry earned his livelihood by farming; the family prospered. Born in 1735, future president John Adams graduated from Harvard College and became a lawyer. At thirty, the imposition of the Stamp Act turned him into one of Massachusetts's most ardent advocates for colonial rights. An early leader of Boston's resistance to Parliament, John Adams was less radical than older cousin Samuel. He had an intensity and commitment to principle that few could match, however. He also had as an inseparable ally in his wife, Abigail Smith Adams, whom John married in 1864. Congregationalist ministers dominated both family trees, and while she was a typical colonial woman in that she never had any formal schooling, Abigail Adams was anything but typical. By devouring the classical texts and of course the Bible, she "became one of the best-educated women of her time in New England, perhaps in all of the thirteen colonies." John and Abigail had seven children (the last was stillborn). Their oldest son, John Quincy, was born on July 11, 1767.[2]

The family moved to Boston when John Quincy was a year old. He grew commensurately with the movement toward independence. No contemporary child could have been more consumed by its passion, or more steeped in its ideology. In this regard his mother's influence was as great as that of his father. While John Adams served as a delegate to the Continental Congress in Philadelphia, on June 17, 1775, Abigail took John Quincy up to the top of Penn's Hill to watch the Battle of Bunker Hill. He was old enough to appreciate its significance and, soon thereafter, his father's contributions to writing the Declaration of Independence and the Model Treaty.

John Quincy was likewise old enough to accompany his father when in 1778 he sailed to France to assist in the negotiations of a Treaty of Alliance. On arrival in Paris the Adamses moved in with Franklin in Passy. Not yet eleven, John Quincy went to school with two of Ben's grandsons, Benjamin Franklin Bache and William Temple Franklin. Whereas the relationship between John Adams and Benjamin Franklin was a rocky one, John Quincy welcomed his time spent with the legend. His later career demonstrates that he fully embraced Franklin's vision of the American empire.

In this manner John Quincy Adams began his diplomatic education. John Adams arrived in Paris too late to participate in the treaty negotiations. His service no longer needed after Congress named Franklin its sole representative to the French court, he returned with John Quincy to the United States. Less than a year later, however, his son in tow, he was back in Europe, first in an effort to reach an accord with the British, then as the minister plenipotentiary to the Netherlands. The younger Adams then trekked with Francis Dana across Germany and the Baltic provinces to St. Petersburg. Congress dispatched Dana to try to convince Russia's Catherine the Great to allow the United States to join the League of Armed Neutrality. The teenage John Quincy translated.

Young John was a seasoned statesman by the time his father signed the treaty that achieved American independence. He remained in Paris for the next two years, with his father, Franklin, and Thomas Jefferson, with whom he became especially close—his son "appeared to me almost as much your boy as mine," John Adams described the relationship to Jefferson a year before their deaths (both died on Independence Day, 1826). Early on John Quincy foreshadowed his characteristic independence, bipartisanship, and intellect. When in 1785 John Adams moved to London as America's first minister to the Court of St. James, John Quincy returned to the United States to attend Harvard. Two years later he graduated Phi Beta Kappa. The *Columbian Magazine* published his senior oration, "The Importance and Necessity of Public Faith to the Well Being of a Nation." The Constitutional Convention was completing its work in Philadelphia.[3]

Although his family had shed the doctrine associated with its Puritan ancestors, stern religious principles remained central to John Quincy's worldview his entire life. His thoughts, actions, and words "emanated from a soul that premised its existence and all of its acts on the presence of a Divine will which had created an immutable moral order." None of the Adamses doubted that John Quincy's place in this immutable order was that of an American statesman. George Washington made sure John Quincy assumed his proper place. In 1794, in the middle of his second term as president, Washington appointed him minister to the Netherlands. Two years later he appointed him minister plenipotentiary to Portugal. John Quincy Adams was just shy of his thirtieth birthday.[4]

Adams moved to Berlin as minister plenipotentiary to Prussia when his father moved into the vice presidency. What marked Adams's early official career as a diplomat was, more than his achievements, the ideas he developed from what he observed. The year 1789 was the inaugural year of the Washington administration and America's government under the new Constitution. Both struggled mightily. Hamilton might have detected "the embryo of a great empire," but the United States received no respect from even the world's feeblest states.

American commerce suffered from the severe restrictions imposed by England and virtually all the Europeans. American exports grew, but only at a fraction of the rate of its imports. This imbalance of trade created skyrocketing debt. Building on Franklin's arguments, in advocating ratification of the Constitution James Madison had written in Federalist No. 10 that by expanding its territory the United States could accommodate an increasing number of competing interests. The result would be greater prosperity for all and the multiplicity of "factions" necessary to prevent any one from acquiring sufficient support to subvert liberty. Pluralism was the antidote to tyranny. Americans did expand. Yet when the federal government proved unable to provide citizens protection from Indians, guarantee them access to rivers like the Mississippi that they needed to ship their goods to markets, or even open up those markets to their goods in the first place, they considered, or in some cases conspired, to shift their loyalties to an empire that could. Merchants and shipbuilders found relief by all but returning to the grip of Britain. What developed were not only factions (i.e., political parties) but sectional divisions.[5]

John Quincy Adams observed this growing domestic strife from across the ocean. His vantage point on international events was much closer. He was an eyewitness to the revival of the French Empire that the French Revolution spawned. The start of his official diplomatic career coincided with the rise of Napoleon. By the time Adams began his residency in Berlin, Napoleon had gained acclaim in France by leading it to victory over Austria. His star and ambition continued to ascend even as he suffered defeat in the Egyptian campaign. Back in Paris in 1799, Napoleon participated in the coup that replaced the French Directory with a Consulate. The next year he was named First Consul; in 1804, emperor. During this time he fought wars against a variety of European coalitions. Except for the short-lived fourth war in 1806–7, these shifting coalitions had but one common denominator: Great Britain.

Adams assessed developments as U.S. minister to Prussia (although a member of the initial coalition that confronted France from 1792 to 1797, Prussia was subsequently neutral until 1806, when it was crushed by Napoleon), as an uncompromising champion of union, and as the son of the U.S. president. Each perspective led to the same conclusion. He supported Speaker of the House Madison and Secretary of State Jefferson in their effort to punish London for its stranglehold on American commerce and its encouragement of Indian resistance to American expansion by enacting discriminatory measures against British trade. He supported Secretary of the Treasury Hamilton in opposing Madison's effort to compensate by calling attention to the 1778 treaties and wooing trade with the French. But he opposed Hamilton's bias toward the British. Adams endorsed not only the Proclamation of Neutrality that Washington declared in 1793, but also the principles that Washington articulated in his 1796 Farewell Address: "The great rule of conduct for us in regard to foreign nations is, in extending our commercial relations to have with them as little political connection as possible. . . . Europe has a set of primary interests, which to us have none, or very remote relation. . . . 'Tis our true policy to steer clear of permanent alliances."[6]

The task of turning Washington's words into deeds fell to John Adams. It cost the second president dearly, and cost his almost son as much. The British effort to strangle the French Revolution ravaged America's economy and political order. Competing definitions of the national interest led political leaders in opposite directions. On one side were the Madison- and Jefferson-led Republicans who insisted on retaliatory legislation—tariffs and prohibitions against trade (nonintercourse)—against the British. Arrayed against them were Hamilton and the Federalists. They argued that the capital needed to pay off the national debt in order to make America solvent required the income that only duties on British imports could produce. Jay's Treaty with Britain in 1794 and Pinckney's Treaty with Spain the next year gave Hamilton's Federalists the upper hand. Britain relaxed some of its trade restrictions, acknowledged U.S. shipping claims, and promised to give up its forts on U.S. territory. And Spain opened up the Mississippi River again to American ships. Moreover, by the time Adams took office in 1797, what sympathy Americans retained for the French Revolution had all but evaporated. This turn against Paris can only partially be attributed to the excesses of the guillotine, although Americans far less conservative that either of the Adamses, including Jefferson, recoiled at the carnage.

At least as important to America's disenchantment were French conspiracies to gain the allegiance and territories of disaffected U.S. settlers in the West; their demands that American diplomats pay a financial tribute for the privilege of negotiating trading rights; and their "undeclared war" on neutral shipping. Federalists insisted that the United States exact revenge for this behavior by waging a real war against France, or at least its Spanish ally. This would both win favor with the British and provide an excuse to conquer Spain's trans-Mississippi holdings and the Floridas. President Adams's hostility toward France was no less intense. He resurrected the army and navy, supported the abrogation of the 1778 treaties, and suspended commerce with France and its colonies. He even undermined the civil liberties for which he had fought so hard by enacting the Alien and Sedition Acts. In America, it was becoming evident, liberty was more relative than absolute.

Adams nonetheless refused to adopt the Federalists' full agenda. Certain that a war would destroy the union and "put the United States back under the shadow of the British Empire," and wary of Hamilton's ambition to become an American Caesar, Adams opted to negotiate a settlement. The Treaty of Mortefontaine liberated the United States from its 1778 Treaty of Alliance with France, required the mutual return of seized ships and reparations payments, guaranteed neutral shipping rights, and accorded both France and America the equivalent of Most-Favored-Nation status. The Federalists, New England's so-called Essex Junto in particular, were "thunderstruck." In the election of 1800 Adams lost the presidency to Thomas Jefferson.[7]

John Adams retired to Braintree. John Quincy Adams returned to resume his law practice. Thomas Jefferson embarked on an ambitious program of boundless expansion. Taking a page out of Franklin's book, Jefferson foresaw a time "when our rapid multiplication will expand itself . . . [to] cover the whole northern, if not the southern continent, with a people speaking the same language, governed in similar forms, and by similar laws." The new president could not even "contemplate with satisfaction a blot or mixture on that surface." John Quincy Adams avidly campaigned in favor of the project. In the service of Jefferson's agenda, he transformed the Irish philosopher Bishop George Berkeley's well-known verse from the seventeenth century into the mantra for American expansion in the nineteenth. "Westward the course of empire takes its way," Adams proclaimed to an audience in Plymouth in 1802, expressing his vision and expectation.[8]

Adams's support of Jefferson and the westward course of America's empire was a turning point in his career and American history. He never begrudged Jefferson his electoral victory over his father. His villains were Hamilton, the rabid Federalists that comprised the Essex Junto in his own New England, and Aaron Burr. Moreover, his relations with Jefferson since their days together in Paris remained close, and his relations with the Federalists had long been distant. He did not expect to reenter either the political or diplomatic arena in the foreseeable future. Yet no sooner had he unpacked his bags and rehung his lawyer's shingle when fate intervened. Responding to the requests of moderate Federalists, his sense of duty, and his own ambition, in 1802 he successfully ran for the Massachusetts State Senate. Shortly thereafter, he unsuccessfully ran for the House of Representatives. He was consequently available when a vacancy opened for the Senate. The party selected John Quincy Adams to fill it.

The year 1803 was a landmark for the growth of the American empire. The story begins with Napoleon, who began to plot his next move shortly after his defeat in Egypt and emergence as the dictator of France. Napoleon formulated a plan by which he could resurrect the French Empire in the Western Hemisphere. Doing so would provide him with more assets for his next round with the British. The linchpin was the island of Santo Domingo (present-day Haiti and the Dominican Republic). The problem was finding a food supply that would enable turning over virtually all the island's land to growing sugar for export. The solution was the Louisiana territory; what Louisiana grew would feed slaves in Santo Domingo. Because he needed time to put his plan into action, Napoleon could ill afford a war with the Americans. Hence he negotiated the settlement with John Adams in 1800. He then coerced Spain into secretly ceding Louisiana to France.

To Jefferson and Secretary of State James Madison, the cession threatened to establish precisely the "blot" on North America's "surface" that they could not "contemplate with satisfaction." They responded forcefully and imaginatively with a three-pronged strategy. They assisted the Haitian rebels, the black pigment of their skin notwithstanding; they publicly floated a plan to relocate the Cherokee, Chickasaw, Choctaw, Creek, and Seminole Indians to the region west of the Mississippi, where they would threaten French setters; and they obtained congressional authority to raise a militia of close to 100,000 men capable of making life miserable for the arriving French. Jefferson even raised the possibility of allying with the British. The effectiveness of these measures cannot be gauged. But they doubtless exacerbated the distress Napoleon encountered in Haiti (caused more by germs than bullets) and the effect of a late winter that prevented his forces from leaving European ports. The combination drove the soon-to-be emperor to change his plans. He arranged a fire sale of his holdings in the Western Hemisphere in order to finance his next war against the British. He instructed his infamous foreign minister, Charles Maurice de Talleyrand Périgord, to tell special envoy James Monroe and Minister to France Edward Livingston that he would sell Louisiana to the United States for a mere 15 million dollars. Jefferson perceived the offer as better than a "noble bargain." It promised to double the size of his Empire for Liberty. To Jefferson, more American land meant more American liberty because more Americans could farm. "Dependance begets subservience and venality," Jefferson famously wrote in his 1787 *Notes on Virginia.* "Those who labour in the earth are the chosen people of God," he explained, "whose breasts he has made his peculiar deposit for substantial and genuine virtue."[9]

The Federalists thought otherwise because they conceived of liberty differently. They identified virtue with commerce and manufacturing. In their view, moreover, the United States could never assimilate this much new territory, and this many new people, relatively few of whom spoke English or resembled what an American should look like, without ripping apart the fabric of society and undermining their definition of republican governance. A more immediate consequence would be a radical transformation in the balance of political power. The Federalists foresaw the new western states allying with those in the South, leaving the states controlled by the Essex Junto but a feeble minority. This perspective put a different spin on the potential of the acquisition of Louisiana to destroy the union. It could precipitate the secession of New England.

Every Federalist in the U.S. Senate opposed the Louisiana Purchase— except John Quincy Adams. He had devoted his diplomatic career to promoting the maritime and commercial interests of paramount importance to New England. Yet if anything his continental vision of territorial expansion was a higher priority. This was not only because such expansion was vital to placating restless settlers on the western frontier in order to cement their bond to the union. It was also because, as Franklin wrote before him and Jefferson adopted as his own belief, God intended the United States to cover North America, from east to west, from north to south. Although differing from many of the expansionists of the 1840s because with the possible exception of Cuba he "harbored little ambition to move American territorial claims beyond the North American continent," Adams anticipated their rhetoric of Manifest Destiny by proclaiming that the continent was America's "natural dominion." No people or nation could stand in the way of Americans transforming 'howling deserts into cultivated fields and populous villages." The acquisition and settlement of the trans-Mississippi region was necessary but not sufficient for fulfilling the nation's destiny. Believing, as did Jefferson, that Divine Providence destined the continent to "be peopled by one nation, speaking one language, possessing one general system of religious and political principles, and accustomed to one general tenor of social usages and customs," the territories had to be organized as states and "associated in one federal union" committed to life, liberty, and the pursuit of happiness. Otherwise, Adams eerily warned, "America like the rest of the earth [would] sink into a common battlefield of conquerors and tyrants."[10]

It was therefore consistent with Adams's belief system that he would support Jefferson's purchase of Louisiana. It was equally consistent that he would not be deterred by his isolation from other Federalists. Always looking to the future, Adams had been assessing the pros and cons of acquiring Louisiana since his tenure as minister to Prussia. At one point his calculations had led him to favor French control. The "natural antipathies of borderers" to alien neighbors would combine with southern opposition to France's "system of liberating slaves and of shackling trade" to "propel the South and West into a closer union with anti-French New England." This would produce dividends until the territory inevitably gravitated to the American orbit, which it inevitably would. But by 1803 Adams concluded that the risk of allowing nature to take its course was too great. His concern now was "keeping Napoleon Bonaparte out of the region for the peace and safety of the United States." Further, although Adams worried along with the

Federalists about America's ability to defend this vast new territory and the immediate cost in influence to his New England constituents, he was confident that in the long term the addition of the Louisiana Territory would produce an "extension of national power and security" that would be "of the highest advantage" to the United States.[11]

Adams's defection from the Federalists over acquiring Louisiana did not signal that he was prepared to align with the Republicans. At issue was liberty, the very liberties that drove Jefferson and Adams's father to declare America's independence. These were the political liberties that transcended vocational and even financial interests. To ensure that the inhabitants of the Louisiana Territory enjoyed all the rights and liberties that came with incorporation into the United States, Adams proposed a constitutional amendment empowering Congress to ensure that U.S. laws protected peoples who did not inhabit America's initial territory and eventually incorporate them into the union. He sought to tie ratification of the treaty by which American purchased Louisiana to adoption of this amendment.

Adams had identified a contradiction that plagued him throughout the remainder of his life. International hostility to the American project and the selfish interests of the American people demanded American expansion to safeguard its liberties. Yet that very expansion endangered those very liberties. Jefferson, Madison, and most of the Senate recognized the problem, but they considered a constitutional amendment too cumbersome and time-consuming a solution. Besides, few believed that the Indians, French, Spaniards, and Creoles who made up the bulk of the Louisiana Territory's population warranted the extension of the rights and liberties that concerned Adams. White Anglo-Saxons did, but it would take decades for them to populate the land. Whereas Jefferson won overwhelming support for legislation that allowed a virtual military occupation of Louisiana, only two senators joined Adams in voting for the amendment. Henceforth Adams refused to support any measures concerning the governance of the territory, likening the authority Congress vested in Jefferson to "the absolute Powers of a Spanish monarch over a Spanish colony."[12]

Adams stuck to his principles and demonstrated his independence. He would do so repeatedly throughout his decades of public service, but most emphatically over the next half-dozen years. In some ways the Louisiana Purchase made America's situation relative to the French and British worse. They resumed their war the year of the sale. Neither side respected the U.S. tenet that "free ships make free goods." The British used their naval superiority in an effort to prevent Americans from feeding and supplying Napoleon's troops by seizing U.S. ships and their cargoes. Napoleon retaliated by promulgating the Berlin and Milan decrees. The first imposed a blockade on the British Isles; the second banned any state in Europe from trading with Britain. Because France lacked the capability to enforce this continental system, however, the British became the primary thorn in America's side.

London's discrimination against American trade had prompted Madison's anti-British commercial legislation in the 1780s and 1790s. Along with Jefferson he now persuaded Congress to enact a ban on British imports. Fearing that depriving Americans of textiles and other valuable commodities would prove too politically divisive, Jefferson delayed implementation. While the president struggled to formulate a less painful strategy, the British upped the ante. They impressed into His Majesty's service sailors on foreign ships that looked like deserters. More than three-quarters of those impressed were Americans. Tensions rose, cresting in June 1807 when the British boarding of the USS *Chesapeake* off the Virginia coast produced more than twenty U.S. casualties, including three deaths. The action unified Americans like nothing since independence. Jefferson could have easily received from Congress authorization to go to war. Yet he realized that the nation was woefully unprepared to fight. Economic coercion seemed the best alternative. Jefferson thus pushed through Congress an Embargo Act that closed all U.S. ports to foreign vessels and prohibited America's own export trade. The initiative made all but moot London's orders of council that further restricted neutral trade.

For Federalists, Jefferson's coercive policies compounded the sins he had committed by winning the presidency and then purchasing Louisiana. They contended that trade with Britain buttered their—and America's—bread. Tolerating British trade practices and even impressments were but a short-term cost for long-term benefits. Again Adams dissented by supporting Jefferson's and Madison's policy. From his point of view, the British disregard of U.S. neutral rights and the impressment of its sailors constituted an attack on America's liberty and independence. To be sure, Adams was far from enthusiastic about the embargo. He appreciated its potential damage to the U.S. economy, especially but not exclusively his New England constituents'. Denying Americans the freedom to trade would be necessarily "distressing to ourselves" and impossible for any length of time "in a great commercial country." Adams also doubted that the measure would be sufficient to bring about a British change of heart. But with the liberty of American commerce and the liberty of American sailors under siege, the national government had to respond forcefully. Americans could afford an embargo more than they could a war. On December 17, 1807, Adams voted with the twenty-one Republicans in the Senate in favor of the embargo. The six other members of his Federalist Party all voted in the negative.[13]

The Federalist opposition represented in Adams's mind the most severe threat to American liberty and empire: a coalition between a disaffected domestic faction and a hostile external power. The result would do violence to the will of God as well as the Founding Fathers. If the Federalists are not "put down," he predicted, spinning phraseology that would soon be linked to Manifest Destiny in a direction sui generis to Adams, "Instead of a nation, coextensive with the North American continent, destined by God and nature to be the most populous and most powerful people ever combined under one social compact, we shall have an endless multitude of little insignificant clans and tribes at eternal war with one another for a rock or a fish pond, the sport and fable of European masters and oppressors."[14]

In voting for the embargo Adams "simply voted his life-long convictions." He had no doubt that this second act of defying the Federalists was the equivalent of political suicide. "I am constantly approaching to the certainty of being restored to the situation of a private citizen," he wrote in his diary. Adams's certainty is understandable; his support of the embargo outraged and enraged the Federalists. Their political influence all but negligible and thus faced with the prospect of following the dictates of what they defined as a cabal from the South and West, they were prepared to separate from the union. Massachusetts Federalists, and in particular its other senator, Timothy Pickering, were exceptionally hostile to the Jefferson government. Pickering's idea was for Massachusetts to secede in alliance with New York. To him and his cohort, Adams's "stand against the Federalists Party's trucking to British policy" revealed him as the worst kind of traitor. Before the end of his term in office, they elected James Lloyd to succeed him as Massachusetts's senator. Adams immediately resigned.[15]

Adams was right when he predicted that the Federalists would oust him from the Senate. He was wrong in thinking he would be "restored" to the life of a private citizen. Adams resigned as Jefferson approached the end of his second administration. As expected, the president cemented the precedent Washington established by deciding against running for a third term. Likewise as expected, James Madison almost tripled the Federalist Charles C. Pinckney's votes in the Electoral College. Before leaving office Jefferson counseled his successor that America's Empire for Liberty, now twice as large with the Louisiana Purchase, should soon envelope Canada, the Floridas, Texas, and even Cuba. No "constitution was ever before so calculated as ours for extensive empire and self-government," he boasted.[16]

Madison did not need convincing. Nor did he need convincing that Adams could contribute vitally to achieving this vision. Madison appreciated Adams's unswerving commitment to placing principle over politics as much as he did his skill and expertise. He also appreciated that Adams was as fervent an advocate of continental expansion as of commercial rights. Indeed, he was publicly on record as critical of Jefferson's and Madison's expansionist policies for being insufficiently aggressive. Their proposed "Two Million Act" aimed at inducing Spain to recognize that Florida and Texas were territories belonging to the United States was a case in point. He denounced Jefferson's apparent willingness to "renounce all our claims upon the western boundary [of Louisiana, i.e., Texas] and pay several millions to get the Floridas." Adams was especially opposed to surrendering the claim to West Florida. "West Florida I consider as our own," he proclaimed. "We have bought and paid for it." Madison could not allow such a forceful proponent of both union and empire to retreat to private life. Without consulting anyone, he appointed Adams minister plenipotentiary to Russia.[17]

Adams considered the assignment "honorable diplomatic exile." He was not altogether wrong, at least at first. After the Emperors Napoleon and Alexander I reached an agreement at Tilsit, in 1807 Russia was an ally of France with neither the capability to contest British naval supremacy nor the will to challenge the French continental system. Yet Russia's potential for affecting their balance remained vast. America needed someone with Adams's experience and expertise on the spot to help determine which way the balance shifted. The posting turned out to be very significant, but not for reasons that anyone predicted.[18]

Arriving in St. Petersburg in 1809, Adams pursued two inseparable objectives. Although Jefferson had lifted the embargo shortly before turning the White House over to Madison, American trade remained crippled. Russia, its alliance with France notwithstanding, was sufficiently distant from Europe to remain beyond the reach of the continental system. Consequently, Adams sought to gain Alexander's support for promoting greater trade with the United States and resisting all infringements on neutral shipping rights. He was successful. The czar went so far as to issue an ukase (edict) that declared Russia's allegiance to freedom of the seas and granted to the United States terms of trade superior even to those of France. Adams's diplomacy overcame the protests of "the most powerful diplomatic representative in Europe, the French Ambassador at St. Petersburg."[19]

The practical effects of Adams's achievements, nevertheless, were negligible. British control of the seas trumped the Russian edict. In fact, concurrent with the headway Adams made in Russia, the British, retaliating against Madison's foolish decision to reopen U.S. ports to French trade but maintain the ban on Britain's, enforced their restrictions and impressed U.S. sailors with greater determination. Congressmen from the West and South demanded that Madison respond. They charged the British with strangling American liberty and prosperity and inciting Indians, such as Tecumseh and his brother, Tenskwatawa the Prophet, to wage war against American frontier settlers. William Henry Harrison's defeat of Tecumseh at the Battle of Tippecanoe bolstered their confidence. America could defeat the British too, thereby putting an end once and for all to Britain's commercial polices, naval practices, and Indian conspiracies. What is more, Henry Clay, John Calhoun, and other "War Hawks" gleefully announced that the first move in this military conflict would be to conquer Canada.

Madison was already a move ahead. Seeking to preempt a British seizure of the Floridas should war erupt, he approved a plan by which between 1810 and 1811 inhabitants in both East and West Florida sympathetic to the United States would stage coups and then request U.S. annexation. That the plot succeeded only in West Florida did not dampen America's war fever. Nor did it diminish the American appetite for East Florida. Satisfying that appetite would just have to wait. In the meantime, Madison collaborated with Congress's War Hawks to declare that Britain's acquisition of Florida from Spain would violate explicit U.S. policy. The "No Transfer" resolution stipulated that the "United States . . . cannot without serious inquietude see any part of the said territory [the Floridas] pass into the hands of any foreign Power."[20]

Adams supported Madison's and the War Hawks' goals. He agreed that Britain's assault on Americans' maritime liberties could not be tolerated. He held that West Florida already belonged to the United States, and for East Florida to remain in foreign control would pose a threat to American security as well as violate nature's laws. Acquiring Canada could present problems for the same reasons that did the Louisiana Territory: constitutional governance. Nevertheless, at a minimum a successful invasion to the north would cement America's claim to valuable fisheries and allow it to hold the remainder of Canada as hostage to British concessions on trade and impressment.

Outweighing a war's potential benefits, however, were the potential costs. Adams doubted that the United States was prepared, and in light of its overlapping political, economic, and even cultural schisms, that it could mobilize resources rapidly enough to compensate. If it could not, the consequences would exacerbate those schisms. Once again American liberty, union, and empire would be at risk. Waging war against the British could easily precipitate a "struggle for the division of the states," he wrote his father. It could also precipitate "changes of administration" and perhaps "of constitutions in our country."[21]

Adams's prescience became evident. Believing that he had run out of diplomatic options, that the public clamor for war was irresistible, and that he could not shirk his responsibility to protect and promote the Empire for Liberty, on June 1, 1812, Madison requested from Congress a declaration of war. He received it, albeit in neither chamber by an overwhelming majority. More ominously, in both chambers the vote went strictly according to party and geographical lines. Madison was certain that the conquest of Canada would compel the British immediately to sue for peace and thereby ameliorate the discord. In the event,

America's invading force suffered a string of embarrassing defeats. Elsewhere the ragtag American military did score some noteworthy victories. Despite Britain's naval mastery, the United States turned back the British on Lake Erie and Lake Champlain, and off the coast of Nova Scotia the USS *Constitution*, "Old Iron Sides," won its legendary face-off with the HMS *Guerriere*. And of course, following up his defeat of the Red Stick Creeks at the Battle of Horseshoe Bend, Alabama, in 1815, General Andrew Jackson triumphed over the British at the Battle of New Orleans.

Strategically none of these victories compensated for the American defeats, and the British retained control of the eastern seaboard. The burning of the White House and many other buildings in the capital dealt a devastating blow to the already reeling national morale, adding impetus to Essex Junto conspirators in New England. At an 1814 meeting in Hartford, Connecticut, they proposed constitutional amendments that would invest them with veto power over questions related to commerce and western expansion. Their allegiance to the United States, they vowed, was contingent on adoption of these amendments.

Adams played a principal role in America's escaping the danger. Virtually concurrent with Congress's approval of Madison's request for a declaration of war, a new British government repealed the onerous orders of council. Even had the news reached Madison sooner, he probably would not have altered his course. Impressment remained Britain's policy, as did its intrigues with American Indians. Further, the opportunity to conquer Canada, which his mentor Thomas Jefferson assured Madison could be accomplished by a "mere matter of marching," was too enticing to pass up. When the plan to attack north crumbled at Detroit and Niagara, however, Madison reconsidered. He was willing to entertain peace talks.[22]

Shortly thereafter the president received from Adams a report of Alexander I's offer to mediate. The same month the United States declared war on Britain, Napoleon invaded Russia. Suddenly Russia's enemy was Britain's, and almost as suddenly Alexander asked Adams about the U.S. government's readiness to accept Russian mediation to end Anglo-American hostilities. The czar wanted London's undivided attention. Without waiting for instructions from Washington, Adams replied that he was sure that Madison would not object and approved

Russia's passing on this judgment to the British. The failure of the American attack on Canada before it reached Canadian soil, which Adams described as a "burlesque upon war" that made America "the scorn and laughter of all Europe," reinforced his pessimistic estimate of U.S. military capabilities. "I can see no good results likely to arise" from the war's continuation, he opined to Secretary of State James Monroe when informing him of the czar's offer. More likely in his view were defeats on the battlefield and "the dismemberment of the American Union." Monroe and Madison concurred. They accepted Czar Alexander's offer without word that Britain had. They then appointed Adams to lead America's negotiating team, naming Secretary of the Treasury Albert Gallatin and Delaware's Federalist senator James Bayard to serve with him.[23]

The British did want to negotiate. They were weary of war and hoped to avoid the expense that sending a major force across the Atlantic would entail. In addition, they were less cocky after suffering naval defeats at the hands of the upstart Yanks. The annihilation of Napoleon's force diminished the urgency of reaching an accommodation with the Americans, however. They also balked at mediation by Russia, which, since the time of the American Revolution, had supported neutral maritime rights. Joined by Gallatin and Bayard in mid-July, Adams waited impatiently in St. Petersburg for instructions. After six months Gallatin and Bayard moved to London to facilitate communications. British foreign minister Robert Stuart, the Viscount Castlereagh, consented to open direct negotiations with the Americans. After further dickering, the parties agreed that the talks would take place in Ghent, Belgium (Flanders). Madison could not act fast enough to confirm the arrangement. He added Henry Clay and Jonathan Russell, like Adams from Massachusetts, to the American commission. Adams, who "knew more about European affairs than any other American," was its chairman. He left St. Petersburg for Ghent at the end of April 1814.[24]

Although frequently rancorous, the negotiations turned out to be something of a nonevent. Their significance to the United States was nonetheless vital. With Castlereagh reserving his strongest diplomats for the conference in Vienna to decide the post-Napoleon configuration of Europe, the American commission bargained with what was essentially Britain's second string, composed of an admiral so undistinguished that the navy had no military role for him, an under-secretary in the ministry of war and colonies, and an admiralty lawyer. That was to the U.S. advantage. It was likewise to their advantage that America's negotiators, Gallatin, Clay, and of course Adams, were capable and willing to take risks. They recognized that the military situation left them without the leverage necessary to expand the American empire. The best they could do was eliminate the fundamental issues that most immediately caused the war, and in fact had poisoned Anglo-American relations for decades: neutral rights and impressment above all. Further, they had to thwart any British gambits intended to chip away pieces of America's current empire or impede its future growth. Adams was especially sensitive to this danger. As a senator he had, over the objections of then–Secretary of State Madison, led the opposition to a proposed settlement of a boundary dispute between Canada and the United States dating to the 1783 Treaty of Paris. Had the treaty been ratified, Britain would have gained direct access to the Mississippi and incorporated into Canada a 150-mile swatch of territory cut from the northern parts of present-day North Dakota, Montana, Idaho, and Washington. For this reason historian Samuel Flagg Bemis called this tract the "Adams Strip."[25]

At Ghent Adams and his fellow peace commissioners refrained from bringing up either Canada or Florida, in the hope that their counterparts would reciprocate by leaving off the table any discussions of boundaries. They planned to concentrate exclusively on maritime issues. The British had other ideas, especially after they received news of the burning of Washington, D.C. They had no intention of making any concessions on either neutral rights or impressment. Further, their set of demands included a favorable adjustment of the northwest boundary but went well beyond it. The American negotiators had to fend off British proposals to lop off chunks of New York and Maine, establish a "neutral" Indian state south of the Great Lakes and bounded by the Mississippi and Ohio Rivers, sanction navigation rights to the Mississippi, and terminate American fishing rights off the Newfoundland coast.

The British commission was no match for the Americans. Castlereagh had so little confidence that he prohibited any member from saying anything without his express permission. Consequently, although their demands provided the British with the initial initiative, they soon forfeited it. The Americans parried each of their thrusts with vigor and imagination. Indeed, more skillful diplomacy was required to keep the peace among the American commissioners than to stymie the British. A dispute between Adams and Clay over what should be a higher priority, retaining American fishing rights off Newfoundland (favored by Adams) or denying British navigation rights to the Mississippi (Clay's fixation) threatened the commission's effectiveness by rendering it hopelessly divided. Gallatin's intervention restored sufficient harmony for the British to conclude they could not crack the American front. Concurrently, the Duke of Wellington, who had commanded the allied forces that defeated Napoleon on the Iberian Peninsula, told Castlereagh point blank that he was more valuable in Europe than in America. Preoccupied with Vienna, the foreign minister instructed his emissaries to offer the United States a peace on the basis of the status quo ante bellum; London and Washington would defer settling most of the outstanding disputes. With the blessing of Madison, Adams was the first of his colleagues to sign the Treaty of Ghent on Christmas Eve, 1814. From his perspective, God had once again protected the American empire. "I cannot close the record of this day," he wrote later that night, "without an humble offering to God for the conclusion to which it has pleased him to bring the negotiations for peace at this place, and a fervent prayer that its result may be propitious to the welfare, the best interests, and the union of my country."[26]

The terms of the Treaty of Ghent resulted more from the environment that Britain confronted in Europe than American diplomacy or divine intervention. Yet regardless of the hierarchy of variables responsible for its final form, the treaty unquestionably served the welfare, interests, and unity of the United States. It cost Americans no territory, and combined with the postwar defeat of the British at New Orleans, it allowed the United States to regain a good measure of its damaged pride. As the historian George C. Herring aptly writes, in the aftermath of the treaty "the United States surged to the level of a second-rank power."[27]

Yet Adams, as always looking to the future, was far from satisfied. With Napoleon defeated, the issues of neutral rights and impressment lost their salience. Moreover, the Hartford Convention turned out to be the Essex Junto's last hurrah. For Adams, accordingly, peacemaking at Ghent was but a way station in his service to the American empire. His subsequent posting in London was likewise. As America's minister plenipotentiary to the Court of St. James from 1815 to 1817, Adams initiated the process of Anglo-American reconciliation that almost a century later provided the framework for the replacement of Pax Britannica by Pax Americana.

This trajectory was not linear. Although Britain and the United States would never again fight a war, they had many close calls. Still, more than any of his predecessors in London, Adams made headway in mitigating historically divisive issues. Only weeks after Wellington's victory at Waterloo ended Napoleon's One Hundred Days campaign to resurrect his empire, Adams, on July 3, 1815, concluded a commercial convention that prohibited discriminatory duties. The convention fell far short of a reciprocal commercial agreement, and it left unmentioned impressment and neutral rights. It was a start nonetheless. In addition Adams laid the foundation for a future settlement that provided for permanent U.S. access to inland Canadian fisheries. His discussions with Viscount Castlereagh, moreover, led directly to the famous deal struck in Washington between Britain's minister to the United States, Charles Bagot, and U.S. acting secretary of state Richard Rush. One of history's few lasting arms control agreements, the Rush-Bagot pact of 1817 demilitarized the Great Lakes. Adams also drafted an omnibus treaty that addressed virtually every outstanding issue. Before it could be consummated, however, in 1817 James Monroe succeeded to the American presidency. He chose as his secretary of state John Quincy Adams.

Adams celebrated his fiftieth birthday shortly before he arrived back in the United States. Short, heavy-set, and bald, he described himself as virtually the polar opposite of Ben Franklin: "I am a man of reserved, cold, austere, and forbidding manners; my political adversaries say, a gloomy misanthropist, and my personal enemies, an unsocial character." Still, no American did more to bring to fruition Franklin's vision of an American empire. That he did was Adams's legacy as secretary of state. Yet his insistence that the American empire truly be one of and for liberty complicates that legacy immensely.[28]

The challenges Adams confronted in 1817 were enormous, as were the opportunities and his ambition to resolve them. His immediate priority was to continue his effort begun at Ghent and carried over to London to eliminate the sources of Anglo-American enmity. He achieved only partial success. His most bitter disappointment was his inability to secure Britain's agreement on commercial reciprocity. In his view, not only was such an agreement vital to the American economy, but also the principle of reciprocity was inextricable from the principles of equality, liberty, and peace. Reciprocal trade was "one of the ingredients of our national independence" Adams expounded. Further, coupled with its cognate, neutral rights, the principle—"founded in justice, humanity, and benevolence" and "enjoined by the Christian precept to love your neighbor as yourself"—promised "a great amelioration in the condition of man."[29]

Despite his failure to obtain his most cherished goal, Adams's orchestration of the Convention of 1818 represents a historic landmark. Completing what Franklin and his father had done, Adams worked with his successor as minister in London, Richard Rush, and his former colleague at Ghent and now minister in Paris, Albert Gallatin, to persuade the British finally to agree that Americans should "have for ever, in common with the Subjects of His Britannic Majesty, the Liberty to take Fish of every kind" off the banks of Newfoundland and Labrador. He settled the long-simmering dispute over America's boundary with Canada west of the Lake of Woods to the Rocky Mountains that denied Britain access to the headwaters of the Mississippi River and confirmed U.S. entitlement to the "Adams Strip." For a ten-year period citizens of both the United States and Great Britain could jointly occupy Oregon Territory, the region that today comprises Canada's British Columbia and the states of Washington and Oregon. The convention also stipulated that with regard to the claims that British soldiers had abducted and or deported slaves from U.S. territory, a neutral third party would determine whether it was Britain's responsibility to provide southern slaveholders with full compensation for the loss of their "private property." At this point in his career Adams was willing to compromise on his opposition to slavery for the purpose of carrying out his duties as America's chief diplomat and smoothing over sectional divisions within the union. That would change. So would his convictions that the conduct of foreign policy should be "strictly an Executive act," and that the extent of Congress's power over it was an "absurdity."[30]

Adams's greatest triumph as secretary of state resulted from his unwillingness to allow any government institution, political dynamic, or, some would say, personal qualm stand in the way of the expanding American empire. What is more, improved Anglo-American relations notwithstanding, Adams vigorously pursued policies to ensure that Britain's hemispheric interests did not handicap, let alone thwart, his imperial design. He set his sights particularly on securing what Madison had failed to achieve in 1811, the annexation of East Florida and the extension of U.S. sovereignty over what was left of the Spanish Empire in North America. British resistance made his task exponentially more difficult.

The behavior of Adams's own countrymen, most notably General Andrew Jackson, exacerbated the problem. The leadership and military skills of "Old Hickory" were invaluable to the young republic, and his victory at the Battle of New Orleans had made him a household name, especially in America's South and West. This victory also fueled his political ambition. Furthermore, the cantankerous Jackson was sure that he knew best about almost anything. He was much better at giving orders than following them. His actions accordingly presented Adams with both obstacles and opportunities. Adams managed the former and exploited the latter.

How the synergy between Jackson and Adams resulted in America's acquisition of East Florida and much more makes for strange and convoluted history. It begins during the War of 1812, when as the commander of the Tennessee militia Jackson led the campaign that crushed the British-assisted Red Stick Creek Indians at Horseshoe Bend. He took for the United States their land, more than twenty-three million acres. The Red Sticks fled south to East Florida but, allying with the Seminoles, continued to conduct raids north into U.S. territory. Madison coveted East Florida. He also heeded the cries for help from white settlers in Alabama and Georgia, both for protection and for the capture of their runaway slaves. Madison ordered Jackson south for all three purposes. The general had to confront three enemies. In addition to the Creeks and Seminoles, there were the Spaniards, who still considered the territory their own and remembered the Americans' earlier efforts to steal it from them. Then there were the British, who had been using the Creeks against the Americans for years. They also for years had supported Spanish control of East Florida in order to deny it to the Americans. Castlereagh had warned Adams that America must stop "pursuing a system of encroachment upon your neighbors."[31]

Jackson was sensitive only to the benefits of annihilating the Creeks and Seminoles and acquiring East Florida. He had received from Secretary of War John Calhoun the instruction to acknowledge Spanish authority "wherever it is maintained" out of fear that a "hostile encounter with Spanish troops might bring the allied powers on us." In tension with that instruction, however, was one to "adopt the necessary measures to terminate a conflict which it has ever been the desire of the President, from motives of humanity, to avoid." Jackson wrote down his interpretation of the instruction in a confidential letter to Monroe: "The Executive government had ordered (and as I conceive, very properly) Amelia Island [off the west coast of Florida, just north of Jacksonville] to be taken possession of; this order ought to be carried into execution at all hazards, and simultaneously, the whole of East Florida seized. . . . [T]he possession of the Floridas would be desirable to the United States, and in sixty days it will be accomplished." Neither Monroe nor Calhoun challenged Jackson's interpretation. Because Indian affairs were the bailiwick of the Department of War, Adams knew nothing of either the instructions or Jackson's interpretation of them.[32]

For Jackson, Monroe's silence meant his consent. He was probably correct, although we will never know for sure. What matters is the chain of events that followed. With a force of some 3,000 men Jackson steamrolled through Florida, smashing all Indian resistance and pursuing the fleeing Creeks and Seminoles to the eastern town of St. Marks, which he occupied. Jackson then deployed his forces to the west, taking possession of Pensacola. The Spanish protested. So should have the British. Along the way, Jackson also captured and summarily executed by firing squad Robert Ambrister, a former British army lieutenant turned mercenary whom Jackson charged (perhaps correctly but never proven) with conspiring with the Indians. Even more egregious was the justice he dispensed to Alexander Arbuthnot, a Scottish trader who Jackson believed was in league with the Seminoles and Creeks. Old Hickory had him hanged.

Jackson had deviated from his letter to Monroe only by taking ten weeks to complete his mission. Attesting to its improved relations with the United States and recognition that the Spanish were powerless to contain American "encroachment," London turned a blind eye to the episode. The only protests that had the potential to undo what Jackson had done came from within Monroe's own cabinet. Secretary Calhoun and William Crawford, Calhoun's predecessor as the head of the War Department but by 1818 secretary of the Treasury, did not object to wresting territory from Spain or executing a few British subjects. They objected to Jackson's responsibility for doing it. Each hoped to be the president after Monroe, and saw the growing legend of Andrew Jackson as a major obstacle. They beseeched Monroe to take him to task. As Adams recounted a cabinet meeting, they excoriated Jackson for acting "not only without, but against, his instructions; that he has committed war upon Spain, which cannot be justified, and in which, if not disavowed by the Administration, they [the president and his cabinet] will be abandoned by the country." They recommended that Monroe restore Florida to the Spanish Crown.[33]

The cabinet's lone dissenter was John Quincy Adams. He also wanted to be president, and as the secretary of state he was by precedent the frontrunner. Jackson was probably the only contender who could derail his candidacy. Adams also considered the rough-hewn general unsuitable to lead the nation. More important to Adams, however, was the growth and security of the American empire, and he recognized that the impetuous general could help him attain both. Before Jackson took matters into his own hands, Adams had begun negotiations with the Spanish minister, Juan de Onís, to acquire Florida as well as the Rio Grande River as the western boundary of the Louisiana Territory. He hoped that the deterioration of Spanish power in the hemisphere, most evident by revolts throughout its extensive South and Central American possessions but manifest in the number of American filibusterers as well, would provide Madrid with the incentive to strike a deal with Washington before Americans took the disputed territory without Spain receiving anything in return. Adams planned to throw into the bargain a U.S. pledge not to recognize the emerging nations south of its border. But he could get nowhere with Onís, whose experience in foreign affairs rivaled that of Adams and who was from the secretary of state's point of view "the first man I have ever met who made it a point of honor to pass for more of a swindler than he was."[34]

If Adams did not outswindle the swindler, he did not miss by much. Frequently a fine line distinguishes a swindler from an effective diplomatist. Putting aside his own ambitions and contempt for Jackson, Adams seized on the invasion of Florida as an opportunity to break the deadlock with Onís. Whereas his fellow cabinet members lambasted Jackson and implored Monroe to censor him, Adams defended Jackson so that he could exploit him. Taking on Calhoun, Crawford, and the others, Adams presented Monroe with his "opinion . . . that there was no real, though an apparent, violation of his instructions; that his proceedings were justified by the necessity of the case, and by the misconduct of the Spanish commanding officers in Florida." To disavow Jackson's conduct would be "a confession of weakness" and a "disclaimer of power in the Executive [that would be] of dangerous example and of evil consequences."[35]

Adams carried the day. With the blessing of Monroe, a week following this momentous cabinet meeting at which these contending opinions of Jackson's actions were expressed, Adams responded to Onís's complaints about Jackson's assault and occupation of Florida. Jackson was reacting, the secretary of state wrote on July 23, 1818, to "a series of events which necessitated and justified the entrance of the troops of the United States upon the Spanish boundary of Florida, and gave occasion to those transactions of the commander of the American forces against which you complain." Adams then combined what the historians Fred Anderson and Andrew Cayton call "just war ideology" with what the historian Richard Drinnon calls the "racism he shared with his countrymen" to articulate a doctrine of the right to defensive war. Adams reminded Onís that Americans living on the "frontier" of Georgia and Alabama "had been exposed to the depredations, murders, and massacres of a tribe of savages, a small part of which lived within the limits of the United States, far the greater number of them dwelling within the borders of Florida." It was Spain's obligation to "restrain them by force" from committing these atrocities. It could not. Hence "the immutable principles of self-defense" justified Jackson's behavior.[36]

Having made his case to the Spanish, Adams presented it to the British in order to preempt any intervention London might be considering and to put it on notice of America's intentions. "The right of the

United States can as little compound with impotence as with perfidy," he wrote in a state paper that he circulated to London in advance. Hence "Spain must immediately make her election, either to place a force in Florida adequate at once to the protection of her territory and to the fulfillment of her engagements, or cede to the United States a province, of which she retains nothing but the nominal possession, but which is, in fact, a derelict, open to the occupancy of every enemy, civilized or savage, of the United States, and serving no other earthly purpose than as a post of annoyance to them."[37]

Adams's argument left Onís defenseless. Britain's tacit approval, or at least acquiescence, to the state paper left Spain isolated. Adams pushed his advantage. With Onís resigned to surrendering (though managing to obtain a pledge that the United States would assume responsibility for the $5 million American citizens claimed as an indemnity from Spain for Indian raids) Florida by ceding the East and dropping its resistance to American occupation of the West, Adams demanded a western boundary of Louisiana that included all of Texas. Onís balked. On the verge of losing all the Spaniards who lived in Mexico, Spain "could not abandon without humiliation" the population of Texas as well. To his "astonishment," Adams received instructions from Monroe to drop the issue. "The President thought it was not a point upon which we should endanger the conclusion of the treaty," a chagrined Adams noted in his memoir.[38]

A concession Adams won without any interference from the White House or "assistance" from Jackson compensated. Based solely on his conviction that American possession of the Oregon Territory was a law of nature, Adams put on the table Spain's claim to it. As a warranty that the United States would not renege on either Texas or the $5 million indemnity, Onís handed Oregon to him—in fact, he handed over all Spanish land north of the forty-second parallel from the Rocky Mountains to the Pacific Ocean without a fight. Spain's "acknowledgement of a definite line of boundary to the South Sea forms a great epocha [*sic*] in our history," Adams proclaimed. His biographer used more flowery language to describe Adams's accomplishment. "It was Adams, and Adams alone, who saw the opening for a break through to the Pacific. It was a brilliant plunge. Oregon was his most massive contribution to Manifest Destiny. Even without Texas the Transcontinental Treaty with

Spain was the greatest diplomatic victory won by any single individual in the history of the United States."[39]

Adams and Onís signed the Transcontinental Treaty on February 22, 1819. Adams had insisted on Washington's birthday. The nation's first president had predicted America's rising empire, and Adams had made good on that prediction. "[I] closed the day . . . with ejaculations of fervent gratitude to the Giver of all good," he rejoiced. Adams probably could have gotten Texas, or at least much of it. Unjustly he received criticism for not doing so. Adams was accustomed to criticism. He knew the truth. He was also certain that the United States would acquire Texas eventually. In time, "The world shall be familiarized with the idea of considering our proper dominion to be the continent of North America."[40]

Because there were those in Spain who thought Onís had given up too much and in the United States who thought Adams had gotten too little, not until 1821 did the treaty go into effect. By that time Adams's disappointment over Texas had lessened considerably. He still believed ardently that it could and should be American property. But he had developed serious misgivings about the dangers acquiring Texas would present to an American Empire for Liberty. The year 1819 turned out to be pivotal in the national debates over both expansion and liberty. Even as Adams negotiated with Onís over Florida, Texas, and Oregon, the Panic of 1819 intensified domestic strife. A concurrent opinion by Supreme Court chief justice John Marshall in *McCulloch v. Maryland* raised the stakes higher. In ruling in favor of the constitutionality of Second National Bank, long opposed by southern and now western constituents, Marshall appeared to confirm that the federal government could exercise power over states sufficient to prohibit slavery, long supported by the same constituents. Southerners perceived their liberty at risk.

Adams's Transcontinental Treaty made the issue more explosive. Juxtaposed with the applications for admission to the union of states carved out of the Louisiana Purchase, what some southerners considered a pernicious trade of Texas for Oregon brought to the fore the precarious balance between pro- and antislave votes in Congress. Elevating these suspicions was the simultaneous battle raging over the admission of Missouri, which would add to the slave state column.

In 1820 Henry Clay temporarily put out the fire by orchestrating the Missouri Compromise. It offset the admission of Missouri with that of Maine (formerly integrated with Massachusetts) and bisected the Louisiana Purchase at 36°30'. There could be no slavery north of that line.

Adams identified slavery as an evil that "pervert[ed] human reason" and "taint[ed] the very sources of moral principle"; he wanted it banned everywhere. For the sake of the union, nevertheless, he hoped the Peculiar Institution would die a natural death. The emotional controversy over Missouri assured that it would not. The controversy that Texas would provoke was sure to be even more emotional, and the consequences much worse. The "greatest danger of this Union was in the overgrown extent of its territory, combining with the slavery question," Adams reflected less than a year after consummating the treaty with Spain. He then spelled out the danger. "Since the Missouri debate, I considered the continuance of the Union for any length of time as very precarious, and entertained serious doubts whether Louisiana and slavery would not ultimately break us up." He did not mention Texas. He did not need to. Adams foresaw that expansion, the putative savior of the American empire, would become its greatest enemy.[41]

Adams's concerns about empire and liberty, and the enemies to both, dominated his second term as secretary of state. At home the economy recovered, but there was no relief from the sectional rancor over slavery that America's expansion had aggravated. Abroad, the upheavals that afflicted the aging empires endangered America's. Many of the same Americans who denied liberty to slaves (and Indians) in America crusaded for Washington's support for states and populations battling for their liberty against imperial oppressors. In eastern Europe the Greek revolt against the Ottomans threatened to consume the Balkans, where Austria's hold was tenuous. Within America's own neighborhood most of the Spanish Empire had already disintegrated. On one level Adams sympathized with the emerging Latin American nations. But he did not empathize. Adams was too convinced of U.S. exceptionalism to equate its revolution with theirs, or to equate their independence with the promotion of liberty. His "mental image of the peoples to the south," conceded Adams's most ardent champion, "reflected an ignorant miscegenated populace benighted by centuries of political and ecclesiastical tyranny, doubtfully capable of self-government, hardly profitable for the communion of free men."[42]

Adams's anxiety transcended ideology and culture. He feared that American intervention on behalf of Latin American insurgents would create geopolitical vacuums that U.S. slaveholders would seek to fill. He also feared the potential of a war, possibly with Britain, which had its own agenda. Consequently, when invited by Congress in 1821 to deliver the July 4 address in the nation's capital, Adams used the occasion to admonish all Americans to curb their enthusiasm over others' revolutions. Adams was obviously not an isolationist. But he was a firm believer in George Washington's caution against international political entanglements. America had to devote its full attention, energy, and resources to cementing liberty within the United States. He waxed grandiloquent: "Whenever the standard of freedom and independence has been or shall be unfurled, there will her [America's] heart, her benedictions and her prayers be. But she goes not go abroad in search of monsters to destroy. She is the well-wisher to the freedom and independence of all. She is the champion and vindicator only of her own. . . . She well knows that by once enlisting under other banners than her own, were they even the banners of foreign independence, . . . [t]he fundamental maxims of her policy would insensibly change from liberty to force. . . . She might become the dictatress of the world. She would be no longer the ruler of her own spirit."[43]

Anxious Americans quoted Adams's words approvingly following the extension of the U.S. empire overseas at the end of the nineteenth century and after. They had less effect at the time Adams uttered them. The dim clamor in favor of providing assistance to the rebellious Greeks was insufficient to garner Monroe's support. But with evidence of the Spanish defeat unambiguous, the president mandated that the United States recognize the new Latin American nations. He rationalized that if the new nations had any chance to develop political institutions and commercial policies compatible with those of the United States, Washington had to guide them. More important, Adams had also reached the judgment that America's passivity toward its southern neighbors might endanger America's emergence as the prevailing power in the hemisphere.

Adams worried that should the United States stay out of Latin America, nations from Europe would move in. He was not imagining the peril. In 1821 Alexander I had issued an ukase claiming Russia's unilateral control of the Oregon Territory, which because of Adams's diplomacy the United States now shared with Britain. Alexander backed off when Adams, with a strong British second, protested. The incident would have been minor were it not for its implications for Adams. The ukase signaled to the secretary of state that foreign nations retained ambitions to stake new claims in the Western Hemisphere, thereby posing a threat to American security and an affront to its destiny and perhaps even its liberty. Hence he unilaterally declared that henceforth the "American continents . . . will no longer be subjects of colonization." At the same time Adams told Stratford Canning, Britain's minister to the United States, that America had no intention of challenging British control of territory to which it was currently entitled to by treaty. "But," he ended the conversation, "leave the rest of the continent to us."[44]

Adams was not overly concerned about the British. The two empires had fought their wars and arrived at something of a modus vivendi. The situation was very different with Russia and other European powers. With the defeat of Napoleon, Alexander had taken the initiative in organizing a Holy Alliance, ostensibly for the purpose of spreading Christian values of peace and justice. By 1822, however, the mission of the alliance, which included now France as well as Austria, Prussia, and of course Russia, was more narrow: the suppression of nationalist revolutions. In its name Austria had intervened to reinstate monarchical rule in Italy, and so had France in Spain. Adams now learned that this conservative alliance was considering intervening in Latin American to restore "the supremacy of Spain over the revolted colonies." Albeit confirmed by the Russians themselves, this intelligence first came to Adams from the U.S. minister to Great Britain, Richard Rush, who had received it from British foreign minister George Canning. Rush also sent along a proposal from Canning. The Americans and British should respond to this threat to the freedom and independence of the new nations of Latin America by jointly announcing that the continent was henceforth closed to European colonization—or recolonization.

To prove their genuine commitment to the principle, each would fore-swear forever any intention of grabbing any more territory.[45]

Monroe, with the approval of both Jefferson and Madison as well as Calhoun and others in his cabinet, thought the offer too good for the United States to refuse. Adams thought it so good that the United States *should* refuse. Canning was less friendly to America than had been his rival Castlereagh, who had committed suicide in August. Brit-ain cared more about Latin America's trade than about its liberty and independence. "The revolution in South America has opened a new world to her commerce," Adams recognized, "which the restoration of the Spanish colonial dominion would close to them." Sharing credit with the British for defending Latin Americans would handicap U.S. efforts to gain a larger share of that trade. Further, his trepidation about America's acquiring Texas notwithstanding, Adams was certain that it would. And it would probably obtain Cuba, too, which by reason of geopolitical "gravitation" would inexorably move toward the U.S. "bosom," much as an "apple severed by the tempest from its native tree cannot choose but fall to the ground." Adams, therefore, coun-seled that it was against the American interest to "tie ourselves down to any principle which might immediately afterwards be brought to bear against ourselves." In addition, a joint announcement would call attention to America's junior status. The United States should make the announcement unilaterally. Adams argued that "it would be more candid, as well as more dignified, to avow our principles explicitly to Russia and France, than to come in as a cock-boat in the wake of the British man-of-war."[46]

On November 23, 1823, Adams once again took on Monroe and the remainder of the cabinet. Once again, the force of his arguments pro-duced a watershed in the extension of America's imperial reach. In-corporating Adams's diagnoses and prescriptions into his December 2 annual address to Congress, the president articulated three principles that collectively became known as the Monroe Doctrine. In both form and substance, nevertheless, the principles were Adams's. The first, which Adams developed initially when confronted with Alexander's I's ukase, declared the Western Hemisphere off limits to "future coloniza-tion by any European power." America would expand its hemispheric preserve, Adams was confident, but not by colonization. A second principle would facilitate this process. "We should consider any attempt on their [the European powers] part to extend their system to any portion of this hemisphere as dangerous to our peace and safety." Hence the United States was no less opposed to the extension of European influence and informal control. The third principle pledged that in return the United States would abstain from involving itself in "matters relating to" European powers in their sphere on the globe. This principle reflected Adams's devotion to reciprocity as well as Washington's Farewell Address. But it was also a device to put an end to the continuing domestic agitation in favor of support for the Greek Revolution.

Adams was no less responsible for the Monroe Doctrine than he was for the Transcontinental Treaty, and he was no less gratified by his accomplishment. Although America would need to rely on British power to enforce the principles, John Bull would perform its deeds on behalf of Uncle Sam's words. What is more, from Adam's perspective the U.S. anticolonization declaration brought the world a major step closer to his interpretation of the meaning of the American Revolution. The "great colonial establishments are engines of wrong" and "cannot fulfill the great objects of governments in the just purposes of civil society," he confided in private letter. "In the progress of social improvement it will be the duty of the human family to abolish them." Their abolition would extend the area of liberty. Thus, certain as he was that continued America expansion was a natural, inevitable, and indeed providentially ordained process, abolishing Europe's colonies was a precondition for the future American Empire for Liberty. Viewed in this light, the Monroe Doctrine "was inseparable from the continental expansion of the United States. It was a voice of Manifest Destiny," as Samuel Flagg Bemis rightly comments.[47]

Notwithstanding the principles espoused in the Monroe Doctrine, by the time Monroe gave voice to them Adams was anguishing over the divergence between Manifest Destiny and the Empire for Liberty. It could not have been otherwise. The more forcefully he demanded the abolition of colonization, the more difficult it became to divorce the expansion of U.S. territory from the expansion of slavery. For this reason Adams concluded that the compromise reached over Missouri had been a grave mistake. The antislavery states should have drawn a line in the sand. Doing so would have provided impetus for their "rallying to their standard the other States by the universal emancipation of their slaves." Theirs would have been a "great and glorious object."[48]

Adams never proposed such brinkmanship. The union would not have survived. He wanted it to survive, and he wanted to be its president. Consequently, his problem with slavery "laid asleep" as he engineered the Transcontinental Treaty and the Monroe Doctrine.[49] His unparalleled successes as secretary of state were a major reason for his capturing the White House in 1824, but not for the reasons that Franklin and the other Founding Fathers envisioned. They held that American expansion would produce a pluralistic society even as it satisfied the multitudinous factions. As attested to by the 1824 election, however, American expansion had produced a society suffused with irreconcilable factions that reflected sectional divisions. Adams received fewer popular votes than Andrew Jackson. But neither received the requisite majority in the Electoral College; Henry Clay and Georgia's William Crawford were also on the ballot. It thus fell to the House of Representatives to decide the winner. Clay, the House speaker, announced his support of Adams. The House voted to elect Adams president.

Adams chose Clay as his secretary of state. Combined with Adams's minority vote, suspicions that the two had made a corrupt deal militated against their taking any bold initiatives. Adams did renew for twenty years the agreement with Britain for the joint occupation of Oregon, and he overcame congressional opposition to U.S. representation at a meeting of the Latin American nations in Panama. It took so long for Congress to appropriate the funds for the delegates to attend, however, that one died en route and the other arrived too late to participate. In addition, persuaded by Clay that acquiring Texas would generate support from the West, and optimistic that he could keep it free of slavery, Adams opened negotiations with Mexico to extend the U.S. southwestern boundary to the Rio Grande or at least the Colorado River. Mexican resistance doomed the effort.

Adams accepted the setback with more equanimity than he had past failures. More empire could wait. The time had come to consolidate and develop the territory already acquired. He promoted an agenda of internal improvements—roads, canals, a national university, and more, paid for through tariffs secured by national banks and stable currency. His "American System" would overcome sectional divisions, unifying the disparate factions. This program of centralization contradicted the emphasis on mass democracy and states' rights that formed the core of Jackson's platform. Adams never stood a chance. After the 1828 election he joined with his father to comprise the fraternity of American single-term presidents.

Depressed as well as disappointed, Adams lamented that "the sun of my political life sets in the deepest gloom." He expected to react as his father did: live out his life in retirement in Braintree (by then Quincy). His congressional district in Massachusetts, dominated by the National Republican and fledgling Anti-Mason parties, had other ideas. Midway through Jackson's first administration, it returned Adams to Washington as the only former president in U.S. history to serve in the House of Representatives. His role in guiding and defining America's empire changed dramatically. By the 1830s Americans competed only with Indians and Mexicans to populate the entire continent. As Franklin before him, Adams believed it was Americans' destiny to win this competition. A civilized, as opposed to savage, nation, the United States had a "moral and religious duty" to develop its lands. But as Jefferson before him, he hoped that Indians would ultimately embrace that destiny and assimilate, at least to the limits of their capability.[50]

From Jackson, with his frontier spirit and take-no-prisoners philosophy, arose a variant on Franklin's and Adams's concept of Manifest Destiny (a term coined by John L. O'Sullivan in the Jacksonian *Democratic Review*). Because God chose Americans to spread liberty and civilization across the continent, Jackson believed and O'Sullivan wrote, it stood to reason that non-Americans, no less than "kings, hierarchs, and oligarchs," were the enemies of liberty and civilization, whom it was the duty of Americans to "smite unto death." For evidence, Jackson had to look no farther than his wars against the Red Sticks and the Seminoles. These Indians identified settlers as trespassers and murdered them. Jackson, consequently, arrived in the White House convinced that Natives to America were irreconcilably hostile to God's design for America. The Indian, he said, "is unwilling to submit to the laws and the States and mingle with their population." His policy was to remove them to land not yet occupied by Americans, or if that was not possible, to annihilate them. In some cases, most notably the Cherokees of Georgia, forced removal meant extermination. Congressman John Quincy Adams was aghast. He indicted Jackson for the "extermination of the Indians whom we have been driving like swine into a pen west of the Mississippi."[51]

The historian Anders Stephanson writes that, juxtaposed with Adams's disappointment in his own presidency, Jackson's policies "open[ed] his [Adams's] eyes" to the perception that American expansion was "no longer the fulfillment of God's promise but a "disgraceful, tyrannical usurpation of the national purpose." Stephanson exaggerates. Shortly before his death Adams was one of a small minority in Congress who as late as 1846 urged the Jacksonian president James K. Polk to reject a northern boundary of the Oregon Territory short of the latitude 54°40'. Congressman Adams remained adamant that the territory was of a single piece, and it was rightfully America's. Britain sought to keep Oregon "a wilderness of savage hunters," he explained. The United States sought to "fulfill the commands of Almighty God to increase and multiply and replenish and subdue the Earth."[52]

Yet Stephanson is more right than wrong. Adams pursued territory in the American Northwest beyond what Polk settled for (the forty-ninth parallel) owing to his confidence that it could be obtained through negotiations. His diplomatic triumphs had all resulted from diplomacy. Further, the Oregon Territory was appropriate for an Empire for Liberty because it was inappropriate for slavery. Hence while its acquisition was dictated by the tenets of Jacksonian Democrats' ideology of Manifest Destiny (in contrast to Adams's ideology of Manifest Destiny), this was an anomaly in terms of their specific expansionist agenda. At the top of that agenda was Texas. The instrument for acquiring it was war. And this war for Texas served the interests of slavery, not liberty. As such it was a "disgraceful, tyrannical usurpation of the national purpose."

A great paradox in U.S. history is that Adams's congressional service is best remembered for his opposition to slavery and the annexation of Texas. He had always opposed slavery. Yet his commitment to union and empire had compelled him to keep his contempt for the institution largely to himself. As for Texas, only on Monroe's orders did he discontinue his quest to include it in the Transcontinental Treaty,

and he had tried to remedy that when he was president. The prevailing political culture caused him to reverse his position on both
issues when he returned to Washington. The year 1831 was also when
William Lloyd Garrison published the first issue of the *Liberator*, and
the Great Religious Revival of that decade generated a groundswell of
support in the North for his abolitionist cause. The abolitionists' call
for immediate emancipation intensified the southern slaveholders' insistence on state sovereignty, which they averred was the purest form
of liberty. At the same time they insisted that their plantation economy
required more land in order to replace the depleted soil in the Southeast and increase their representation in Congress to ward off abolitionists dedicated to destroying that economy. They coveted Texas as
the solution to each of these problems.

The pivotal year was 1836. Over the previous dozen or so years,
thousands of Americans, along with thousands of their slaves, had
emigrated to Texas in search of cheap land. By so great a margin did
they outnumber the Mexicans that Mexico's dictator, Antonio López
de Santa Anna, abolished slavery and reinforced his federal authority
by eliminating the state legislature. In 1835 the Texans rebelled. After
following up their heroic stand at the Alamo with a smashing victory
at San Jacinto the next year, the Texans gained their independence.
Meanwhile, in Washington the slavery issue took an ominous turn.
Congress had received a growing stream of petitions demanding the
abolition of slavery in the nation's capital. John C. Calhoun proposed
that the Senate refuse to consider any of them. He thundered that
slavery's future was an issue for the states to decide, not the federal
government. The Senate would not go as far as Calhoun wanted. But
it did enact a "gag rule." It would avoid a vote on whether to accept a
petition by voting on whether it should vote to accept the petition. The
House followed suit in May by enacting a somewhat less convoluted
measure. It would receive the abolitionists' petitions but take no action
on them.

Approaching his seventieth birthday, nominally a Whig but always
independent, Adams had yet to denounce slavery publicly. Union and
empire always took precedence. The conjunction of Texas's declaration of independence, which evoked immediate calls for annexation
from the South and the West, and this legislative assault on Americans'

civil liberties forced his hand. "Am I gagged or am I not?" he famously shouted from the House floor. Then, as the debate continued, Adams, earning the nickname "Old Man Eloquent" (to some he was the "Massachusetts Madman"), expressed what was really on his mind, and on the minds of his fellow representatives and their constituents. He charged that the proslavery forces that controlled the White House and Congress would stop at nothing to ensure the abomination's continuance. Because the intention of both the gag rule and the annexation of Texas were to achieve this end, they were inseparable, intolerable, and symptomatic of an empire gone wrong. "Are you not large and unwieldy enough already? Have you not Indians enough to expel from the land of their fathers' sepulchre?" he intoned. Further, Adams predicted that the slaveholders' aggressive effort to annex Texas could well lead to war, definitely with Mexico, probably with England, perhaps with France. "Mr. Chairman," Adams asked Speaker of the House and future president James K. Polk, from Jackson's home state of Tennessee and a slaveholder himself, "are you ready for all these wars? A Mexican war? A war with Great Britain, if not with France? A general Indian war? A servile war? And, as an inevitable consequence of them all, a civil war?"[53]

Polk was ready. It took a decade more and his presidency for America to wage war with Mexico, and fifteen years after that for America's Civil War to erupt. Adams lived long enough only for the former. But that was sufficient time for him to define his life as a failure. No one had done or would do more than John Quincy Adams to create an American Empire for Liberty. For him, spreading liberty was integral to God's design. It was also integral to American power. "Liberty is power," Adams proclaimed in his first annual message as president. "The nation blessed with the largest portion of liberty must in proportion to its numbers be the most powerful nation upon earth." This premise framed his behavior and attitudes as a congressman decades later. In 1845 Adams referred to President John Tyler's use of a joint resolution of both congressional chambers to effect the annexation of Texas despite the refusal of the Senate to ratify the treaty as "the heaviest calamity that ever befell myself and my country."[54]

President Polk's manipulation of Congress a year later, after Mexicans and Americans exchanged fire on the banks of the Rio Grande, to induce it to recognize that a state of war existed (he never requested a declaration of war) confirmed for Adams that the United States had become weak. The subject of multiple resolutions in the House that he "be brought to the bar to receive the severe censure of the Speaker" for his refusal to concede to the gag rule, in 1846 he was one of but fourteen in that chamber to vote against recognizing that America was at war with Mexico.[55] Adams never voted to withhold appropriations from the soldiers, but neither would he vote even once to decorate or honor them. On February 20, 1848, news reached Washington that several weeks earlier a treaty to end the war had been signed at Guadalupe Hidalgo, north of Mexico City. By its terms Mexico would acknowledge America's annexation of Texas and sell to the United States territory that comprises present-day California, Arizona, New Mexico, Nevada, Utah, and parts of Colorado and Wyoming. The next day Adams prepared to cast his final vote against a resolution to commend America's victorious generals. While waiting for his name to be called, he slumped over his desk. At age eighty, he had suffered a massive stroke. Adams died two days later, his body never having left the capitol building.

CHAPTER 3

William Henry Seward Reimagines
the American Empire

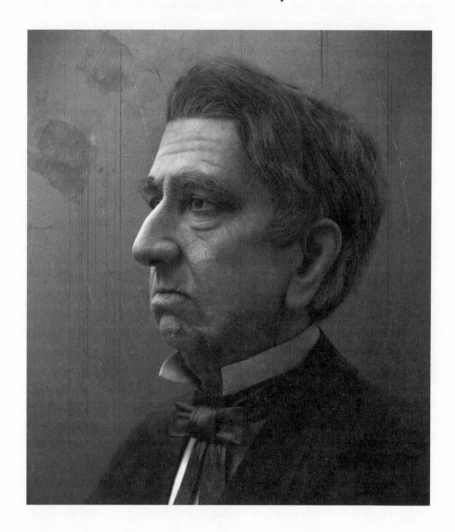

J OHN QUINCY ADAMS was the most resolute and celebrated opponent of "Mr. Polk's War" of conquest against Mexico. Yet in
contrast to most of the domestic battles he waged as secretary
of state, in this case he had staunch allies. Recognizing that he would
probably not live long enough to witness the climax of America's current conflicts, particularly that over slavery, Adams encouraged a select cohort of young disciples to carry on the cause. In addition to
his son Charles Frances, chief among them were Charles Sumner, the
senator from his home state of Massachusetts, and a junior congressman from New York named William Henry Seward.

Within the context of the Mexican War each would proudly serve
as Adams's standard bearer, but it was Seward who subsequently re-
vived, albeit in a different form, Adams's ideal of an American empire.
Considered by many scholars second only to Adams in the pantheon
of American secretaries of state, he was "the pioneering figure before the Civil War to recast territorial empire into a commercial" one.
Seward's successors accomplished much more than he did. But "none
could approach his vision of American empire." Seward was confident
that along with its material goods the United States would export its
values and principles. In this way expanding "not by force of arms, but
by attraction," America would become a true Empire for Liberty.[1]

Although in terms of background, pedigree, and demeanor the two
men could hardly have been more different, Adams was Seward's
model and inspiration. "I have lost a patron, a guide, a counsellor, and
a friend—one whom I loved scarcely less than the dearest relations,
and venerated above all that was mortal among men," he eulogized his
fallen hero. The next year he became Adams's first biographer, dedicating his volume to the "friends of equal liberty and human rights
throughout the world." That the slender, dishevelled, beak-nosed, cigar-
smoking, highly partisan, and monotone-speaking Seward would forever be linked to the indomitable, aloof, and slightly rotund "Old Man
Eloquent" appears incongruous but speaks volumes about the early
American Republic's political culture. In contrast to Adams, nothing
about Seward's personal history or early life provided even a hint of the
extent to which he would influence the course of America's empire.[2]

Born on May 16, 1801, shortly after Jefferson's inauguration signaled the end of the Federalist era and the beginning of America's

explicit quest for an Empire for Liberty, Seward grew up in the small village of Florida in Orange County, New York. Samuel, his father, was a Jefferson Republican who occupied a number of low-level political positions while pursuing with moderate success a variety of careers ranging from physician to land speculator. Harry, as Seward was called, was only fifteen when he went north to Schenectady to attend Union College. Taking time off to travel to Georgia, where for a short while he taught school in Savannah, he took a somewhat cavalier attitude toward his studies. Seward nevertheless graduated Phi Beta Kappa in 1822, after which he returned to Orange County to read law in Goshen. Admitted to the New York bar two years later, in 1824 he married Frances ("Fan") Adelaide Miller, the daughter of his law partner, Judge Elijah Miller. They settled not far from Buffalo in Auburn, where when not in Washington Seward lived for the rest of his life.

The young Seward paid scant attention to politics. Even the War of 1812 had little effect on his worldview. Perhaps influenced by his father-in-law, however, in 1824 he abandoned his Jeffersonian heritage and supported John Quincy Adams for the presidency. Seward liked Adams's promotion of education and internal reforms, which he believed would benefit upstate New York. More important in explaining Seward's conversion was ambition, on the one hand, and, on the other, his contempt for Martin Van Buren. To Seward, Van Buren's New York Democratic machine, the so-called Albany Regency, was thoroughly corrupt.

With Adams's defeat in 1828 Seward, like the former president, gravitated toward the Anti-Mason Party. The first formal "third party" in U.S. history, the Anti-Masons, loosely united by its conspiratorial concern with the subversive influence of secret societies (like the Freemasons) on the government, had been founded in New York in 1827. Because it represented the most effective opposition to the Albany Regency, it quickly became a force in the state. Opportunistically tying his fortunes to the journalist Thurlow Weed, Seward rose to a position of leadership. He became acquainted with Adams as a consequence. When the no-less politically amorphous Whigs consumed the Anti-Masons in 1834, Seward and Weed became the kingpins of the New York Whigs. In 1838, two years after Van Buren captured the White House, New Yorkers elected the Whig William Henry Seward their governor.

During his campaign Seward boasted that under his governorship the Hudson River would become "the true and proper seat of commerce and empire." Not even the candidate appreciated the significance of his rhetoric. Moreover, during Seward's two-term tenure in Albany he paid little attention to either commerce or empire. He owed his election to the blame Van Buren received for the financial Panic of 1837 and the efforts of the incumbent governor, the Democrat William Marcy, to dampen New Yorkers outrage over the *Caroline* affair. An American-owned steamer used to provide men and supplies to the Canadian rebel William MacKenzie on the northern side of the Niagara River, the *Caroline* had been burned and tossed over the falls by a group of British and Canadian Royalists. The attack caused the death of Amos Durfee, a U.S. citizen, producing intense anti-British sentiment throughout upstate New York. Seward's posture during the campaign was to avoid taking any side, thereby leaving Marcy to squirm between the two.[3]

What role the *Caroline* affair played in the election's outcome cannot be precisely established. What can is that Seward distinguished himself more as a politician than as a statesman. Further, while in office, more important than managing the *Caroline* affair's fall-out was Seward's resistance to efforts by Secretary of State Daniel Webster to insert the federal government into what Seward insisted was a state affair. Under Seward's watch in 1840 a New York grand jury indicted the Canadian Alexander McLeod for Durfee's murder, and the state Supreme Court directed him to stand trial in Utica. Britain's foreign secretary, the imperious Lord Palmerston (Henry John Temple), demanded McLeod's release on the grounds that New York lacked the authority to try a Canadian (i.e., British) citizen. The Anglophile Webster sought to have the charges dropped lest they poison Anglo-American relations. Seward scored points with the New York electorate by insisting on the state's prerogative. He won the skirmish, but there really were not any losers. McLeod was tried but promptly acquitted.

For Seward the primary consequence of the *Caroline* affair and subsequent events was to accelerate his alienation from the Whigs in Washington. Indeed, albeit impossible to predict at the time, the dynamics within the Whig Party were to profoundly affect Seward's career—and American history. In particular, the death of President William Henry Harrison a month after his inauguration in 1841 brought to the White House John Tyler, a Virginian who opposed internal improvements and a national bank and supported slavery and the annexation of Texas. At the national level Webster, in contrast most notably to Henry Clay, supported Tyler. The Whig Party began to fracture. Seward, a proponent of internal improvements and the national bank who had long been cool toward Webster, would have sided against Tyler regardless. The controversy over McLeod's trial reinforced this predisposition. The strife within the Whigs forced Seward for the first time to confront the issue of slavery and, by extension, the tension between American expansion and human liberty.

Like any American, especially any American politician, Seward was not agnostic about slavery. Although in practice he did not believe in equality between blacks and whites, in principle he believed that blacks and whites shared equal rights. On an ethical level he considered "human bondage as a great moral and political evil." As early as the 1820s Seward expressed his support for federal legislation aimed at emancipating slaves. Racial prejudice pervaded upstate New York, however, and during his initial years as a politician Seward thought it prudent to keep his distance from the antislavery cause.[4]

By the time of his election as governor, the abolitionist movement had gained momentum and increased its power in New York, especially in the central and western counties that constituted Seward's base. He deemed the time right to go public with his views. Seward garnered much national attention by resisting the efforts of the governor of Virginia to surrender to that state three black sailors from New York accused of helping the escape of Virginia slaves. He declared that New York did not recognize their behavior as a crime. Moving beyond the current position of the Supreme Court, Seward asserted that regardless of race no man could "by the force of any human constitution or laws be converted into chattel or a thing in which another being like himself can have property." Soon the controversy spread as other states came to Virginia's support. Seward attracted the support of the New York legislature and, more important in the long term, John Quincy Adams and leading abolitionists. Seward's stance on slavery gained him his initial national prominence.[5]

Because Seward's conflict with the Virginia governor over the fugitive slaves coincided with his conflict with Tyler (and Webster) over the charges against McLeod, the New Yorker ascended to prominence as a perceived leader of the liberal, antislavery Whigs. This was the early 1840s, a time when the juxtaposition of the "doctrine" of Manifest Destiny and the intensification of the debate over slavery challenged the premises of the American empire. Overlaying the deepening sectional divisions produced by this dynamic was a radical political realignment. With his star rising nationally, New York's political complexion ambiguous, and the state's fiscal health uncertain (in no small part due to Seward's spending on internal improvements), Seward decided against seeking a third term in 1842. While he remained largely on the sidelines practicing criminal and then patent law, New York politics, mirroring the national trend, ruptured. The state's Democrats divided into the proslavery Hunkers (William L. Marcy and his allies) and antislavery barnburners (led by Van Buren). The parameters of Whig factionalism were less defined. Seward was associated with the "progressive" (i.e., supportive of the rights of blacks and immigrants) Whigs identified with Weed and his fellow journalist Horace Greeley. He contributed in large measure to this reputation by defending (unsuccessfully) two black men accused of murder. Arrayed against them were more conservative Whigs like Millard Fillmore, who were tied to New York's wealthy elite. Another Whig faction, moreover, never forgave their brethren for turning from Henry Clay to William Henry Harrison in 1840.

The Whig's nomination of Clay to head the national ticket in 1844 while Fillmore ran for New York governor allowed Seward to focus on the national scene. He campaigned almost exclusively for Clay, staying in New York but developing a stump speech that reflected both his personal principles and his pragmatic conviction that slavery was "now henceforth and forever among the elements of political action in the Republic."[6]

Taking his cue from Adams, Seward drew the connection with Texas and empire. "The reckless folly of the Administration in regard to Texas and the unprincipled adoption of it by our opponents have loosed our tongue stays," he wrote during the campaign. He delivered the same speech over and over. The "security, the duration, the extension of slavery," Seward lectured, "all depend on the annexation of Texas." Wading into the waters of foreign policy for the initial time, save for the *Caroline* affair, which he framed in domestic terms, he then warned that to annex Texas would mean a war with Mexico, an "unjust" action fought to extend the "slave trade," a war that would bring dishonor on the United States. Seward would soon make explicit his support for American expansion, for American empire. But this was not the way to achieve it. "I want no enlargement of territory, sooner than it would come if we were contented with a 'masterly inactivity,'" he said. "I would not give one human life for all the continent that remains to be *annexed.*"[7]

Clay lost the election—not because Americans gave their mandate to the Democrat James Polk and his expansionist platform (the "Re-annexation" of Texas and "Re-occupation of Oregon," or "54°40' or Fight"), but because many antislavery Whigs defected to James Birney and his splinter Liberty Party. New York's thirty-six electoral votes proved pivotal to the outcome. Polk won New York by 5,000 votes; 15,000 New Yorkers, doubtless almost all disaffected Whigs, voted for Birney. Although his party was defeated, Seward won national acclaim. Further, because he anticipated that the nexus between slavery and empire would henceforth be the driving force behind American politics, Seward would ride the wave of history.

Small wonder, then, that John Quincy Adams anointed Seward his standard-bearer. And shortly after Adams's death Seward seized his idol's position at the center of Washington's political drama. Polk had set the stage. After threatening war with Britain over the Oregon Territory by campaigning on the slogan "54°40' or Fight" and then unilaterally terminating the joint occupancy, Polk in 1846 compromised by agreeing to a treaty in 1846 that set the boundary between the United States and Canada at the forty-ninth parallel. Seward disagreed with Adams and agreed with Polk on both the ultimatum and the compromise. But as a private citizen he expressed his resolute opposition to Polk's declaration of war with Mexico, continually portraying what he called a "bastard war" as an instrument of the proslavery forces.[8] For that reason Seward was devastated when the Whigs nominated the Mexican War hero and Louisiana slaveholder Zachary Taylor for president in 1848, and added insult to injury by giving the vice presidential nod to Seward's most recent New York bête noire, Millard Fillmore. Many who shared Seward's opposition to slavery backed the hastily formed Free Soil Party that ran Van Buren and John Quincy Adams's son, Charles Francis. Although tempted, Seward had learned his lesson about third parties with the Anti-Masons, and he could never give his blessing to Van Buren. He campaigned for Taylor, proclaiming that as the leading party in opposition to the Democrats, the Whigs had to be the leading party in opposition to slavery. With Fillmore removed from Albany, moreover, the Whigs, recapturing control of the New York legislature, sent Seward to Washington as the state's senator in 1849. There he remained a fixture for the next quarter-century.

Not yet forty-eight years old, Seward was a freshman senator in 1849, junior to the Democrat Daniel Dickinson. Yet to no one's surprise his behavior was remarkably precocious. While for the first time holding national office, Seward was an established public figure and Adams's heir among the antislavery Whigs. He had repeatedly spoken out against the war in Mexico, which in 1849 remained the political fault line. What is more, while Polk's vacating the White House after fulfilling the fundamentals of his platform brought to an end the period of rabid Manifest Destiny in the United States, he left unanswered an incalculably important question: What was the future of California? Mexico had ceded California to the United States as a critical component of the Treaty of Guadalupe Hidalgo. To some Americans it was the greatest prize of, if not the raison d'être for, the Mexican War. At issue, then, were the form by which it would be governed and the date when it would receive statehood. In 1849 United States, the most emotionally charged debates were over the adjectives that modified states: slave or free.

Seward immediately threw himself into the debate as if America's—and his—future depended on it. Both did; the stakes could not have been higher. He was well prepared. Seward was on record as averring that slavery should be prohibited from all new states admitted to the union, and through an evolutionary process, ended in those states where it currently existed. His outlook had its origins in the 1820s and had crystallized in the 1840s. Also in the 1840s, but from sources impossible to pinpoint, Seward developed coherent ideas about American expansion and empire. Perhaps Seward studied the "early" Adams more closely than contemporaries realized. Perhaps the ethos of Manifest Destiny permeated his political consciousness, as it did so many others'. Or perhaps Seward was simply farsighted in identifying America's national interest.

Whatever the origins, Seward's conception of the future course of the American empire was highly developed by the time he went to Washington. He had entitled his 1844 address to the Phi Beta Kappa Society at his alma mater, Union College, *Elements of Empire in America*. Employing rhetoric that a politician from any party would embrace, Seward proclaimed, "Expansive Territory inseparably belongs to the idea of National Greatness." He continued, "The passion of Territorial aggrandizement is universal as well among nations as individuals," as the growth of America attested. Choosing his words carefully, Seward emphasized that since its birth the United States has "attempted to subjugate, or rather to liberate, British North America." It offered non-Americans "an invitation to perfect security and unbounded popular liberty, with a guaranty of Republican Institutions (the heart's desire of mankind) forever." Seward left no doubt about his confidence that it would continue—both to expand and to liberate. He never lost this confidence.[9]

Like Franklin and Adams before him, Seward believed that America was destined for greatness and power, and without explaining why, he linked the expansion of liberty to both. Like them as well, he saw the American empire locked in inexorable competition with that of Britain for global supremacy, with America's victory preordained. More than either Franklin or Adams, however, Seward envisioned how the competition would play out. Even as Polk was engaging Britain in brinkmanship over the Oregon Territory and provoking war with Mexico over Texas (and more), Seward recognized the limitations of defining the American empire in terms of territory acquired. Franklin's population table must no longer drive expansion, nor must his and Jefferson's ideal of the yeoman farmer. Primarily because of the foundations laid by Adams during the Monroe administration, within a few short years the United States would reinforce its security and provide living space for its burgeoning population by enveloping the entire continent. Britain, let alone Mexico, could do nothing to threaten the United States or impede its growth. What Americans must focus on, then, was its future prosperity and power, and the key to both lay in commerce—specifically, in the establishment of a commercial empire. Seward took it for granted that the Spanish would cede to the United States its remaining influence in the Western Hemisphere. Hence the key global contest would be with the British over the Far East. "The battle between Britain and America is to be fought if not in at least for Asia!" Seward wrote Thurlow Weed while Polk was still in the White House. "It will come off when we have grown strong and England has begun to decline."[10]

For Seward the United States was not yet sufficiently strong to wage the battle effectively. The discord over slavery was a major reason. The United States had first to put its own house in order. But as Abraham Lincoln would soon declare, that house was divided. The United States also suffered from geopolitical liabilities. In particular, notwithstanding its recent seizure of unilateral control of the Oregon Territory (most importantly a secure outlet to Puget Sound via the southern half of the Juan de Fuca Strait) and all of California, it remained in a strategically inferior position to Britain with regard to competing for the Asian market. California, with its magnificent port of San Francisco, was thus pivotal. Indeed, to Seward California was now America's most valuable real estate. Its immediate and full integration into the union was imperative. That meant that California must receive statehood as soon as possible. Its population, swollen after the discovery of gold in 1848 by the influx of new settlers, applied for admission as a free (nonslave) state. Their balance in Congress thereby threatened, representatives from the slave states circled their wagons. At stake for Seward was his vision of America, the current continental empire and the future commercial one. For reasons of power and principle, he demanded that both be empires for liberty. To explain the reasons, on March 11, 1850, he delivered his first speech to the Senate. Its contents if not Seward's delivery were worthy of John Quincy Adams's disciple.

The precise catalyst for the speech was a proposal by Henry Clay for a series of measures intended to placate both the slaveholding and free states. Subsequently brokered by Stephen Douglas, Abraham Lincoln's future rival, this soon-to-be-called Compromise of 1850 sought to use the concept of "popular sovereignty" to regulate the spread of slavery in the newly acquired territories even as it balanced the abolition of slave auctions in the nation's capital and the enactment of more severe fugitive slave legislation. Seward solidified his credentials as the leading antislavery Whig by his impassioned advocacy of admitting California as a state without ceding any ground to the supporters of compromise, let alone slavery. Seward fused his allegiance to liberty with his promotion of empire.

As an orator Seward paled in comparison to Daniel Webster, who just four days earlier backed up Clay by speaking for more than three hours in favor of compromise. Acknowledging his shortcomings, Seward relied exclusively on the power of his words, and he harnessed that power. As one historian writes, "Seward wrote speeches, not treatises; advocacy, not analysis. . . . [He was] more salesman than theoretician, more attorney than philosopher." And indeed, having spent weeks crafting the speech, for the most part he simply read its dozens of pages of text in a subdued monotone and without gesticulating for effect. By the time he finished he had nonetheless captured the rapt attention of his audience.[11]

Seward began by extolling at great length the virtues of California, which he described as "the youthful queen of the Pacific, in her robes of freedom, gorgeously inlaid with gold." When campaigning for governor a decade before Seward had referred to the Hudson River as the "true and proper seat of commerce and empire"; he now bestowed that title on California. "There are silver and gold in the mountains and ravines of California," he said. "The granite of New England and New York is barren." Because it "bounds at once the empire and the continent," California would prove both a magnet and outlet for America's expanding population as well as a window opening up on the Pacific. Seward concluded this section of his speech with a flourish that imagined the American empire as it was and could be:

> The world contains no seat of empire so magnificent as this; which, while it embraces all the varying climates of the temperate zone, and is traversed by wide expanding lakes and long branching rivers, offers supplies on the Atlantic shores to the over-crowded nations of Europe, while on the Pacific coast it intercepts the commerce of the Indies. The nation thus situated, and enjoying forest, mineral, and agricultural resources unequaled, if endowed also with moral energies adequate to the achievement of great enterprises, and favored with a government adapted to their character and condition, must command the empire of the seas, which alone is real empire.[12]

For Seward "real empire" was "the empire for the seas." As a real empire, the United States would not only bring greatness and prosperity to its own citizenry, but it would also, through example and contact, contribute to "renovating the governments and the social constitutions" of Europe, Africa, and Asia. Yet Seward made clear that a "real empire" had to be "endowed with moral energies." A real empire was an empire for liberty. And while "California brings God and commerce as well as freedom," the other components of the compromise, such as dividing the Texas territory into multiple slaveholding (and slave-voting) states and then disregarding the Wilmot Proviso (an unsuccessful effort to ban slavery from U.S. territory acquired through the Mexican War), or strengthening the fugitive slave laws, undermined the essential moral energy and as a consequence undermined the empire. This would be the case even if, as Webster proclaimed, the sanctity of the U.S. Constitution was preserved. "There is but one law for all, namely, that law which governs all law; the law of our Creator, the law of humanity, justice, equity, the law of nature and of nations." This is "a higher law than the Constitution." The American empire must follow that law.[13]

In fundamental respects this maiden speech of Seward's, published as a pamphlet and distributed widely by antislavery societies, expressed the precepts of an American empire that he would enlarge and seek to make operational over the next quarter-century. It was an uphill struggle from the start. Over Seward's protests Congress admitted California as part of the Compromise of 1850. Almost simultaneously President Taylor, who counterintuitively had become Seward's ally, succumbed to acute gastroenteritis. His successor, Millard Fillmore, and the new secretary of state, Daniel Webster, were Seward's political enemies. Although without an expectation of success, Seward spent the remainder of this blundering decade hammering home his prescriptions.

In doing so, Seward, once known almost exclusively as a champion of domestic causes, evolved into America's foremost apostle of oversees expansion. As he did, incrementally and perhaps unconsciously, he shifted his priorities from opposing slavery to promoting commerce. This was unavoidably the case following the Civil War. The transition began prior to 1861, however, and was concurrent with Seward's increased attention to the parameters, concept, nature, and purpose of an American empire. Indeed, the basis for the transition is evident in

Seward's "Higher Law" speech of 1850. His evolving views on empire signal his and many of his allies' most profound beliefs about the relationship of slavery to an Empire for Liberty.

Seward emerged on the national stage as a vocal and ardent opponent of slavery in the early 1840s, the era when the debate over the annexation of Texas joined with the Democratic Party's doctrine of Manifest Destiny to link slavery and expansion inextricably. Polk's success in fulfilling most of his platform intensified the debate by reinforcing the link. The result was the conviction of Clay, Webster, Stephen Douglas, and a majority in Congress that the survival of the union required a compromise. Seward delivered his famous speech in 1850 to challenge that conviction but at the same time urge the immediate admission of California as a state.

This juxtaposition reveals in outline Seward's still inchoate but progressively more internally consistent thinking about the nexus of empire and liberty. He opposed slavery and favored liberty. He embraced the concept of an expanding American empire but insisted it be an empire both of and for liberty, consistent with his faith in the inexorable improvement of the human condition and confidence that mankind was progressing toward "an ultimate and glorious destiny." Resolute in his belief that "no ignoble race can enlarge or even retain empire," Seward held that Americans must banish slavery from their entire territory, not just half of it. Liberty was inviolate; it could not be compromised. He took it as axiomatic, as his biographer stresses, that the "existence of an institution that consigned millions of its citizens to servitude, forbade them opportunity for social and economic progress, and denied the democratic principle by its tolerance of an aristocratic, slaveholding class . . . [challenged] America's claim as the home of freedom and equality and its right to a position of world leadership."[14]

Yet it was one thing to identify the incompatibility between liberty and slavery and another to believe that all people were capable of sustaining liberty. Seward assumed sustaining liberty required appreciating if not contributing to liberal institutions. He believed that all the inhabitants of the American empire deserved the blessings of liberty equally, but he did not believe that all inhabitants of the American empire were equally blessed. Put another way, while "liberty was the rightful heritage of all men," an empire for liberty had to be populated by people capable of contributing to and exploiting that liberty.[15]

Seward's direct experience with African Americans was limited. Nevertheless, he had serious doubts about the race's suitability for citizenship in the American empire. As was common among the Whig Party's opponents of slavery, Adams included, Seward considered the innate superiority of especially Anglo-Saxon but also Germanic and Norman Americans incontestable. Blended together, they could offer the world something very special—true liberty. Indeed, liberty was their "peculiar prerogative." For this reason, from Seward's perspective an American empire free of slavery was necessary but not sufficient. It also had to envelop the right kind of people. Hence although he considered Andrew Jackson's policy of forcibly removing Indians from their lands abhorrent, he operated on the premise that over time Anglo-Saxon Americans would so overwhelm Native ones that the latter would disappear as a result of some combination of disease, their inability to adapt to American-style civilization, or war. Moreover, when Polk and allied Democrats objected to the terms of the Treaty of Guadalupe Hidalgo because they perceived an opportunity for the United States to acquire all of Mexico, Seward recoiled in horror. The All-Mexico movement not only presented the possibility for slavery to expand, but incorporating such a large population of Catholic Mexicans would also threaten the institutions on which American liberty depended. For Seward, the All-Mexico movement exposed in bold relief the contradiction between empire and liberty.[16]

Unable to resolve this tension, John Quincy Adams had put further American expansion on hold. William Seward refused to accept this tether. As he argued in his 1850 speech, empire could not wait. The reasons for his impatience were complicated. Seward's support for immediate statehood for California cannot be attributed solely to its intrinsic value. Texas was likewise valuable. Nor was the determinant factor the California constitution, which prohibited slavery. That positive was subsumed within a larger dynamic—the rapid expansion of America's Anglo-Saxons, the harbingers of liberty, across the continent.

There is no evidence that Seward was familiar with Franklin's predictions about America's demographic explosion. He did not claim that the population would double every twenty years. By using what he labeled "well established political arithmetic," nevertheless, he presented his Senate colleagues with a parallel table. Stipulating that America's population in 1850 was 22 million, according to his calculations in 1870 it would grow to 28 million, in 1900, to 80 million, and in 1950, to 200 million. That Americans would populate the entire continent was therefore a certainty. Integrating California into the republic sooner rather than later would ensure that it was an inviting environment for Anglo-Saxon Americans to migrate to and republicanism to flourish. Seward projected California as America's new frontier, and anticipating the received wisdom of the late nineteenth century, he proclaimed that it provided an atmosphere "not only of health, but of liberty and freedom."[17] He explained at length:

> The population of the United States consists of natives of Caucasian origins, and exotics of the same derivation. The native mass rapidly assimilates to itself and absorbs the exotic, and thus these constitute one homogeneous people. The African race, bond and free, and the aborigines, savage and civilized, being incapable of such assimilation and absorption, remain distinct; and owing to their peculiar condition, they constitute inferior masses, and may be regarded as accidental if not disturbing political forces. The ruling homogenous family . . . is seen continually and rapidly spreading itself westward year by year . . . and thus extending this great political community, . . . having a common origin, a common language, a common religion, common sentiments, interests, sympathies, and hopes. . . . If, then, the American people shall remain an undivided nation, the ripening civilization of the West . . . will, in the circuit of the world, meet again and mingle with the declining civilization of the East on our own free soil, and a new and more perfect civilization will arise to bless the earth, under the sway of our own cherished and beneficent democratic institutions.[18]

Seward accordingly dared not postpone California statehood lest it impede the expansion of Anglo-Saxonism. The promotion of liberty was as contingent on this expansion as it was on the abolition of slavery. Yet Seward's concern with the march of liberty demanded that he look beyond America's continental limits. This concern drove him to envision—and advocate—a commercial empire even before the United States had resolved the slavery question. This empire would extend across the Pacific to Asia, consequently completing the "circuit" essential to establishing a "new and more perfect civilization."[19]

Like Franklin, Adams, and so many before him, Seward identified the progress of civilization with the spread of liberty, and prosperity, or the opportunity to prosper, was a fundamental ingredient of liberty. More than his predecessors, however, Seward took it as an article of faith that commerce would create the most opportunities for the greatest number of Americans. Even as the forces for and against slavery battled for control over America's land, Seward proclaimed commerce the "the chief agent of its [America's] advancement in civilization and enlargement of empire."[20]

Without suggesting that Seward's interest in the elimination of slavery diminished during the 1850s, by word and deed he demonstrated that already by this time he was at least as interested in promoting an American commercial empire. Beginning almost immediately after his delivery of his "Higher Law" address, Seward, who served on the Committee on Commerce virtually from the moment he arrived at the Senate, drove home the theme of commercial expansion in almost all of his public rhetoric. The nation that "draws the most materials and provisions from the earth, fabricates the most, and sells the most of productions and fabrics to foreign nations," he told his colleagues in the upper chamber, "will be the great power of the earth." More precisely, Americans must come to dominate "the commerce of the world, which is the empire of the world." Time and again Seward stressed that "political supremacy follows commercial supremacy," or words to the same effect. And the acquisition of political supremacy would allow the United States to spread its ideals and institutions along with its products. He estimated that this "expansion of American influence, ideologically and commercially, would have far-reaching consequences. . . . As the United States became the strongest power in the world, and as its influence promoted the spread of democratic institutions, its geographical limits would be steadily enlarged."[21]

Not only did Seward during this decade develop his vision of an Empire for Liberty, but he also formulated a strategy for realizing that vision. The vision was one of an American empire that exploited commercial relationships and the values that accompanied them to stretch its influence. Unlike the growth of the empires of the past, U.S. expansion would be achieved not by war but by "a process of osmosis, selective in character." It was Americans' mission and responsibility to "take up the cross of republicanism and bear it before the nations." He imagined a United States with "commanding sway in the world" and with borders, figuratively speaking, that greeted "the sun when he [*sic*] touches the tropics, and when he sends his gleaming rays toward the polar circle." To the Senate in 1855 Seward said, "I would not seize in haste, and force the fruit, which ripening in time will fall of itself into our hands. I know nevertheless that the stars will come out even if the moon delays its rising. I have shown you then that a continent is to be peopled, and even distant islands to be colonized by us."[22]

Two years earlier, in fact, Seward had spoken of an American empire that "shall include even distant islands in either ocean." Seward meant islands primarily in the Pacific but also in the Caribbean. Seward frequently looked enviously at British possessions in Central America, concurred with Adams's belief that someday Cuba would become part of the United States (albeit opposing Democratic efforts to acquire it lest it add to their total of slave territory), and he was certain that the exercise of "paramount influence in the affairs of the nations situated in this hemisphere" was vital to American security and prosperity. Nevertheless, in his judgment Asia was the greatest "prize" and "the chief theater of events in the world's great hereafter." So avidly did Seward champion America's reaching across the Pacific, most manifest in his applause for Admiral Matthew Perry's coercive "opening" of Japan in 1854 to American trade, that his advocacy earned the epithet "Seward Doctrine." The United States "must continue to move on westward," he said, "until the tides of the renewed and the decaying civilizations of the world meet on the shores of the Pacific Ocean."[23]

In this regard Seward added a new dimension to "Go West Young Man," the mantra of his erstwhile New York political ally, Horace Greeley (Greeley and Seward split in the 1850s). In Asia Americans would find the materials, markets, and human resources to revolutionize global civilization. This was their true manifest destiny. What made Seward still more enthusiastic about this prospect—not that he needed to be more enthusiastic—was his ready synthesis of this vision of a global empire with the Whig agenda of internal improvements that he, and the party, inherited from Adams. Seward's platform of providing free land for settlement, funding education for agricultural development, protecting industry and encouraging inexpensive immigrant labor through a high tariff, and promoting applications for statehood would produce the kind of synergy that promoted strength and cohesion. Most important, Seward pushed for building a transcontinental railroad. It would unite "the American East and West" even as it afforded "a means of providing national communication with the Orient." Along with constructing a canal through the Central American isthmus, which Seward also advocated, and the acquisition of the previously mentioned "distant islands," the railroad would facilitate the transportation of American produce and manufactures across the continent and thereby ensure American penetration of the Asian market. The railroad's completion, he wrote, would turn San Francisco into the "Constantinople of the American Empire."[24]

As the conflict-ridden decade of the 1850s approached an end, Seward approached this sixtieth birthday. His frustration and impatience intensified. He wanted an America consistent with the ideals of its founding, and the foremost of those ideas was "freedom in the pursuit of happiness." He wanted an American empire that extended the sphere of this freedom throughout the United States and the world. The continuance of slavery on American soil impeded the achievement of all three goals. Seward responded in October 1858 by reprising his condemnation of the efforts to reach a compromise with proslavery Americans in 1850. But this time he used words that came ominously close to sanctioning the use of force to banish the institution from U.S. soil. The United States suffers from "an irrepressible conflict between opposing and enduring forces," he famously asserted a year before John Brown's raid on Harper's Ferry. The country "must and will, sooner or later, become either entirely a slaveholding nation, or entirely a free-labor nation. . . . It is the failure to apprehend this great truth that induces so many unsuccessful attempts at final compromise between the slave and free states, and it is the existence of this great fact that renders all such pretended compromises, when made, vain and ephemeral."[25]

Seward's lament reflected the grief he felt over the failure to abolish slavery or even prevent its expansion. It reflected no less his campaign to secure his party's nomination for the president. On the one hand Seward explicitly indicted the Democrats as "inextricably committed to the designs of the slaveholders."[26] On the other hand, he struggled to position himself as the candidate who both represented the centrifugal forces that comprised his party, the newly formed Republicans, and stood the best chance of winning a national election. With his election to the Senate Seward instantly became a party leader, but his party was dying. Proslavery Whigs defected to the Democrats, and antislavery Whigs divided over internal improvements, the tariff, land policy, and above all, nativism. Seward could not stomach the Know-Nothings, but found himself in bed with them regardless with the birth of the anti-Democrat Republican Party. With much anguish Seward withdrew from the hunt for its nomination in 1856 after concluding that John C. Frémont was more popular among both moderate opponents of slavery and the Know-Nothings.

When James Buchanan beat Frémont (and trounced former president and Seward's New York rival Millard Fillmore, who ran as a Know-Nothing, or American, as the party called itself officially), Seward set his eyes on 1860. Recognizing that his talk of commercial grandeur would sway few electors, he delivered his 1858 "Irrepressible Conflict" speech in Rochester as a tactic in his strategy to secure a Republican victory in the New York gubernatorial election, thereby energizing as well as confirming his base. The Republicans won in New York, and Seward emerged as the party's front-runner in 1860. But although Seward came out ahead on the first ballot of the convention, he was defeated on the third.

The Know-Nothings preferred Abraham Lincoln, about whom they knew little other than that he was not Seward. Considered more moderate than Seward on the issue of slavery, and less associated with the abolitionists, Lincoln, the conventioneers thought, also held greater appeal among the border states. While Seward's effort to move more toward the political center on slavery cost him the allegiance of Horace Greeley and his influential *New York Tribune*, he was unable to shed the label of radical. With the southern Democrats turning to John Breckinridge rather than supporting Steven Douglas, and John Bell running as a Know-Nothing (now the Constitutional Union Party), Lincoln secured the election with 40 percent of the popular vote (albeit with 180 of the 303 electoral votes).

Seward was bitterly disappointed. Yet as events turned out the unexpected result of the 1860 Republican Convention enabled him to focus his energies for much of his remaining life on pursuing his dream of an American empire. It is doubtful that Abraham Lincoln had paid close attention to Seward's remarks about expansion and commerce. He may not even have fully appreciated the New Yorker's efforts on his behalf during the 1860 campaign. Seward predictably focused many of his remarks on the evils of slavery, but he also interjected numerous comments portraying westward expansion as the engine of liberty and democracy and predicting that soon the center of power in the United States would inexorably move west along with its population—and trade. Lincoln did fully appreciate Seward's talents and, more important, the power he exercised within the Republican Party. He invited Seward to join the administration as secretary of state. Seward hesitated; he had grown to like the Senate. Still, the position of secretary of state remained the prime stepping stone to the presidency. Moreover, Seward, who initially perceived Lincoln as incompetent as well as unqualified, was confident that he would wield the real power in the administration. He accepted the president's offer.

Seward's stewardship of the Lincoln administration's foreign affairs during the Civil War provided little hint of his historical stature among U.S. secretaries of state and his robust influence on the growth of America's empire. Especially early in his tenure, his prescriptions verged on bizarre, understandable only in the context of the unprecedented environment in which he was operating. Notwithstanding the implications of his choosing the words "irrepressible conflict" to characterize America's polarization in the 1850s, Seward's loyalty to the union drove him to try desperately to avoid a civil war. Following the principle that "the enemy of my enemy is my friend," he concluded that the only way to halt the momentum toward a war between the states was to shift the attention of both North and South toward an external enemy. A war against any or all of the European powers would, he predicted, "unite the country in a burst of patriotic fervor."[27]

As a consequence of this misguided judgment, when Seward learned at the end of March 1861 that Madrid and Paris were colluding to take control of Santo Domingo and Haiti (France had a scheme for Mexico as well), he presented Lincoln with "Thoughts for the President's Consideration." Criticizing the administration for lacking "a policy that is either domestic or foreign," he recommended that Lincoln exploit Spanish and French interference in the hemisphere by "demanding explanations categorically" from both of them. He suggested that the president also demand from the British and Russians an estimate of their likely response in the event of an insurrection by the southern states. Unless each replied satisfactorily, a virtual impossibility, Lincoln should request from Congress a declaration of war, or at a minimum institute a blockade, Seward counseled.[28]

Lincoln dismissed the recommendation as the outlandish proposal that it was. Doubtless Seward expected this response. He probably also expected what happened less than two weeks later. On April 12 forces of the Confederate States of America fired on the forces of the United States of America garrisoned in Fort Sumter, South Carolina. Seward's irrepressible conflict erupted into the Civil War. Somewhat ironically, rather than continue to seek to provoke a war with the British, Seward devoted the majority of his time and energy over the next four years to deterring the British from intervening to assist the Confederacy. The incentives for London to provide Richmond with assistance were robust. British relied on Southern cotton for its textile industry even as it competed with manufacturers in the American North. In addition Seward, who was Anglophobic to begin with, could imagine grinning Britons as they contemplated the crippled American empire that would result from its house permanently dividing into two.

Seward's instinct was to caution the British against even recognizing Confederate independence. In the end, however, his threats were less consequential than the abilities of the secretary of state's handpicked ambassador to the Court of St. James, his friend and John Quincy Adams's son, Charles Francis Adams, to keep British sympathies for the secessionists in check. The combination of Adams's diplomatic skill, British opposition to slavery juxtaposed with Lincoln's Proclamation of Emancipation, and the tide of battle after the Confederate forces retreated south following Antietam proved sufficient to deter British intervention. Relations between London and Washington were frequently tense. Crises arose over the Union's blockade of the Atlantic coast south of the Chesapeake Bay, the capture of Confederate emissaries James Mason and John Slidell aboard the British *Trent* as it—and they—steamed toward Europe, and the success that British-built Confederate cruisers, most notoriously the *Alabama*, had in damaging union merchant shipping. Nevertheless, the South's "King Cotton Diplomacy" failed. In large part because it did, the American empire survived.

Had the British intervened, the French would have been right by their side. Napoleon III was even more eager for the Confederacy to succeed, and not only because France, which lacked an alternate source such as Britain's Egypt, desperately required King Cotton. Perhaps more important, as a vital dimension of his effort to support his problematic claim that he was Napoleon Bonaparte's nephew by returning France to its imperial glory, Napoleon III concocted a plan to bring Mexico into the French sphere. With the United States weakened, owing to the successful secession of the Southern states if not Americans' preoccupation with fighting among each other, the French emperor thought he could capitalize on Mexico's palpable instability. By the time of the Confederate attack on Fort Sumter, the chronic unrest that characterized Mexico since its independence from Spain had "greatly expanded into a sanguinary civil war." Ostensibly to protect the lives and property of their nationals, Napoleon III proposed that along with Britain and Spain, France intervene to restore order and ensure that the Mexicans repaid their debts. In the process he would "re-establish the monarchical principle in the New World, check the advance of republicanism and democracy, and oppose [i.e., establish] a barrier to the commercial and territorial expansion of the United States in the Western Hemisphere."[29]

Although the threat of such a collective intervention persisted for the initial years of the Civil War, the British nonintervention sounded its death knell. In part this was because of the potential complication of the Confederacy enveloping Mexico within a slave empire. Perhaps in greater part, London's reluctance to concert with Paris evolved from its appreciation of Napoleon's ambitions, and it had no intention of assisting its historic rival to regain an imperial foothold in North

America. Hence Napoleon in 1863 turned to Plan B. With the assistance of Mexican conservatives and the Catholic Church, which opposed the rule of Benito Juárez, a Zapotec Indian, he seized Mexico City, engineered a plebiscite that proclaimed Mexico an empire, and convinced the out-of-work Habsburg archduke Maximilian, the brother of Austrian emperor Franz Ferdinand, to accept the crown. The naive Maximilian encountered resistance from Mexicans both on the left and on the right virtually from the moment that he landed at Veracruz in 1864. After Robert E. Lee's surrender Napoleon III urged Maximilian to abdicate. He would not, claiming that he could not desert his supporters. Left high and dry by the French, Maximilian was captured by Juárez's forces and executed by firing squad in June 1867.

Despite his bellicose posture at the start of the Civil War, Seward opposed proposals that the United States deploy its forces to Mexico. By the end of the Civil War, he was less concerned with the threat of a French proxy-empire in Mexico than with rejuvenating America's, which in his eyes would not include Mexico, at least not immediately. That the United States survived the ordeal of the Civil War confirmed the belief of many Americans that its destiny was exceptional. That Seward survived a personal ordeal doubtless provided him with even greater motivation to pursue that destiny.

In early April Seward had broken his jaw when thrown from his carriage. He was recovering in bed the evening of April 14 when Abraham Lincoln attended a performance in Washington, D.C., of *Our American Cousin* at Ford's Theater. As John Wilkes Booth fired the shots that killed the president, his fellow conspirators attacked Seward. Unlike the president, the secretary of state recovered from his wounds. Afterward he seemed even more determined to give special meaning to his additional years on earth. Building on his prewar rhetoric, Seward would dedicate his life, he told Charles Frances Adams, to bringing America, and through America the world, to "a higher state of civilization." Commerce would be the vehicle. In an 1802 address in Plymouth Massachusetts, Seward's hero John Quincy Adams famously expressed his vision for America by quoting the seventeenth-century Irish philosopher, Bishop George Berkeley. "Westward the course of empire takes its way," went Adams's modification of Berkeley's verse.[30]

After the Civil War Seward began to express his vision by quoting a different poem:

Our nation with united interests blest,
Not now content to poise, shall sway the rest;
Abroad our Empire shall no limits know
But like the sea in boundless circles flow.[31]

Having formulated his concept of a commercial empire prior to the Civil War, Seward lost no time attempting to bring his concept to fruition. In his mind the time was right. Previously Americans and non-Americans had used the construction *the United States are*; the defeat of the Confederacy meant that *the United States is*. Further, with the Thirteenth, Fourteenth, and Fifteenth Amendments to the Constitution abolishing slavery and confirming that in principle all former slaves were voting citizens of the United States, Seward could believe in the American ideal of an Empire for Liberty without the complication of conflating liberty with equality. Filling in missing blanks from his 1850 "Higher Law" address to the Senate, shortly after the surrender at Appomattox, assassination of Lincoln, and ratification of the Thirteenth Amendment, Seward energetically turned against the Radical Reconstructionists. "The north must get over this notion of interference with the affairs of the South," he wrote. "I have no more concern for them [the "negroes"] than I have for the Hottentots. . . . They are not of our race."[32]

Seward's "belief in the black man's inferiority" and conviction that "peace and harmony between the white populations of North and South" was a prerequisite for the post–Civil War "glorious era of national greatness" reinforced one another. Together they generated momentum for his empire-building efforts even as they contributed to a domestic environment that repeated frustrated them. In many cases Seward simply overreached. In the aftermath of the Civil War the United States lacked the instruments to secure oversees possessions, however limited their number. If this constraint was not enough, Americans predictably turned inward. Still, Seward was in fundamental ways his own worst enemy. For the Radical Republicans, his lack of concern for freedmen, combined with his advocacy of leniency toward the former rebels in the South and alliance with Andrew Johnson, transformed him into traitor. The obstacles he confronted, consequently, were more political than strategic or economic.[33]

Anticipating the strategies associated with his protégé John Hay a quarter of a century later, and even more so Woodrow Wilson a quarter-century after that, Seward compounded these obstacles by challenging orthodoxy. While he was, as one historian labeled him, the "central figure of nineteenth century imperialism," Seward never defined himself as an imperialist. Much as he did not recognize the contradiction between his certainty about Anglo-Saxon superiority and his opposition to the enslavement of black men, Seward was convinced that the expansion of the American empire need not entail military conquest or the subjugation of indigenous peoples. Either phenomenon would in his mind weaken the United States by forcing it to incorporate inassimilable, inferior, and likely ungovernable populations (parallel to the Native and African Americans). Seward's conception of a commercial empire avoided these dangers. America's ideals, resources, and products, not its soldiers, guns, and bullets, would constitute the means to its global ends. "Commerce has largely taken the place of war," he explained. The acquisition of some territory would be necessary. But Seward recommended that America choose what to acquire selectively on the basis of strategic need, that it acquire new territory without the resort to military force, and that it keep to a minimum the number of nonwhite peoples over whom it exercised control.[34]

Seward called this phenomenon of pacific expansion that he predicted would be welcomed by indigenous peoples as much as Americans a "process of political gravitation." At his suggestion, Andrew Johnson used this term in his third annual message to Congress. Before then, however, Seward had provided Johnson with a far-reaching but integrated program that would drive that process and demarcate its end point. With the reunification of the states achieved, a transcontinental railroad built, and the western lands settled, the strength and promise of the continental United States would be unparalleled. Seward was confident that in the decades ahead even Mexico would open "herself as cheerfully to American immigration as Montana and Idaho are now," reaching a juncture when, like California in 1850, its population met the racial criteria for U.S. statehood. Long before that, he predicted, the "ingenious, enterprising, and ambitious people" of Canada would have built "excellent states" that would surely be admitted to the union. Ben Franklin's vision and Quincy Adams's fundamental goals would be achieved; America would have extended the sphere of liberty.[35]

America's greater destiny, nevertheless, required its establishing the commercial empire he had imagined years earlier. This empire would assure peace and prosperity for Americans and bring the best of its civilization to others. For this purpose Seward proposed to Johnson the acquisition of strategically situated islands, or merely their ports, that would create a network of observation posts, policing "headquarters," and way stations for America's transoceanic commerce. He also pursued the construction of a canal thorough the Central American isthmus, the development of a communications system that spanned the continents, and the widespread acceptance of the dollar as *a* if not *the* global currency. Seward did not expect to achieve all of his plan immediately. He did expect to make progress. In the meantime he would use international negotiations to establish a global environment of cooperation that allowed for equal opportunity for all nations—a concept that policymakers decades later dubbed the Open Door.

So that the United States was prepared for a spectrum of contingencies, Seward concurrently advocated enhancing U.S. military, especially naval, capabilities, and signaling America's willingness to use force to buttress its diplomacy. The operative word was *signal*, however. Seward considered the employment of force but a tactic in a diplomatic strategy, a last resort to be used reluctantly and judiciously. Seward was not modest in his ambition for America. In addition to securing stepping stones across the Pacific and island outposts sufficient to turn the Caribbean into an American lake and safeguard an isthmian canal, he envisioned an American empire that eventually stretched across all of North America, including Canada and Mexico. Achieved through commercial ties and political gravitation, however, the empire's cost to America's lives, treasure, or ideals, liberty above all, would be negligible.

If judged by his specific accomplishments, Seward's record between 1865 and 1868, his final year in office, was dismal. His greatest success was the purchase of Alaska. But even that triumph resulted from luck and chicanery. Although Alaska had long been on Seward's wish list, the real estate was never of particular interest to him. Rather, along with the Aleutian Islands Alaska could serve as a "drawbridge" that spanned the Pacific, "an entrepot in the Northwest" for trade with Asia. This perspective drove Seward to introduce a bill to survey the Bering Strait as early as 1852. The Senate killed the bill, but it gained the attention of Edouard de Stoeckl, who arrived in the United States as the secretary to the Russian legation and worked his way up to chargé d'affaires and then minister.[36]

The "Baron," as Americans called Stoeckl, and Seward became fast friends, more so during the Civil War. Notwithstanding Seward's attention to countering King Cotton diplomacy, thwarting Napoleonic empire-building, and so much more, he devoted vast amounts of time and energy to gain congressional funding for an Alaska-Siberian telegraph line. Also known as the Collins' Overland Telegraph after its originator, Perry McDonough Collins, the line's purpose was to establish a communication link north from California through British Columbia, across Alaska via the Bering Strait to Siberia, and then onto Europe. Seward could not contain his enthusiasm. Not only would it increase America's influence, he lobbied Congress, but the telegraph line would also serve as a conduit to spread "throughout the world American ideas and principles of public and private economy, politics, morals, philosophy and religion."[37]

Seward obtained Russian approval and Britain's permission to run the line through British Columbia. While the House passed a bill supporting the venture, it would not appropriate the necessary funds. The completion of Cyrus Field's transatlantic cable in 1866 doomed the project. Its demise made Seward more determined to use Alaska as a gateway to Asia. The end of the Civil War, moreover, convinced Stoeckl that the time had come to sell Alaska. Russia had turned its attention increasingly to China, its defeat in the Crimean War made it even more wary of sharing an indefensible border with Britain, and it was acutely aware of Americans' reputation for overrunning sparsely populated territory. With minimal haggling on March 30, 1867, he and Seward settled on a price of $7,200,000 (Stoeckl was prepared to accept $5 million). Although the cost still represented a bargain for acquiring territory twice the size of Texas, Seward confronted intense congressional opposition. Few shared his vision of Alaska as a commercial asset, some worried about the cost of defense outweighing any possible benefits, and many detested the secretary of state simply because he served a president that they detested. They lampooned Alaska as "Seward's Folly," "Seward's Icebox," and a "Polar Bear Garden," among other infelicitous epithets. In the end, nonetheless, Seward had the last laugh. Apparently in part because Stoeckl "had greased palms liberally," in July 1868 the House appropriated the funds. What only mattered to Seward was that the deal was done.[38]

The domestic environment proved less poisonous with regard to Alaska than it did to Seward's other initiatives, forcing him in the end to accept an American empire with significant limits. Alaska was Seward's northernmost "connector" to Asia, and as a consequence, it was not at the top of his list of priorities. More appealing were the southern routes: one directly west from California, the other west from the Atlantic Coast but dipping south through the Caribbean and passing through Central America via an isthmian canal. Especially with the construction of the Transcontinental Railroad well under way (California governor Leland Stanford drove in the ceremonial golden spike on April 10, 1869), sailing across the Pacific Ocean from California seemed the most viable route. Securing the port of San Francisco for this purpose had been a primary motive for coveting California in the first place, and rail travel reduced the time needed to transport goods from coast to coast from six months to six days.

Yet without coaling stations steamships could not make the journey across the Pacific. During Seward's tenure the United States did annex Midway Island, a small and barren atoll discovered in 1859. But its port was too small, and its distance from California too great, for it to serve as a linchpin of a commercial empire. Seward thus set his sights on the Hawaiian Islands, then known as the Sandwich Islands. In light of Hawaii's majority, nonwhite population, annexing the islands while the United States was in the throes of Reconstruction was out of the question. So Seward negotiated with Hawaii's King Kamehameha V a treaty of reciprocity as a first step in gaining U.S. control. The opposition of domestic sugar growers stymied ratification during an era when public attitudes toward expansion were indifferent at best. Not until a decade later would the acquisition of Hawaii signal the arrival of a new American empire.

Seward's frustrations in the Caribbean were greater, and from his perspective, more difficult to accept. Hawaii was far away, and until the mouth of the Pearl River could be dredged (ultimately producing Pearl Harbor), it lacked an accommodating port. Closer to home and of greater immediate value were islands in the Caribbean, several of them. They would be crucial to Seward's projected southern route to Asia as gatekeepers for the isthmian canal, whenever and wherever it was built. And in the interim such outposts would support America's commerce with South America. While this trade's potential was not as vast as Asia's, it was vast, and as far as Seward was concerned, largely untapped, except by the British. This enhanced its appeal, because for Seward gaining wealth and influence at the expense of the British was inherently of great value to America's rise to global dominance. To him, Britain would always remain the most severe threat to his American empire. It was also to serve as an inspiration and model. "Wise Old England," Seward commented near the end of his life, betraying his bounded notion of liberty. "How she fortifies her island Realm, and yet all the while develops and improves the energies of her people, while she does not hesitate to undertake the regulation of the world! She knows, moreover, when and where and how to establish the necessary police stations."[39]

In the Caribbean Seward identified two such police stations: the Danish West Indies and the Dominican Republic. In both cases Seward sought to purchase islands whose harbors he considered hospitable for U.S. naval and commercial ships and which were well placed in terms of their proximity to South America in general and the Central American isthmus in particular. In 1867 Seward successfully negotiated with Denmark a treaty that would have transferred what are now called the Virgin Islands to the United States for $7.5 million. "When St. Thomas and St. John are brought under the jurisdiction of the United States," he wrote the Radical Reconstructionist Charles Sumner, "they will constitute a halfway station for our national commerce with South America and the Pacific coast, an entrepot for our trade with the tropical regions, and a relay for our squadrons of war or apprehended disturbance of general peace." Concerned with the consequences of the purchase for America's racial composition, however, and preoccupied with the imminent impeachment of President Andrew Johnson, led by Sumner the Senate refused to ratify the treaty.[40]

Seward made less progress toward acquiring the Dominican Republic. Along with his son Federick, Seward had visited the Dominican Republic shortly after he recovered from the wounds he suffered the evening of Lincoln's assassination. He returned to the United States convinced that Samana Bay on the island's eastern end was ideal for sheltering American ships en route to South America and, soon he hoped, passing through a canal to Asia. In this instance, exacerbating the racially and politically motivated opposition that had killed the deal with Denmark was the corruption of Seward's intermediaries with the Dominicans and the island's endemic instability. The best Seward could do was to persuade the succeeding administration of President Ulysses S. Grant to continue the efforts he had begun. Grant did, and he failed.

After nearly a half-century in public office, Seward returned to New York a private citizen in 1869. He would have liked to have remained secretary of state, but Grant did not offer him the job. Nor did he offer it to Charles Francis Adams, whom Seward recommended as an alternative. Seward was confident that he could trust his legacy to his friend and John Quincy Adams's son. Although Grant may have turned his back on their legacy, America's successor leadership did not. Dying in his Auburn, New York, office in 1872, Seward left for them not only a road map but an ideology of an American empire. As his biographer wrote, Seward "was a follower in the footsteps of John Quincy Adams and like him dreamed of those places 'where the strange roads go down.'" Seward was unquestionably frustrated, but he left footprints almost as big as Adams's. All that was really new about the new American empire that took form at the end of the nineteenth century was "the means and politically favorable conditions for realizing Seward's future advantages." And no one was more instrumental in promoting both those means and politically favorable conditions than Henry Cabot Lodge.[41]

CHAPTER 4

Henry Cabot Lodge and the New American Empire

S EWARD NEVER WROTE DOWN a blueprint for his successors. Notwithstanding the imperial vision that pervaded so many of his public addresses, those who followed in his wake had to infer from his behavior the specifics of the American empire that he imagined—with its isthmian canal and strategically situated island outposts facilitating the spread of American products, ideas, and ideals to Asia and elsewhere. There were exceptions, successors who had more direct knowledge of Seward's vision. In addition to his son Frederick, who served as his father's assistant secretary of state, and Charles Francis Adams, his longtime friend and blood-disciple of John Quincy, Seward took into his confidence John Hay, Lincoln's secretary. Seward became Hay's patron, launching his career in foreign policy by appointing him secretary to the U.S. legation in Paris and then chief of the U.S. mission to Austria. Decades later, as secretary of state to Presidents William McKinley and Theodore Roosevelt, Hay's conduct was so faithful to Seward's design that some historians conceived of America's imperial growth in genealogical terms. The "new empire of 1900," in the opinion of one, "deserved to be known as the Adams-Seward-Hay empire."[1]

Yet however closely he walked in Seward's footsteps, the mild-mannered, good-humored Hay was not representative of the muscular empire-builders who shepherded America to global dominance in the late nineteenth and early twentieth centuries. Of these, no one was more muscular, better situated, or more instrumental in America's imperial rise than Henry Cabot Lodge. As captured in a famous portrait by John Singer Sargent, Lodge projected America's growing confidence—and arrogance. Almost a caricature of the Boston Brahmin, his breeding, personality, and physical appearance contrasted starkly with Seward, much as Seward's contrasted with Adams. He was tall and wiry, with a full head of hair that curled elegantly and a well-groomed Vandyke beard. Lodge appeared to be vain because he was. He could also be austere and aloof. Albeit a lifetime politician, glad-handing and back-slapping were not his style. Even a friend like the prominent historian James Ford Rhodes commented about Lodge's "unconscious, supercilious manner." Juxtaposed with his partisanship, his "combative, uncompromising, sometimes cynical aggressiveness" won him few converts to the causes he championed. As if to mock his

Harvard accent, moreover, the high pitch of his voice was so irritating as to evoke the sensation produced by chalk scratching a blackboard. In short, gaining political prominence in the ethos of the backroom deal-making during America's Gilded Age, Lodge possessed few of the attributes likely to "make him popular within the Senate's convivial precincts."[2]

Lodge was nonetheless a pivotal force in driving America's rise to global dominance. In retrospect this role was unexpected; not unlike Seward, Lodge focused his early career almost exclusively on domestic affairs. In part the explanation for his huge influence on the growth of the American empire lies in his intelligence, energy, and political acumen. But in larger part the explanation lies in who Lodge was and where he came from. An avid nationalist who interpreted America's survival of the bloody Civil War as proof of its exceptionalism and global mission to promote liberty and civilization, Lodge epitomized the earliest iteration of America's "Best and the Brightest."

Born in Boston on May 12, 1850, Lodge grew up across the street from George Bancroft, America's leading historian in the first half of the nineteenth century as well as a statesman in his own right. Bancroft knew all about Lodge's lineage. The first Lodge had arrived in America in 1791, when Giles Lodge, a commercial agent, emigrated to escape the slave revolt in Santo Domingo. The Cabots were of older New England stock. Great-grandfather George Cabot had been a Boston ship owner and merchant before entering politics. Elected to the Senate from Massachusetts the year Giles Lodge came to Boston, he was one of Alexander Hamilton's most trusted allies and a friend to George Washington. With the election of Thomas Jefferson and the escalating tensions with the British, Cabot became a leader of the Essex Junto. During the War of 1812 he presided over the Hartford Convention, one dimension of his heritage that the patriotic Henry Cabot Lodge did not boast about.

Lodge did boast about his Federalist pedigree. He identified that party, and by extension the Republican Party, with American greatness and grandeur. He also believed that the Republicans remained true to the Federalists' measured understanding of liberty. His hero was John Cabot's most powerful ally, Alexander Hamilton. Hamilton's conservatism, distrust of mass democracy, and confidence in federal power appealed to Lodge for intellectual and dispositional reasons. He later described Hamilton as blessed with the "greatest constructive mind in all our history, and I should come pretty near saying, or in the history of modern statesmen in any country." Lodge found even more attractive Hamilton's nationalism, a nationalism that was as physical as it was mental. Lodge would have been an avid nationalist regardless of the circumstances of his youth. Still, the most salient circumstance was the Civil War, which Lodge later called an "overshadowing experience" that exerted a "great educational force" on his worldview. Not only did it teach him that in politics as in life there was "a right and a wrong," but the tragic bloodshed produced by the evil of slavery combined with the weak leadership of the Democrats (the party of Jefferson) during the Blundering Decade also reinforced his perception of Hamilton's brilliance. Hamilton was never wrong, nor was he ever weak. In contrast to the "inconsistent, supple, and feminine" Jefferson, Lodge wrote, "Hamilton was consistent, strong, masculine, and logical."[3]

Lodge's first book was a biography of Hamilton, at it should have been. Lodge wrote history because he was compelled to tell a story about American strength and greatness. In this story Hamilton starred as the strongest and greatest American. Although he received one of the first three Ph.D.s awarded in the United States, Lodge was never a scholar. Enrolling at Harvard in the aftermath of the Civil War, he excelled in a class taught by the newly arrived medieval historian Henry Adams, Charles Francis Adams's son and John Quincy Adams's grandson. Lodge enjoyed the subject matter immensely, and he and Adams became lifelong friends. Yet when he returned to Harvard after spending the year after his graduation touring Europe with his new bride, Anna Cabot Mills Davis ("Nanny," a distant cousin), it was to start law school. In his first year, nevertheless, he accepted Adams's invitation to serve as his assistant editor on the *North American Review*. Lodge soon became coeditor, prompting his decision that concurrent with his study of law he would pursue a Ph.D. in political science (which at the time was the equivalent of political history), writing a dissertation on Anglo-Saxon land law. Lodge received a law degree in 1874 and a Ph.D. in 1876, just as America celebrated its centennial.

Henry Adams brought with him to Harvard the rigorous German methodology that transformed the study of history into a professional discipline. Lodge learned this methodology well, but he rejected Adams's dictum that the historian should strive for objectivity. Lodge conducted research with painstaking care, but he used the evidence to construct a partisan narrative. His historical writings served his politics. Within a decade and a half of earning the Ph.D., during which time he launched his political career, Lodge wrote biographies of Hamilton, Washington, and Daniel Webster for the popular American Statesmen series and edited, in nine volumes, Hamilton's papers.

Lodge used history as an instrument to inform the present and provide lessons for contemporary leaders—U.S. leaders. He wrote about Federalists whose assumptions about America's greatness exhilarated him. Repeatedly he cited Washington's references to the United States as an "infant empire" with a glorious "imperial future." He was enthralled by Gouverneur Morris, who bragged that "the proudest empire in Europe is but a bauble compared to what America will be." Lodge's heroes were flawless, larger than life. Of Hamilton, Lodge wrote with shades of deep purple, his "blood was hot with the new strong wind of revolution, risking his life and what he loved probably much more, his influence and his popularity on behalf of law, order, and mercy." As one student of Lodge explained, "For his distrust of democracy, his favoritism toward the propertied classes, his belief in a strong central government at the expense of the states, and *his drive to establish an American empire*, Hamilton was Lodge's political model." Another Lodge scholar generalized from this particular: Lodge's "methodology was ever the servant of his purpose and science was never a purpose in itself." His "history had a didactic and utilitarian quality. History was a substitute for philosophy."[4]

Lodge's careers as historian and politician were inextricably intertwined. Further, history was his entrée to politics and exercised a robust influence on his career trajectory. Ironically, given his role in young Lodge's decision to study history, Henry Adams was equally pivotal to a more mature Lodge rejecting the academic life. Concluding that the ineffectual and corruption-ridden administration of President Ulysses S. Grant violated the values of the Republican Party that he held so dear, Adams recruited Lodge to support his effort to establish the Independent Party. The endeavor foundered when Adams's chosen standard bearer, Carl Schurz, deemed the 1876 Republican presidential nominee, Rutherford B. Hayes, sufficiently reformist to warrant his allegiance. Adams disagreed; so did Lodge. After wavering for months, Lodge for the only time in his life cast his vote for a Democrat, Samuel Tilden.

After Tilden lost, Lodge remained with the Independent Party for several more years. But his experience in 1876 convinced him that his future lay in politics, and that the Independent Party did not have a future. In 1879 he ran for the Massachusetts House as a reformist Republican. He won, and two years later he ran for the state senate. This time he lost. His period out of office provided him with the opportunity to write his Hamilton biography and immerse himself in the business of building up Massachusetts's Republican Party. Because of both ventures he came to know a young New Yorker who likewise graduated from Harvard and had political and scholarly aspirations, Theodore Roosevelt. After Lodge's intervention led to Roosevelt's writing biographies of Thomas Hart Benton and Gouverneur Morris in the New Statesmen series, they developed a rapid, some might say rabid friendship.

In the early 1880s Lodge and Roosevelt united to form a political team. The catalyst was a fissure within Republican ranks parallel to the one that emerged in 1876. In the contest for the GOP nomination, James G. Blaine, the former Speaker of the House who had run for president twice previously and served as secretary of state under James Garfield, defeated Chester Arthur. Arthur had succeeded Garfield after the latter's assassination in 1881. Unlike many of the party's reformers who had concerted with him and Adams to organize the Independent Party, Lodge was willing to back Blaine, despite his reputation for corruption. "Blaine is obnoxious," Lodge said in retrospect, and supporting him was "the bitterest thing I ever had to do in my life." He had "stood by the party." For that he paid a price. Lodge stuck with Blaine in order to ensure his selection as the GOP candidate for the House from Massachusetts's Sixth District, on the North Shore (the Lodges summered in Nahant). He won the nomination but lost the election by a margin so razor thin that it required a recount. The tipping point was probably the defection of former allies in the Independent Party who would not forgive him for supporting Blaine. More than a decade later many of these "Mugwumps" became the fiercest "Anti-Imperialists" who opposed Lodge's global agenda.[5]

Roosevelt remained in Lodge's camp, thereby solidifying their personal friendship and political alliance. Neither had any idea of how vital both would prove for America's international ascendancy. In 1886 Lodge's assiduous work for the Republicans paid off; he won a seat in Congress. Thus began almost forty consecutive years in national politics, a tenure that only Lodge's death in 1924 brought to an end. The stature and seniority he attained enabled him to contribute to the making of the American empire like no other American politician, with the possible exception of his friend TR. It also enabled him to contribute like no other American politician to preventing Woodrow Wilson from recasting that empire—in the name of liberty.

Lodge's power stemmed as much from the personal relations that he cultivated as from his base in Congress. Moving to Washington, he bought a home around the corner from Henry Adams and his neighbor, John Hay. At the Adams's house they formed something of a salon (the convivial Hay had an affair with Nannie Lodge, which everyone knew about but Cabot Lodge). Teddy Roosevelt still lived in New York (the year of Lodge's election Roosevelt lost the race for New York City mayor), but he visited often enough to gain membership in the Metropolitan Club. Lodge, Adams, and Hay were also members, as were many others soon labeled America's first "imperialists," including Elihu Root, George Dewey, Alfred Thayer Mahan, and Stephen Luce. Lodge likewise became fast friends with foreign diplomats who helped pave the way for America's entry into the galaxy of great powers. Chief among these was Britain's Cecil Spring Rice. Over the subsequent decades Spring Rice, "by merely being himself probably did more to strengthen Anglo-American friendship than did any other single person."[6]

In the 1890s everyone within Lodge's circle assumed a leading role in America's political, commercial, and military (especially naval) expansion. Lodge's position at the forefront of this movement was foreshadowed by his first major public speech. "We are at the very prime of life as a nation," he proclaimed when running for the Massachusetts legislature in 1879. Americans, he continued, were "vigorous, powerful, rich and masters of a continent. . . . We have built up an empire so great that, whether for evil or good [not that this was in question], it is a chief factor in the affairs of civilized mankind and of the world."[7]

Lodge's attention to the American empire in 1879 is misleading. At the start of his career in national politics he was preoccupied with domestic matters. Like many of his erstwhile allies in the Independent Party, he campaigned for civil service reform. Other priorities were traditional Republican ones, such as a high tariff and sound currency. In some areas Lodge was more progressive than many in his party, notably in promoting voting rights in the South. America's political culture was probably as responsible for Lodge's agenda as his personal preferences. William Seward's experience provided an object lesson about the national temper. The legacies of Reconstruction and requisites of reunion still dominated the political landscape.

That landscape began to change at the precise time that Lodge came to Washington. He was well suited for the emerging zeitgeist. Endowed with the fierce patriotism produced by his pride in his pedigree and his interpretation of the Civil War as a triumph of good over evil, and sensitive to the role that overseas trade had played in his family history, Lodge's attraction to the concept of an ever-growing navy that could both pioneer and support U.S. overseas initiatives and thereby enable America to gain dominion over far-flung places was instinctive. Imperialism became fashionable for great powers in the late nineteenth century, and Lodge never doubted that America should follow the fashion. The consequence resulted in an irony that the historian in him doubtless appreciated: "Lodge, who stood for so many traditional and reactionary principles, became a principal animator of a genuine revolution in American foreign policy."[8]

Equally ironic, the appointment of the Republican Party's bête noire James Blaine as secretary of state marked the shift toward the aggressive global posture that portended America's emergence as an overseas empire. It also complicated claims that America's empire stood for liberty. Elected to Congress initially in the midst of the Civil War, Blaine's career paralleled, or really mimicked, Seward's. Although he came from neither an industrial nor commercial background, he identified the expansion of industry and commerce as the keys to America's future. Further, like Seward Blaine developed into the GOP's leading member of Congress. He was Speaker of the House for three terms before his election to the Senate. Also like Seward he would never fulfill

his ambition to be president, but as consolation he was appointed secretary of state—by Garfield and then Benjamin Harrison.

In this capacity Blaine pursued Seward's global agenda. Indeed,
with regard to extending U.S. influence in and building commercial
ties to Latin America, he eclipsed Seward. Blaine did not resurrect
efforts to acquire island bases in the Caribbean (he did try to lease a
port in Haiti), realizing the political impossibility of doing so. He failed
in his attempt to revise the 1850 Clayton-Bulwer Treaty in order to
provide the United States with the authority to construct an isthmian
canal. But by flexing America's growing post–Civil War naval muscles,
he used both coercion and conciliation to induce the Chilean government to apologize for the behavior of its sailors when their brawl with
the USS *Baltimore's* crew outside Valparaiso's True Blue Saloon led to
three American deaths.

Again similar to Seward, Blaine preferred to rely on nonmilitary
instruments to promote U.S. interests and influence. He arranged and
presided over the first Pan American Conference, which in 1889 the
United States hosted in Washington. His vision of a hemispheric customs union and system of arbitration that would facilitate trade and
remedy the chronic inter- and intrastate conflicts foundered because
of Latin American distrust. As a fallback strategy Blaine negotiated
so many treaties of reciprocity with individual nations that they collectively came to be known by the gendered title "Big Sister Policy." In
the Pacific Blaine's behavior was more masculine. He interjected the
United States into the international rivalry over control of the Samoan
archipelago that produced in 1889 a joint American-German-British
protectorate and by the end of the century left America controlling the
group of eastern islands that included the valuable port of Pago Pago.
Although his deteriorating heath forced Blaine to resign from office
prematurely, he set in motion a chain of events that led to the Hawaiian Revolution in 1893 and soon thereafter America's annexation of
the islands.

Lodge's support of Blaine for president in 1884 was a watershed
in his political career. From a fledgling congressman immersed in domestic matters, he became the face of American imperialism. Lodge
never considered Blaine a friend. He came to admire "Jingo Jim,"
however, particularly with regard to his championship of America's

interests abroad, which Lodge equated with championship of American nationalism and its correlate, American greatness. Although Lodge, largely because of his relationship with Roosevelt, came to be identified with America's advocates of war, he admired Blaine as one of the few statesmen who understood the proper balance between force and diplomacy. Blaine held that the promotion as well as protection of U.S. overseas commercial and strategic interests required military preparedness—naval strength above all. Lodge thus situated Blaine historically as an heir to Hamilton. He wisely rejected the Jefferson's "utopian" postulates that nations were inherently equal and that each "in pursuit of self-interest would see the folly of war and be prepared to make its economic contribution to the betterment of all." To Lodge, the "Jeffersonians' gossamer theories had been 'crushed in the iron grasp of facts.'"[9]

Lodge in the late 1880s lacked a sophisticated "theory" or "philosophy" about imperialism. Unlike Franklin, he did not pay close attention to America's population growth. As a Bostonian he was a booster of commercial expansion, but unlike Seward, he did not fixate on it. He was comfortable labeling the United States an Empire for Liberty, yet he hardly ever spoke in those terms. Indeed, for Lodge liberty was never more than an abstraction. He gravitated toward imperialism for the same reason he wrote history. In his worldview international affairs was a function of power: power to command respect, power to safeguard security, power to signal pride and greatness. At its root, Lodge's imperialism sprouted from his "romantic belief in America's destiny, which he saw foreshadowed by the great figures of its past" about whom he wrote.[10]

There was more to Lodge's imperialism than romanticism. As the author of an intellectual history of Lodge's foreign policy argues, "Lodge's imperialism was but a gloss on his conception of the nature of international relations and of how foreign policy ought to be conducted." Congressman Lodge applauded Blaine for supporting the buildup of the U.S. Navy and identifying it as the pivotal instrument of statecraft. Securing peace required the willingness to risk going to war. Hamilton understood this, and, as Lodge interpreted America's bellicose posture toward Mexico in 1861, so did Seward. Lodge accordingly awarded Blaine high marks for his brinkmanship in Samoa and Chile. Yet in the latter case it was Blaine who demonstrated to Lodge—and President Harrison—how skillfully to draw a line between effectively manifesting resolve and needlessly provoking hostilities. Blaine, whose support for Peru in the War of the Pacific inflamed Chilean anti-Americanism, threatened to resign if the administration did not withdraw its ultimatum to the Chileans. After Harrison backed away the Chileans apologized and offered to pay restitution for the killed Americans. The United States achieved peace through its strength.[11]

Lodge followed intently yet remained at a distance from Blaine's statecraft. When elected to Congress he had tried to gain an appointment to the House Committee on Foreign Affairs. The party leadership passed him over in favor of more senior representatives. He did serve on the Naval Affairs Committee, however. In addition, Lodge's involvement in America's international affairs increased exponentially after he took his seat in the U.S. Senate in 1893. This was the year of the Hawaiian Revolution, and as a consequence, a year that inaugurated a new chapter in the history of the American empire. As a fierce advocate for and defender of the Senate's prerogatives in the arena of U.S. foreign affairs, Lodge ensured Congress's contribution to this history.

No one from a family of Massachusetts merchants was unaware of the value of the Hawaiian (formerly the Sandwich) Islands to America's China trade. Still, there is no evidence that Lodge dwelled on the kingdom's strategic significance until he arrived in Washington. But he had written a biography of Daniel Webster. As John Tyler's secretary of state, Webster had been the force behind promulgating the little-known Tyler Doctrine. Declaring that the United States would make a "decided remonstrance against" the policy of any nation that impinged upon Hawaiian independence," this doctrine, in one historian's words, "virtually [established] an American 'sphere of influence'" enveloping Hawaii. That is an exaggeration; the domestic opposition that doomed the Treaty of Reciprocity negotiated by Seward after the Civil War underscored that a small minority sought to embrace Hawaii. Yet the Grant administration did bring Seward's Reciprocity Treaty to fruition, and as U.S. trade with Hawaii expanded dramatically over the following years, so did American influence—and annexationist sentiment. Hawaii became America's "economic colony."[12]

By removing the preferential status the Reciprocity Treaty accorded Hawaiian exports to the United States (for example, domestically produced sugar received a two-cent-per-pound advantage over that imported from Hawaii), the protectionist McKinley Tariff threatened to sever the relationship and thereby jeopardize America's exclusive right to Pearl Harbor (which was still a work in progress). Thus in his waning years Blaine conspired with John L. Stevens, his colleague on Maine's *Kennebec Journal* whom Blaine appointed minister to Hawaii, to oust Queen Liliuokalani and bring to power the minority of Hawaiians (most of whom were immigrants from America) who advocated annexation. Liliuokalani intended to reassert the political control of Hawaii's indigenous peoples at the expense of the pro-American planter class and descendents of American missionaries. She possessed, Stevens warned, "extreme notions of sovereign authority" that could play into the hands of rivals for influence in Hawaii, particularly the British, Japanese, and Russians. Besides, the minister gushed, "The Hawaiian pear is now fully ripe, and this is the golden hour for the United States to pluck it." Blaine agreed. In one of his last official actions (poor health forced Blaine to resign) he met with Lorrin Thurston, who represented Hawaii's "Annexation Club."[13]

Lodge monitored these developments attentively, out of interest in America's Pacific trade, naval strength, and ascendance as a global power. Not until he moved from the House to the Senate in 1893 did his involvement become direct, however. But once involved he became enthusiastically involved, and that involvement radically affected the course of his career and U.S. history. In January, her palace surrounded by a "Committee of Safety" led by Thurston and his proannexation allies and supported by some 160 marines from the USS *Boston*, the queen surrendered to "the superior force of the United States of America, whose Minister Plenipotentiary, His Excellency John L. Stevens, has caused United States troops to be landed at Honolulu and declared that he would support the said Provisional Government." The next month Stevens proclaimed Hawaii a U.S. protectorate, and within weeks Blaine's successor, John W. Foster, negotiated a treaty of annexation. Harrison promptly submitted it to the Senate for its advice and consent. Because Harrison was by then a lame duck, the Senate deferred action until its next session, when Grover Cleveland would return to the White House.[14]

An incoming senator, Lodge expected to vote in favor of ratification. It would take five years for him to receive the opportunity. After an investigation into the circumstances of the revolution revealed evidence of U.S. culpability and improper behavior, Cleveland withdrew the treaty from Senate consideration. As if to remind Americans that the United States expanded in the name of liberty, he rejected this affront to Hawaii's sovereignty "as not only opposed to our national policy, but as a perversion of our national mission."[15]

Lodge was aghast. Despite his freshman status, he emerged immediately as a leader of the "Imperialists" in a debate that in fundamental respects mirrored that which had climaxed John Quincy Adams's career and catapulted William Seward's a half-century earlier. Joined in a battle over America's proper relationship to the world beyond its borders, in both instances each side claimed for itself the role of promoter of the national interest, representative of the public virtue, and interpreter of the American mission. In both instances race was a pivotal variable and a revolution produced a government that reflected a nonindigenous minority dedicated to annexation. Unlike the 1840s, however, the debate in the 1890s focused on America's acquisition of an island chain not contiguous to the United States and considered by annexationists and antiannexationists alike as inappropriate for statehood. In contrast to the gains from the Mexican War, Hawaii's destiny was that of an American colony, challenging the very construct of an Empire for Liberty.

Lodge did not mince his words in arguing the imperialists' case. As the legendary historian Julius Pratt wrote, "No senator had attacked more bitterly [than Lodge] Cleveland's Hawaii policy." The president's objections to the treaty of annexation, and his proposal to restore the authority of the "semi-barbarous" Queen Liliuokalani, were "grotesque & miserable." Lodge understood the economic issues, particularly those of Hawaii's sugar interests. Many of the planters were of New England stock. But in his mind military and strategic concerns were paramount. These concerns were inseparable from America's national character, what Lodge referred to repeatedly as the "character of force." He likened the Hawaiian Islands to Gibraltar, only the stakes, control of not just the Mediterranean Sea but also the entire Pacific Ocean, were higher. America must not "play the part of dog in the manger," Lodge intoned. In 1894 he introduced a Senate resolution to investigate Cleveland's decision to remove U.S. warships from the Hawaiian Islands.[16]

When nothing came of it and the treaty of annexation continued to lay dormant, Lodge escalated his rhetoric. In 1895 he delivered a series of speeches that dismissed all objections to America's acquiring the islands: that the population was racially unfit for incorporation into the United States, that the annexation of the islands would violate the integrity of a continental nation, that Hawaiian sugar would undermine the domestic sugar industry, and more. Lodge did not feel the need to explicitly counter these arguments because from his point of view they were irrelevant. So were considerations of the native Hawaiian's liberty. All that was relevant was that because the islands "lie there in the heart of the Pacific," it would be "madness" to allow powers such as Britain and Japan to take them. Upon "these islands rest a great part of the future commercial progress of the United States," he explained. For these reasons (and lest anyone doubt their salience, Lodge brought to the Senate chamber a large map to illustrate Hawaii's location with regard to Britain and Japan as well as America), the United States should annex them even "if they were populated by a low race of savages, even if they were desert rocks." But more important still was what annexation would represent in terms of America's pride and power. "We are a great people; we control this continent; we are dominant in this hemisphere; we have too great an inheritance to be trifled with or parted with. It is ours to guard and extend." Equally significant, "I cannot bear to see the American flag pulled down when it has once been run up, and I dislike to see the American foot go back where it has once been advanced."[17]

Although a senator for only two years, by 1895 Lodge had emerged as the Senate's "point man for American imperialism." He was the most prolific propagandist for the "large policy." Along with his speechmaking, Lodge wrote numerous articles beseeching Americans to reject Cleveland's "Blundering Foreign Policy." Lodge made explicit that the "large policy" he advocated extended well beyond the annexation of Hawaii. It included assuring that the United States had unassailable supremacy over the Western Hemisphere, solidifying American influence in Samoa and expanding it in Cuba, building an isthmian canal, and acquiring "at least one strong naval situation" in the West Indies. In short, the large policy followed the imperial vision of Seward, and to a lesser extent that of Adams. In contrast to them, however, Lodge wore his label of American imperialist as a badge of honor. "We have followed the teachings of Washington," Lodge boasted in *The Forum*. As a result, "We have a record of conquest, colonization, and territorial expansion unequalled by any people of the nineteenth century." Reviving the dream of adding Canada to the union, he proclaimed that "from the Rio Grande to the Arctic Ocean there should be but one flag and one country." Lodge paid homage to the high trinity of motives: commerce, security, and prestige. But, displaying his pride and prejudice, he aimed higher. "The great nations are rapidly absorbing for their future expansion and their present defense of all the waste places of the earth," read his article for *The North American Review*. "It is a movement which makes for civilization and the advancement of the race. As one of the great nations of the world, the United States must not fall out of the line of march." Lodge was advocating a "scheme of annexation and colonial empire," charged the Democrat from Delaware George Gray. Lodge accepted this verdict without the slightest guilt or misgiving.[18]

Two primary causes motivated Lodge's imperialist impulses. First, he came under the spell of Alfred Thayer Mahan. As a captain Mahan had been among the Naval War College's first four faculty members when it was established in 1884; two years later he succeeded his patron, Admiral Stephen Luce, as its president. In this capacity he became close friends with a visiting member of the faculty, Teddy Roosevelt. Roosevelt encouraged Mahan to publish his lectures. The results were *The Influence of Sea Power upon History, 1660–1783* (1890), and *The Influence of Sea Power upon the French Revolution and Empire, 1793–1812* (1892). Capturing the ethos of the time, both books attracted a broad readership in Europe as well as the United States, and Mahan's thesis became the conventional wisdom for leaders on both sides of the Atlantic. The explanation is easy to understand. Mahan argued that sea power had determined the outcome of the contest for global primacy between the British and French empires. Not only was control of the seas decisive in war, but, providing a neomercantalist twist by extolling England as a model, it was also decisive to commercial supremacy. No one who read Mahan could doubt the importance to the United States of Hawaii, bases in the Caribbean, and an isthmian canal. And no one could doubt the synergy between a powerful navy, colonial outposts, national power, and pride.

Lodge read Mahan. So did Roosevelt, who, reviewing *The Influence of Sea Power upon History* for the *Atlantic Monthly*, could hardly contain his enthusiasm. "Captain Mahan," he exclaimed, "has written distinctly the best and most important . . . book on naval history which has been produced on either side of the water for many a long year." It may have been at Roosevelt's urging that Mahan sent Lodge a copy. Lodge's reaction was equal to that of his friend. Unlike Roosevelt, and notwithstanding the marriage of one of Nanny Lodge's sisters to one of Stephen Luce's sons, Mahan and Lodge had no personal relationship. Lodge's behavior in 1894, nevertheless, attests to the extent to which Mahan had already been welcomed into the senator's inner circle. Resenting the publicity generated by the *Influence of Sea Power Upon History* and critical of the captain's scholastic priorities, Rear Admiral Henry Erben, Mahan's superior on the USS *Chicago*, wrote a fitness report so devastating that it jeopardized Mahan's future assignments in the navy and opportunities for promotion. Lodge pled Mahan's case before Secretary of the Navy Hillary Herbert. His intervention at a minimum ensured that Mahan did not suffer from the report and thus retained the standing appropriate for a senior lecturer at the Naval War College. Subsequently the two became friends and partners, with Mahan providing an intellectual foundation for Lodge's emotional expansionism.[19]

The second cause for Lodge's emergence as the Senate's leading voice for imperialism in the 1890s was the outbreak of a crisis over Venezuela. The precipitant was a long-standing dispute over the boundary between Venezuela and the colony of British Guiana, exacerbated by the discovery of gold. Venezuela severed diplomatic relations with Britain during the first Cleveland administration, and by the time he returned to the White House in 1893, a resolution seemed no closer. Venezuela appealed to Washington for help. Cleveland had demonstrated his antipathy to imperialism by opposing the treaty of annexation with Hawaii. But in this instance the issue was a British colony in the Western Hemisphere. Further, the British claims jeopardized American access to the Orinoco River, the main commercial artery of the northern third of South America. More generally, they threatened to make a mockery of the preeminent influence in the Western Hemisphere that the United States had claimed since the era of James G. Blaine.

The political culture in 1895 mandated that the United States not remain a bystander. Cleveland instructed Richard Olney, a lawyer who was attorney general before being appointed secretary of state following the recent death of Walter Q. Gresham, to articulate the U.S. position. Proud of the instrumental role he played in the violent suppression of the Pullman strike in Illinois a year before, Olney did so with gusto.

Anything affecting the hemisphere affected the United States, Olney wrote in a memorandum of such length and force that it earned the moniker "Twenty-Inch Gun." By this logic it was Washington's prerogative to broker a settlement that London must accept. Indeed, to the surprise and chagrin of the British, who for more than a half-century had held sway south of the Rio Grande, Olney upped the Monroe Doctrine's ante by proclaiming the corollary that the United States was "practically sovereign on this continent, and its fiat is law upon the subjects to which it confines its interposition." When British prime minister Lord Salisbury (Robert Cecil) thumbed his nose at Olney's impudence and dismissed the Monroe Doctrine as well as Olney's corollary as so much hot air, Cleveland raised the specter of war. Salisbury took notice of America's new self-confidence. With the Jameson Raid signaling the potential of a second Boer War in South Africa, Britain agreed to a compromise. In 1896 London and Washington agreed to abide by the findings of an arbitration committee. Four years later the commission recommended a settlement favorable to the British. It did not consult the Venezuelans.[20]

The incident further energized Lodge. Having indicted British behavior for violating the Monroe Doctrine in an article published a few months before in the *North American Review*, he found Olney's justification for his corollary particularly appealing. It resonated with his own beliefs and predispositions. At the start of the crisis Lodge, his eyes glued to Europe's contemporary imperialist ventures across both oceans, warned, "If Great Britain can extend her territory in South America without remonstrance from us, every other European power can do the same and in a short time you will see South America parceled out as Africa has been." Olney had put Salisbury on notice by writing that America's "infinite resources combined with its isolated position render it master of the situation and practically invulnerable as against any or all other powers." The juxtaposition of Olney's analysis and what he had just learned from Mahan about the influence of sea power and a great navy reinforced Lodge's confidence and pride. He discovered confirming evidence in England. By coincidence Lodge was visiting London when Olney's "Twenty-Inch Gun" arrived. He was impressed by Salisbury's aggressive response. It reflected the sense of self, indeed the conceit, that he wanted Americans to emulate. He was more impressed by the respect accorded to him by the Britons he met, including Joseph Chamberlain, the colonial secretary. In his mind this respect was a function of his representing American power. It demonstrated that the British recognized that "we are a great nation and intend to take a nation's part in the family of nations."[21]

Lodge made it his mission as a U.S. senator to promote policies that would demand that all the great powers recognize what the British recognized. In the late nineteenth century, fulfillment of this mission required that the United States build an empire, or more accurately, a new and different empire. Lodge understood the economic benefits that would accrue, and he was certainly a champion of greater American security. But neither was paramount in framing his perspective. To the contrary, during the Venezuela Crisis he complained about the "materialist complacency" that he feared had become an insidious force in America's industrial society. "The moment any question arises in which the honor of the country is involved and patriotism aroused, the opposition seems always to come from bankers and capitalists," he wrote in private letter. In another he provided his take on "security." "War is a bad thing no doubt," Lodge opined, "but there are worse things both for nations and for men." More generally, Americans concentrate too much of their attention on "small matters," Lodge grumbled, "and too little attention to those great and far-reaching issues on which the future of the republic depends." What motivated Lodge's thinking and behavior more than anything was his insatiable appetite for showing and proving America's national greatness. The historian Ernest May famously argued that in the 1890s the United States had "greatness thrust upon it." Lodge spent the last quarter-century of his life ensuring the reverse: The agent for American greatness was America.[22]

For Lodge the imperialist project was a test of the national character. The abortive treaty of annexation with Hawaii represented a failure; the bellicose standoff with Britain over Venezuela was a great improvement. But agreement to arbitrate a settlement over a boundary dispute to which the United States was not a direct party did not satisfy his overarching goals. Passing the test required that the United States demonstrate its willingness and resolve to take risks, to accept sacrifice, and to shed blood, all in the name of honor and country. Urbanization, immigration, industrialization, depression, and other contributors to the politics, society, and culture of post–Civil War United States challenged the makeup and moral fiber of the America of Lodge's imagination, the America that he wrote about in his books and articles. Among contemporary citizens there seemed a potentially fatal absence of the civic virtue and commitment to the notion of nationhood—and thus for Lodge manhood—that he associated with Washington and Hamilton.

Lodge defined the acquisition of colonies, the construction of a two-ocean navy, even the jump in trade with far-off, exotic lands as achievements calculated to recapture the American spirit and revive America's national character. Frank Ninkovich writes that in the 1890s Americans' "subjective worries about self-definition and identity provided more than enough energy and motivation for the imperialist outburst." Henry Cabot Lodge epitomized these Americans. For him, borrowing from Ninkovich again, "the chance to pursue seductive and self-flattering visions of the nation's new standing in the world became the chief force behind the adoption of an imperial identity." To put it another way, Lodge envisioned an aggressive foreign policy as a "a means of curing America's political and social ills." Unlike the consistency and logic that underlay Seward's expansionist agenda, Lodge's imperialism was consequently "eclectic and opportunistic."[23]

Of course for America in the 1890s to recapture the national character that defined its founding and to distinguish its identity from the world's other empire-builders, its imperialism had to serve nobler ends than the aggrandizement of wealth and power. It had to civilize, uplift, and spread the American ideal of liberty. This was the American way, and with the election of Ohio governor William McKinley in 1896, Lodge rose to a position where he could exercise the requisite influence to move America in this direction. In part he owed this influence to his stature within the Republican Party and the Senate. In part he owed it to his relationship with McKinley. That relationship was not close in the sense that Lodge was close to Roosevelt. Lodge had wanted Speaker of the House Thomas Reed to receive the GOP nomination. But he knew that McKinley depended on his support and would listen sympathetically to him. He exploited that dynamic to increase his influence further. He asked McKinley as a "personal favor" to appoint Roosevelt assistant secretary of the navy. McKinley was no fan of Roosevelt. Yet he did Lodge the favor.[24]

From his first day as president McKinley listened as Lodge counseled that the United States should take up arms in support of the Cuban insurrection against Spain. So, too, did his colleagues in the Senate, and for that matter America's attentive public. They had little choice; no one in Washington was a more vocal proponent of U.S. intervention in Cuba than Lodge. His rationale shifted. Sometimes he stressed commercial motives, sometimes strategic ones, and sometimes humanitarian. On occasion, with the proper audience, he appealed to the partisan interests of the Republican Party. Most frequently, and to almost any audience, he used the language of the Revolution, summoning Americans to live up to their destiny. By standing with the Cubans, Lodge proclaimed, the United States was fulfilling "a great movement which has run thorough the centuries. . . . [W]e represent the spirit of liberty and the spirit of the new time, and Spain . . . is mediaeval, cruel, dying. . . . If the principles that we stand for are right, then the principles of which Spain has been the great exponent in history are utterly wrong." The United States was "capable of greater things" than allowing the Cubans suffering to continue. "The responsibility is ours; we cannot escape it."[25]

Thus Lodge appropriated the rhetoric of an American Empire for Liberty for his own purpose. As attested to in his private conversations with Roosevelt, he cared much less about liberty and even Spanish cruelty than he did about American power and America's image. While McKinley agonized over how to respond to the deteriorating situation in Cuba, Lodge and Roosevelt developed a wish list for American expansion. Despite talk about liberating the Cubans, the list included making them subjects of America. In fact, enumerating the annexation of Hawaii, the unilateral construction and control of an isthmian canal, the purchase of the Virgin Islands, and more (such as acquiring all of Canada), the list paralleled the objectives of the "large policy" with which Lodge was by then identified.

Lodge did not specifically mention the Philippines as integral to his large policy. His behavior and attitude toward the archipelago, nevertheless, was entirely consistent with the conceptual context of that policy and the strategic context of the war with Spain. In encouraging Congress to authorize military intervention in Cuba without requesting a formal declaration of war, McKinley had been extremely precise and excruciatingly nebulous about U.S. motives and aims. The United States had to take up arms "in the cause of humanity," he said, "and to put an end to the barbarities, bloodshed, starvation, and horrible miseries now existing" in Cuba. Reversing John Quincy Adams's admonition, McKinley called upon America's to go abroad and destroy the monster (Spain). What would follow he left unsaid. That was because he did not know.[26]

Neither did Lodge. Over the preceding years he had advocated U.S. expansion primarily in the abstract. Only when applied to Hawaii was the prospect of acquiring territory concrete. Congress's official declaration of war on April 25, 1898, presented Lodge with multiple options. He had his wish list, but it was not ordered according to priorities. He had concentrated much more on moving the United States toward war than determining the gains that war would achieve. This focus was understandable because he envisioned the true gain to be recognition and power as measured in terms of reputation and glory. Wealth and security would accompany this power, but they were not goals in and of themselves. In short, Lodge lacked a plan. He advocated that the United States "take" whatever it could "get." He was "gratuitously imperialistic."[27]

The Philippines became for Lodge something that the United States should take because it could. Moreover, the Philippines became the instrument for annexing Hawaii, bringing to fruition Lodge's five-year quest. In order to send the right message to the other global powers and to ensure that Spain could not redeploy its Pacific fleet to the Caribbean, prior to the outbreak of hostilities in February 1898, Roosevelt cabled Admiral George Dewey instructions that he should sail to Hong Kong. From there, in the event the United States declared war, he should undertake whatever measures were necessary to make certain that Spain's Asiatic fleet never left the Asian coast. Roosevelt lacked any authority to issue this instruction. The navy's secretary, John D. Long, was out of the office. But Lodge was there.

As if to bestow Congress's blessing on Roosevelt's preemptive move should the administration not support it, Lodge looked over Roosevelt's shoulder as he sent the telegram. And he took as much satisfaction as did his friend from Dewey's destruction of the Spain's fleet and installations in Manila Harbor in May 1898. This display of military might signaled America's right to stand at the center of the global stage even as it assured a resounding U.S. victory in what Lodge's neighbor and then-secretary of state, John Hay, called the "Splendid Little War." Further, it brought that much more pleasure to Lodge, because the logistical requirements of an American naval presence in Manila provided an object lesson in the strategic value of Hawaii. Seizing the opportunity, days after America's navy inflicted the fatal blow on Spain by destroying its Caribbean naval force in the bay off of Santiago, Cuba, the Massachusetts senator executed a "clever parliamentary maneuver." By attaching a joint resolution to annex Hawaii as a rider to the War Revenue bill, he accelerated its passage. When the House enacted a parallel resolution a week later, in August 1898 the linchpin to Lodge's large policy was finally in American hands.[28]

Lodge favored the United States wrapping its hands around every Spanish possession that it could. Having as recently as 1895 pronounced America's obtaining Cuba a "necessity," he was resigned after the war to the Teller Amendment's precluding its annexation. He was cheered, however, by the prospect of America's exercising control through its military occupation, and he voted enthusiastically in 1901 for the Platt Amendment that transformed Cuba into a virtual U.S. protectorate. Lodge likewise applauded the provision of the Treaty of Paris that transferred Puerto Rico from Spain to the United

States. We "mean to have it," Lodge assured the Rough Rider Roosevelt. Possession of the island would help to secure America's stake in the Caribbean even as it denied one to any other nation. It would also help to safeguard the projected isthmian canal. Symbolically, moreover, Puerto Rico's acquisition was another notch on America's gun. It represented a conquest; it represented power. The same held true for Spain's ceding Guam to the United States. Where "the flag once goes up it must never come down," Lodge explained. It made little difference where that flag actually flew.[29]

The Philippines was different. Because of its geography, the drama associated with Dewey's victory, and the great difficulty and sacrifice that the United States experienced securing that victory, for Lodge the Philippines signified what he hoped would be a wholesale revolution in America's role and status in the world. The very fact that the Philippines was so far removed from the continental United States, and for that reason appeared so exotic, made it emblematic of a revolution. It gave tangible meaning to the concept of a "large policy." Further, along with Hawaii U.S. control of the Philippines would require that America construct and maintain a fleet capable of projecting U.S. power worldwide even as it vested in the office of the presidency and other components of government the authority to exploit that power more effectively. In doing so, Americans would need to accept their position as a global force with a responsibility to project its greatness. Because inherent in this projection of greatness was the projection of U.S. values and ideals, America's was inherently an empire for liberty. Lodge thus saw U.S. imperialism as a "model imperialism" by which Americans behaved as "agent[s] of international reform" and "political mentors to their charges." This "workable fusion of American power and American idealism' in the international arena, in turn, would "elevate and enlarge the whole tone and scope of our politics." For Lodge, U.S. imperialism became a means to bolster, or he would argue to reinvigorate, American nationalism and identity. It was "a challenge whose acceptance could portend a new era in American history."[30]

A decision by President McKinley to pay attention to anti-imperialists and leave the Philippines in Spanish hands would signal a refusal to accept the challenge. Summoning the power of his convictions for which he had become famous and would become more so, Lodge threw himself into preventing, in his words, this "simple infamy." He campaigned for membership on the commission charged with negotiating the Treaty of Paris but was too junior to make the cut. That the treaty nonetheless transferred possession of the Philippines delighted him. That major elements in the United States continued to oppose the transfer worried him. The Senate ratified the treaty in February 1899, but with but one vote to spare. His worries intensified as, beginning almost simultaneously with the Senate vote, insurgent Filipino nationalists engaged the United States in a brutal war over control of the archipelago. As the war claimed an ever growing number of American lives (ultimately more than 4,000; a fraction of the Filipino losses) and, some argued, likewise claimed American morals, the anti-imperialists gained adherents to their cause.[31]

The anti-imperialists were a diverse lot, spanning a spectrum from the author Mark Twain to the industrialist Andrew Carnegie to the Republican senator George Hoar and Democratic presidential aspirant William Jennings Bryant to the philosopher William James to the patrician intellectual and scion of America's first family, Charles Francis Adams, Jr. They opposed the U.S. project in the Philippines for reasons as diverse as their constituencies: America was refuting its anticolonial heritage, violating its Constitution, jeopardizing its security by provoking international rivalries, and ingesting racial minorities that were ill-equipped for democratic governance and could reproduce societal divisions reminiscent of the antebellum era. The list continues, but a comment by one anti-imperialist captures its eclecticism and the centrality of the Philippines to the debate: "Dewey took Manila with the loss of one man—and all our institutions."[32]

Lodge appreciated the difficulties America confronted. "The people whom we liberated down there have turned against us," he commented as reports of Filipino resistance to American poured in. That concession notwithstanding, he rejected every one of the anti-imperialist arguments. Not for one moment did he fret over the risk to America's institutions. To the contrary, the insurrection reinforced his conviction that the vitality if not the survival of America's institutions required its embracing empire, global empire, transoceanic empire. To retreat in the face of opposition, he explained, would make it "inevitable that we should sink out [sic] from among the great powers of the world."

Conversely, if we "follow the laws of our being," laws that, his interpretation of U.S. history underscored, had guided Americans since at least the time of Jefferson's acquisition of Louisiana, "we shall stand in the front rank of the world powers." America owed it to its people and all of mankind to stand in that front rank. "I do not believe that this nation was an accident," Lodge proclaimed. "I do not believe that it is the creation of blind chance. I have faith that it has a great mission in the world—a mission of good, a mission of freedom."[33]

Perceiving no contradiction in defining America's mission as one "of freedom" yet acknowledging that those people whom America had freed opposed it, Lodge harnessed the reality of American power to the ideal of an Empire for Liberty. Taking charge of the political agenda during the debates first over ratifying the Treaty of Paris and then America's conduct during the war by chairing the Senate's Committee on the Philippines, he demonstrated a remarkable facility for intellectual gymnastics. Lodge turned the anti-imperialists' constitutional and racial arguments on their heads. A historian of his ilk had no difficulty dispensing with the contention that the U.S. government lacked the authority to take possession of the archipelago. Jefferson had settled that question when purchasing Louisiana, he declared. Should doubts linger, Lodge cited another of his heroes, the "great" John Marshall— "clarum et venerabile nomen." Marshall reified Jefferson's judgment when during the Jackson administration he ruled in *Cherokee Nation v. Georgia* that the United States could exercise jurisdiction over a "domestic and dependent nation."[34]

For Lodge the Constitution was less of an issue than the Declaration of Independence, with its reference to "consent of the governed." He was more than prepared to provide an answer to all those who questioned the compatibility of this clause and the denial of sovereignty to the Filipinos. Again using the history of Jefferson's acquisition of Louisiana as the appropriate reference, Lodge maintained that the same axiom applied in the Philippines: The indigenous people were as "incapable of self-government as children." Hence just as Jefferson defined bringing civilization to the frontier as a responsibility, so Lodge considered America responsible for bringing civilization to the Philippines (a farther western frontier). "The taking of the Philippines does not violate the principles of the Declaration of Independence, but will spread them among a people who have never known liberty and who in a few years will be as unwilling to leave the shelter of the American flag as those of any other territory we ever brought beneath its folds," lectured Lodge at great length to the Senate in March 1900.[35]

Providing what one historian labeled "the most detailed brief" in defense of U.S. imperialism, Lodge argued that acquiring the Philippines was the culmination of a logical and inexorable process that began with the Ohio River Valley and Louisiana and extended through Florida, Texas, California, and Alaska. Consistent with these precedents, the United States can "give to those people [Filipinos] a larger measure of peace and happiness, of freedom and prosperity, than any other nation in the world," he asserted. It must "not fail in its duty." This duty, he stressed, was to Americans as well as Filipinos. "I believe that these new possessions and these new questions, this necessity for watching over the welfare of another people, will improve our civil service, raise the tone of public life, and make broader and better all our politics," he explained.[36]

Lodge's arguments rested on racial premises that in the course of the controversy over the Philippines emerged as pivotal to his thinking about America, and about America and the world. These premises underlay his paternalistic perspective. Perhaps more salient in terms of his future thinking and behavior, they framed his defense of America's performance during the Filipino-American War. Always the partisan, Lodge on the one hand mocked the Democratic anti-imperialists' sudden "tenderness for the rights of men with dark skins in the islands of the Pacific." He contrasted this sensitivity to the "harsh indifference which they have always manifested toward those American citizens who 'wear the shadowed liver of the burnished sun' [former slaves] within the boundaries of the United States." On the other hand, Lodge's explanation for the atrocities committed by U.S. soldiers rested on his own racism. In the crucible of war, he stated bluntly, white Americans emulated the behavior of their nonwhite enemy. "I think I know why these things ["these atrocities which we all so much regret and over which we sorrow"] have happened," Lodge told the Senate. "I think they have grown out of the conditions of warfare, of the war that was waged by the Filipinos themselves, a semi-civilized people, with all the tendencies and characteristics of Asiatics, with the Asiatic indifference to life, with the Asiatic treachery and the Asiatic cruelty, all tinctured and increased by three hundred years of subjugation to Spain."[37]

From the time of his youth during the Civil War, Lodge, while proud of his conservatism, considered his views on race progressive. Like Seward he did not believe in the equality of races. Yet he was confident that nonwhite races, when properly tutored, would be carried along by white America's march toward power and greatness. He advocated an ever-growing American Empire for Liberty without worrying, like many of his contemporaries from both parties, that nonwhite populations would undermine it. Without a second thought he had seized the opportunity to take the Philippines under America's imperial umbrella.

Yet beginning early in the 1890s, as Lodge migrated from the House to the Senate and established himself as the upper chamber's leading imperialist, his perspective on race, as he defined race, evolved. This was the decade during which the trickle of "new immigrants" to the United States turned into a flood. They came from Russia, Poland, Hungary, Italy, even Japan. Many were Jews. The potential consequences worried Lodge. Long ago he had accustomed himself to the integration of the Irish into Boston politics, and to a lesser extent society, a position congruent with the one he held about African Americans: inclusive albeit separate and unequal. Still at a time when America's industrialism, urbanization, and attendant economic distress caused massive dislocation and political unrest, Lodge feared that the influx of a population that spoke as well as looked different would prove difficult to assimilate and potentially erode Americas' sense of self—their sense of greatness and exceptionalism. That these aliens brought with them such subversive ideas as socialism and anarchism exacerbated the threat.

Lodge consequently emerged as the Senate's most recognizable voice opposing immigration as well as promoting empire. For conceptual reasons the former affected the latter. Lodge's interpretation of historical processes, of change over time, led him to arrive at a definition of race that, he conceded, challenged that of contemporary science. He posited that the evolution of the nation-state and a hierarchically structured global order rendered concepts of race based on genetically transmitted physical characteristics less relevant if not obsolete. Lodge never subscribed to the eugenics movement of the era. Anticipating certain dimensions of present-day cultural anthropology, however, he equated race with ethnicity and, more precisely, nationality.

By the early twentieth century Lodge had concluded that the "races" that mattered most were the "artificial races, that is, races like the English-speaking people, the French, or the Germans—who have developed as races by the operation during a long period of time of climatic influences, wars, migrations, conquests, and industrial development. . . . It is by these conditions and events that the races and nations which to-day govern the world have been produced." Skin color or hair texture were less germane than the "stock of ideas, traditions, sentiments, modes of thought," and, most important of all, "moral characteristics" that determine the "social efficiency" of a "people." Lodge agreed with the many Americans who sought to limit if not exclude immigrants because they created an unsustainable surplus of unskilled workers, caused hazardous overcrowding in cities, and otherwise taxed U.S. institutions. But his concerns were more fundamental. "Alien to the body of the American people," the new immigrants threatened to generate "a great and perilous change in the very fabric of . . . the English-speaking race that our history, our victories, and all our future rest."[38]

Opposition to immigration was Lodge's signature issue from the aftermath of the war in the Philippines through America's entry into World War I. Demonstrating little concern for the words "huddled masses yearning to be free" inscribed on the Statue of Liberty in 1903, he supported literacy tests and other instruments to curb the dilution of America's "racial purity." Largely because of Lodge, the Senate in 1917 overrode President Woodrow Wilson's veto and established a literacy requirement for immigrations and banned immigration from most of Asia. This legislation provided the basis for a National Origins Act, enacted in 1924, the year Lodge died, that correlated quotas on immigrants to the census of 1890 (before the inflation of new immigrants). In short, the passionate beliefs about American greatness that Lodge held since his youth led to an obsession with "American-ness" (or "Whiteness") in his later years. He personally undertook a demographic study that, juxtaposed with Frederick Jackson Turner's treatise on the American West, provided the basis for his argument that the

British race, "Americanized" on the "crucible of the frontier," was responsible for the best in U.S. development and its national character.[39]

This fixation on the American "race" and concomitant anxiety over its contamination did not turn Lodge against empire. He never converted to anti-imperialism. During the Rough Rider Roosevelt's tenure as president he enthusiastically served as his friend's lieutenant. Lodge fully approved of America's "taking" the Panama Canal in 1903, and he cheered when Roosevelt promulgated his corollary to the Monroe Doctrine a year later, proclaiming the U.S. authority to exercise "police power" throughout the Western Hemisphere. In 1912 he added his own corollary, which prohibited any "corporation or association" that was "not American" from gaining possession of "any harbor or other place in the American continents."[40] Lodge even proposed to Roosevelt that the United States acquire Greenland, and he never entirely gave up his interest in annexing Canada. He exulted over the president's showing off America's sixteen battleships by sending them around the world in 1907.

Yet the racial dynamics that drove Lodge's perspective on the war in the Philippines and immigration to the United States caused him to reign in his ambitions. No longer confident that less evolved peoples would or could embrace American values or even tutelage, he began to think in terms of an Empire *of*, in contrast to *for*, Liberty. In contrast to his views on Cuba and the Philippines, he shied away from advocating intervention let alone colonization in pursuit of America's historic mission. As did Roosevelt, Lodge wondered whether insisting that the United States take possession of the Philippines had been a mistake. He never doubted that the United States should project its power throughout the world. He seriously doubted, however, that the United States could export its national character, and he was certain that only Americans could be Americans.

This modification in thinking explains his behavior throughout the climactic chapter of his life and career, World War I and the battle over the Versailles Treaty. When in 1909 William Howard Taft succeeded Roosevelt in the White House, he asked Lodge to become his secretary of state. Lodge declined. He preferred to hold onto his base in the Senate, where he remained a force on the Committee on Foreign Relations. Unlike Roosevelt, moreover, he never broke with Taft. He was more disposed toward Taft's domestic conservatism than Roosevelt's progressivism. He also sympathized with Taft's efforts to substitute "dollar diplomacy" for military force as a means to exercise global influence, whether close to home in Latin America or far away in Asia. In his view effective management of the American empire required carefully calibrating means and ends. Although it pained him, Lodge stayed neutral throughout the 1912 Republican Convention. After losing the nomination to Taft, Roosevelt ran on his own Progressive Party ticket. Lodge stuck with the original.

The split within the GOP was for Lodge a catastrophe. He had put party over friendship. Worse, the Republicans lost. Worse still, Woodrow Wilson won. A respected political scientist whose scholarship eclipsed that of both Lodge and Roosevelt, Wilson, whose road to the White House passed through Princeton University and the New Jersey governor's mansion, was a virtual unknown to Lodge. Nevertheless, his roots were in Virginia, he became a progressive, and he was a Democrat. Hence for the Massachusetts senator the president had three strikes against him. In addition Wilson, a devout Calvinist certain he correctly interpreted God's will, was even more arrogant and irascible than Lodge. The two began as rivals but rapidly turned into bitter enemies. In 1915 Lodged confided to Roosevelt, "I never expected to hate anyone in politics with the hatred I feel towards Wilson."[41]

In 1915 the source of Lodge's ire was Wilson's resistance to helping Britain and France. The animosity developed much sooner, however. Domestic policy played a role. Lodge suspected that Wilson's New Freedom program constituted political pandering of the worst kind. Wilson has "no intellectual integrity at all," Lodge wrote. "A man can change one or two of his opinions for his own advantage and change them perfectly honestly," Lodge wrote, "but when a man changes all his well considered opinions of a life time and changes them all at once for his own popular advantage it seems to me that he must lack in loyalty of conviction."[42]

Foreign policy influenced Lodge's assessment of Wilson even more. That the president would entrust the State Department to William Jennings Bryan, the populist and anti-imperialist who headed the Democratic ticket in both 1896 and 1900 and was an innocent in matters of global affairs, was to Lodge an outrage. That Wilson ineptly as well as unwisely intervened in the Mexican Revolution with military force was to Lodge a calamity. He viewed Mexico's president Victoriano Huerta as no less an enemy of freedom and democracy than did Wilson. No longer an Empire for Liberty enthusiast, nevertheless, he had reservations from the start about committing U.S. forces to remedy these defects. What turned these reservations into open hostility was Wilson's commitment of a force unprepared for resistance and incapable of overwhelming it. To Lodge, a commitment of force required sufficient force to ensure victory. When Mexicans commanded by Pancho Villa launched attacks against U.S. property in New Mexico and Arizona, prompting Wilson to send Major-General John J. ("Black Jack") Pershing across the border in a futile effort to capture Villa, Lodge recoiled in horror. Wilson's incompetence had showed America to be weak and called into question its greatness.

In truth Wilson was as convinced of and determined to put on display America's greatness as Lodge. He was likewise as dedicated an apostle of empire. Their definitions of American greatness differed, however, and unlike Lodge, Wilson remained devoted to an Empire for Liberty. His reading of American history combined with the failed excursion into Mexico to confirm in his mind that what made America great was not its power, as represented by the wars that it won and the territory that it had conquered. It was its ideals, as represented by the values of its people and institutions of its government. Its mission was to spread these values and institutions, not by force but by commerce, education, and example. Synthesizing what he considered the most positive dimensions of the visions of Franklin, Adams, Seward, and even Lodge, Wilson envisioned a reformed, indeed a revolutionized international system in which all nations, some sooner than others, accepted American leadership and adopted American norms and principles. Pursuit of this Empire for Liberty would produce an Empire of Liberty. Wilson would ultimately call this empire a "League of Nations." The name signaled consent, equality, and the right to self-determination, but he never doubted that America would dominate. This global architecture would institutionalize U.S. security, U.S. prosperity, and U.S. greatness. The boundary between American idealism and self-interest would evaporate.

The catalyst for Wilson's epiphany and then revelations was the run-up to and eruption of World War I. The shooting began in August

1914. In the preceding years the collapsing Austrian and Hungarian empires had allied with Germany's powerful new one. In response, Great Britain, France, and Russia had formed their own alliance, the Triple Entente. A Serbian nationalist's assassination of Austria's Archduke Franz Ferdinand in June triggered mass mobilization on both sides. August brought declarations of war, attacks and counterattacks, and bloody stalemate. The empires that had ruled the world since the seventeenth century all faced destruction. Wilson, presiding over the newest and most ambitious empire, looked on with horror.

The president, determined to keep the United States out of the war, declared a policy of neutrality. Having written hundreds of admiring pages about Britain's parliamentary tradition, and acutely sensitive to the cultural and economic bonds between London and Washington, Wilson's sympathies were self-evident. In private he made explicit his view that a victory by the authoritarian and brutish Germans would endanger the entire civilized world. On these basics Lodge fully agreed. He could not countenance, however, the bungling, and in Lodge's view supine, mediation efforts of Secretary of State Bryan, whom Wilson, grieving over his wife's death and still focused on domestic reforms, granted free rein over U.S. diplomacy.

Lodge wanted a policy of neutrality that ensured an allied victory. Bryan's proposed mediation without the precondition that Germany withdraw from Belgium and northern France. Worse, to Lodge Wilson's neutrality was wrongheaded, reminiscent of Jefferson's posture during the era of Napoleon. Americans must be "too proud to fight," said the president. Americans must be prepared to fight, thought Lodge. The only effective neutrality was a "strong neutrality" that signified that the United States was "ready to strike the first nation, no matter which it was, that dared infringe it." Because Wilson refused to back his diplomacy with a capable force, Lodge opined, he forfeited America's "privilege of being neutral."[43]

On April 2, 1917, Wilson did request a declaration of war. Four days later Congress voted overwhelmingly in favor. For more than a year the president had been tilting policy inexorably toward the Triple Entente by sanctioning loans and arms sales, protesting only meekly the British blockade of Germany, and acquiescing to its mining of the North Sea. The German decision in February 1917 to abandon all restraints on its submarine and consider U.S. ships enemy targets was for Wilson the final straw. Not only did he consider the U-boat a barbaric contravention of international law, but he also had issued a public ultimatum to the Germans to cease attacking U.S. vessels or face the consequences. There was no turning back. At least as important, Wilson had concluded that civilization's future required all nations to adhere to U.S. principles. Only by joining the war could it influence the peace. "The world must be made safe for democracy," rang the words of his speech to Congress. "Its peace must be planted upon the tested foundations of political liberty."[44]

Wilson did not call his vision an Empire for Liberty. But that was his vision. He distinguished his goals from those of the Triple Entente (known by Americans as the Allies) by declaring that the United States would enter the war as their "Associate." The Fourteen Points he announced on January 8, 1918, made explicit that his prescriptions for a just and durable peace, idealistic as they were, would replace the imperial structures imposed by the traditional empires over the centuries with liberal tenets that would eliminate all constraints on American political and economic expansion. "Absolute freedom of navigation upon the seas," the removal of "all economic barriers and the establishment of an equality of trade conditions among all the nations consenting to the peace and associating themselves for its maintenance," and "free, open-minded, and absolutely impartial adjustment of all colonial claims, based upon a strict observance of the principle that in determining all such questions of sovereignty the interests of the populations concerned must have equal weight with the equitable claims of the government whose title is to be determined" were not selfish principles. Their effect, nevertheless, would be to open doors to Americans that the belligerents on both sides of the war had kept shut. Wilson's fourteenth point, the establishment of a "general association of nations," would function similarly to the federation of U.S. states. Washington, D.C., would play the same role in both.[45]

Wilson's Fourteen Points formed the foundation for his peacemaking—and the German surrender in October 1918. Millions of Europeans greeted him as their savior when he arrived in Paris the following January. He was greeted very differently by his counterparts when he arrived in Versailles. Some 100,000 Americans died on the battlefields of World War I. France lost over a million of its soldiers, and the United Kingdom only slightly fewer. Wilson had called for a peace without victory. As victors, the French and British wanted revenge. They also wanted to retain their colonies and protect their economies. They chipped away at Wilson's proposals. But they gave Wilson his association, which they agreed to call the League of Nations. As the president learned when he returned to Washington, however, for Lodge the League was like red meat.

By the Great War's end Lodge's hatred for Wilson, and Wilson's toward him, had grown so intense that the two would have clashed regardless of the terms of the treaty. That Wilson made ratification a partisan issue and failed to consult Lodge, who following the 1918 election fulfilled his ambition of becoming chair of the Senate Committee on Foreign Relations and Senate majority leader, fueled their fire. Lodge's objections to the treaty were nonetheless substantive, especially with regard to the League. He feared that it would undermine policies and programs, such as the Monroe Doctrine and restrictions on immigration, that he had championed for years. The League could "bind us to all kinds of things which the country would not hold to," he said. Lodge worried even more about Article 10. It pledged each League member "to respect and preserve as against external aggression the territorial integrity and existing political independence of all Members of the League." Lodge feared the article could commit the United States to take military actions against its will, without Congress's declaring war, and with inadequate capabilities.[46]

Most generally, he had always preached American greatness, American exceptionalism. Although Lodge for practical reasons would not rule out an Anglo-American alliance, he was in principle a unilateralist who would entrust the American empire only to American power. "I have loved but one flag," he pronounced on the Senate floor. "I cannot share that devotion and give affection to the mongrel banner invented for the League." Like Wilson, Lodge combined American self-interest with American idealism, but he did so in a way that portrayed the League as a calamity for both. "The United States is the world's best hope, but if you fetter her in the interests and quarrels of other nations, if you tangle her in the intrigues of Europe, you will destroy her power for good and endanger her very existence. Leave her to march freely through the centuries to come as in the years that have gone."[47]

Lodge turned the Senate Foreign Relations Committee into a forum for denouncing the League—and Wilson. Many seized the opportunity, ranging from conservatives like Lodge, to former Progressives (dubbed "Irreconcilables") who perceived the League as an instrument to defend aging empires, to isolationists. Then, calculated for their symbolic value, Lodge proposed Fourteen Reservations to Wilson's League Covenant. He predicted that the uncompromising Wilson would reject them. The president did not disappoint. Instead of agreeing to any revisions, he took his case directly to the American public. Following a speech in Pueblo, Colorado, in September 1919, Wilson collapsed; several days later he suffered a massive stroke. While he recovered the Senate rejected the treaty, first with Lodge's reservations attached, then without them. Wilson sought the Democratic nomination in 1920 in order to transform the national election into a referendum on the League. He failed. The Democrats rejected him as their nominee, and the electorate chose the Republican Warren Harding as their president. When Wilson died in 1924, the prospect of American participation in the League died with him. Lodge died nine months later. Neither man's vision of empire reached fruition.

CHAPTER 5

John Foster Dulles and
the Conflicted Empire

I N CAMPAIGNING FOR THE PRESIDENCY in 1920, GOP candidate War- ren G. Harding pledged to return the United States to "normalcy." What that meant was evident to no one. More important, while Harding won, the 1920s turned out not to be normal by any definition. For most Americans, the decade roared—then went bust. A decade later they went back to war.

From the point of view of those who guided America's international policies and conduct, the 1920s and beyond would have challenged any sense of "normalcy" even had Babe Ruth, bathtub gin, and the rampaging stock market not dominated the headlines. Despite Lodge's apparent defeat of Wilson's vision, soon known as Wilsonianism, their ideological battle over the soul of the American empire was far from over in 1924, the year that each died. Further, notwithstanding the robust role of partisanship in the Senate's failure to ratify the Treaty of Paris and the electorate's rejection in 1920 of Wilson's "referendum" on U.S. participation in the League of Nations, his multilateral inter- nationalists and Lodge's unilateral internationalists came from both sides of the aisle.

For almost half a century John Foster Dulles represented and re- flected the tension between the two visions. Dulles was, in a very real sense, a child of the American empire, particularly Lodge's American empire. Born in 1888, his formative years paralleled America's ascent as an international power, with worldwide possessions and interests. Americans elected as their president in 1888 the Republican Benja- min Harrison, whose great-grandfather had signed the Declaration of Independence, whose grandfather had defeated Tecumseh at Tippe- canoe and then won election as president, and whose father had rep- resented the state of Ohio in the U.S. Congress. A brevetted general during the Civil War, Harrison shared the same intense nationalism as did Lodge and others whose loyalty and devotion to the union only escalated during that bloody conflict and its tortuous aftermath. Har- rison selected as his secretary of state James G. Blaine. It was Blaine's expansionism that laid the foundation for Lodge's imperialism. When Blaine fell too ill to continue in office, Harrison replaced him with John Watson Foster—the grandfather of John Foster Dulles.

Not uncommon for this era, Foster's direct experience in interna- tional affairs was limited. He rose to prominence in the Republican

Party as a newspaper editor in Harrison's home state of Indiana, playing a pivotal role in swinging the state to Ulysses S. Grant in his 1872
campaign for reelection. Recognition for his service took the form of
an appointment as U.S. minister to Mexico. Subsequently Foster was
also minister to Russia and Spain. Between these assignments he
helped to negotiate several treaties of reciprocity intended to elevate
America's global economic and political influence. While still a novice
in statecraft, Foster was sensitive to and supported the expansive aspirations of late-nineteenth-century America.

Foster consequently acted with purpose and dispatch with regard
to the revolution in Hawaii that occurred shortly after he took office
under Harrison. In February 1893 the fledgling secretary of state delivered to the president a treaty hastily negotiated with Hawaii's white
minority that provided for U.S. annexation of the islands. Harrison
requested the Senate's immediate ratification. By this time already
a lame duck, having lost his bid for reelection to Grover Cleveland,
he had little leverage. Moreover, the Senate's Democrats refused to
allow the Republicans a last-minute triumph. The anti-annexationist
Cleveland's decision to withdraw the treaty from Senate consideration
presented Lodge with an issue on which he would build his career
as a leading U.S. imperialist. Foster assumed a much less public and
bellicose posture. Nonetheless, he was no less committed to an American empire, and he remained extremely active in the international
arena. One of the founding members of the Carnegie Endowment for
Peace, Foster advised the State Department during both the McKinley
and Theodore Roosevelt administrations. He also counseled the Chinese government during the negotiations following the1894–95 Sino-
Japanese War, and afterward accepted as clients numerous other
foreign governments and U.S. business concerns with overseas interests. The defense or promotion of liberty, whether American or not,
was not a high priority for Foster.

John Foster Dulles was born to Foster's daughter Edith on February 25, 1888, the eve of his grandfather's climb to prominence. Edith
received an internationalist upbringing. She accompanied her father
to his ministerial posts in Russia and Spain, and at the age of seventeen she made her formal debut at a glittering ball in St. Petersburg.
While traveling in Paris a few years later, she met the Reverend Allen

Macy Dulles, whose interest in global affairs equaled those of his future wife. His family roots extended to colonial America, and Allen Macy Dulles's father, John Wesley Dulles, served as a missionary in Madras, India, before settling in Philadelphia. John Wesley Dulles sent his son to study first at Princeton University, and then in Leipzig and Göttingen. Allen was returning from a trip to the Middle East when he encountered Edith Foster in Paris.

Edith gave birth to Foster, as John Foster Dulles was always called, in Washington, D.C., where John Watson Foster lived. This circumstance was appropriate. Foster would mentor his eldest grandson throughout his childhood, instilling in him the values of a former secretary of state and international lawyer who had contributed zealously to the growth of the new American empire and its concomitant: the restructuring of the global system.

Competing for influence with his grandfather's cosmopolitan worldview and sense of U.S. exceptionalism was Dulles's father's religiosity, which mixed theological liberalism with austere devotion (John Wesley Dulles died during Foster Dulles's infancy). The pastor of Watertown, New York's First Presbyterian Church during Dulles's early years, the Reverend Dulles mandated a regimen by which the children (Dulles had three sisters and a brother, Allen Welsh Dulles, who grew into a legend as director of the Central Intelligence Agency) awakened every day to a cold bath and hymns. On Sundays they would parade to church in order to attend three services as well as Sunday school. Their education continued when they returned home, where the Reverend Dulles examined them on the sermon and required each to recite a passage from the scripture memorized the preceding week. Dulles's son Avery, who later converted to Roman Catholicism and advanced to the position of cardinal, attested to the rigor of his father's religious upbringing. Avery Dulles referred in his own writings to reports that Foster Dulles "committed the entire Gospel of John to memory." Weekdays were hardly more relaxing. The children would convene for breakfast around a table with hardwood benches. Their father would then deliver a brief sermon, after which, prior to leaving for school, together they would kneel to pray.[1]

If concern for his children's souls drove the Reverend Dulles's asceticism, his liberalism reflected an intellectualism that he hoped would feed their minds. It did. His father's skepticism over the Bible's "inerrancy" (i.e., its literalism) and acceptance of more secular, indeed scientific explanations for human behavior influenced his son's disposition to appreciate complexity. In the final decades of his life, most notably during his tenure as secretary of state in the 1950s, John Foster Dulles gained a reputation as a fire-and-brimstone Presbyterian moralist with an inflexible, in fact calcified, mind. While Dulles certainly held strong convictions, he projected this image in large part for public consumption. Behind the scenes he was invariably careful and deliberate. As a young man, moreover, he proved an exceptional student, studying political science (under Woodrow Wilson) and philosophy at Princeton. He found the latter especially appealing, and after graduating valedictorian he earned a fellowship to study at the Sorbonne with the Nobel Prize–winning philosopher Henri Bergson. Under the brilliant Bergson Dulles developed a lifelong devotion to the inherent benefits of championing dynamism and change. This devotion, especially when coupled with Dulles's utilitarian concept of spirituality, was congruent with his evolving concept of an American empire.

Dulles's career in public affairs, specifically in diplomacy, began prior to his graduation from Princeton. He grew up in an environment of high politics. Young Dulles spent his summers in Henderson, New York, on Lake Ontario, where he hobnobbed with the likes of William Howard Taft, John W. Davies, and Bernard Baruch. Also visiting the Dulles cottage was New York lawyer Robert Lansing. Lansing married Dulles's aunt, Eleanor Foster Lansing. He also became secretary of state to Woodrow Wilson following the resignation of William Jennings Bryan. Dulles's perspective evolved in fundamental opposition to that of "Uncle Bert," a conservative Anglophile. That contrast made him no less proud of the family connection. When Dulles became secretary of state portraits of his grandfather and uncle flanked his desk at Foggy Bottom.

The line connecting family and career was more linear still. In 1907 the Chinese government appointed William Foster its representative to the Second Hague Peace Conference. Excused by Princeton from his spring semester, the nineteen-year-old Foster Dulles accompanied his grandfather as the delegation's secretary-clerk. The experience hooked him on international affairs. Having once considered following in his father's footsteps, he now preferred his grandfather's.

Immediately after returning from his year's study at the Sorbonne, he moved into the Foster home in Washington and began studying law at George Washington University. Despite working part-time for his grandfather's law practice, Dulles graduated in but two years with, legend has it, the highest grades in the school's history. He passed the bar in 1911. Foster then exploited his connections to land his grandson a position with Sullivan & Cromwell, the titan of international law. The firm's founding partner, Nelson Cromwell, had played a pivotal role in the decision by Lodge, Roosevelt, and their allies to alter the route of a projected isthmian canal so that it cut across Colombia's state of Panama instead of Nicaragua. Sullivan & Cromwell was not directly in the business of building empires. But it provided expert assistance to those who did.

Dulles remained with Sullivan & Cromwell for the next almost forty years, much of that time serving as executive partner. He made lots of money, and he spent lots of time among the power brokers within the United States and beyond its borders. His passion for wealth and the law never equaled his passion for global affairs, however, and he frequently received extended leaves of absence from the firm in order to engage in international politics. These intervals of government service began with the Great War. Shortly before replacing William Jennings Bryan as the head of the Department of State, Dulles's Uncle Bert, at the time the department's counselor, asked his nephew to come to Washington as an informal advisor. Through Sullivan & Cromwell Dulles could provide better intelligence on foreign governments than could Lansing's official sources. As the war went on and Lansing took over as secretary of state, Dulles's responsibilities increased. He went to work for the War Trade Board, from which Vance McCormick plucked him to serve on his committee to oversee Soviet-American relations in the aftermath of the Bolshevik Revolution. On the committee's recommendation in October 1918 President Woodrow Wilson established the Russian Bureau, Inc. Owned in its entirety by the U.S. government, the bureau's mandate was to assist Czech forces and their sympathizers who were fighting the Bolsheviks in Siberia. John Foster Dulles became its secretary-treasurer.

A new chapter opened in Dulles's career. While at the time he could not possibly appreciate the implications of his position on the Russian

Bureau, his subsequent reputation depended heavily on his role in the clash of Soviet and American empires. More immediately, Dulles's political, or more precisely his ideological, identity became tied to that of Woodrow Wilson. Virtually at the same time that he created the Russian Bureau, Wilson appointed Bernard Baruch, the wealthy financier who had frequently vacationed at the Dulles's cottage at Henderson Harbor, to head the U.S. delegation to the Commission on the Reparation of Damage. The conferees at Versailles had established the commission to determine what financial penalty to exact from Germany for its role in the Great War. Baruch selected Dulles to serve as his legal advisor. In this capacity Dulles received a lesson in great-power politics that he would never forget.

Dulles later wrote that assessing reparations "proved, perhaps, the most troublesome single problem of the Peace Conference." His case was solid. The associate powers that had fought alongside the Americans, the British, and French above all, insisted that Germany compensate them for the total cost of arms, munitions, and supplies expended throughout the war. They insisted also that Germany pay to replace whatever public or private property had been lost or destroyed during the fighting. The estimated initial price tag was in the neighborhood of 300 billion contemporary U.S. dollars. Dulles, in concert with the other Americans, objected vociferously. In their collective view, imposing this kind of punishment on the Germans would not only cause a degree of resentment that would destabilize Europe for decades to come but also cripple Germany's capacity to recover. A destitute Germany would take France, Britain, and the other European nations down with it. The United States could not hope to remain immune from this domino effect.[2]

Dulles did all he could to contain the vengeance. Largely by drawing on his legal maneuvers, the U.S. delegation chipped away at its counterparts' most Draconian demands. The conferees did compel the Germans to accept ultimate responsibility for the outbreak of the war and the ensuing destruction it caused. The cost to Germany produced by this acceptance of "war guilt" came to around $32 billion (again, in contemporary dollars). Dulles managed, nevertheless, to incorporate into the treaty the caveat that the "ability of the German Government and nation to make such reparation is limited to such an extent as will render the making of such complete reparation impractical." Although this loophole became moot when the Lodge-led U.S. Senate refused to ratify the treaty, it did lay the foundation for the progressive scaling back of the reparations figure during the 1920s.[3]

In fact, a report written under the leadership of General Electric president Owen Young with the help of J. P. Morgan and other giants of U.S. business and banking (Dulles provided minor assistance) recommended in June 1929 that Germany only be required to pay about one-third of its reparations bill, with the remainder postponed until its capacity increased sufficiently. This moment never came. By the time the Allied Powers adopted the Young Plan in 1930, the U.S. stock market had crashed and the world economy was spiraling into depression.

By this time Dulles had also become increasingly convinced that Britain and France, the great empires that had supervised the international system for centuries beforehand, had, because of their mismanagement of Germany and the damage this mismanagement caused, forfeited their global standing. Indeed, much like Wilson, Dulles rejected the paradigm of competing or even equal empires accepted by Franklin, Adams, Seward, and Lodge. No longer did he believe what he had learned from his grandfather: that although the balance among them shifted, the world's great empires created sufficient equilibrium to produce a stable international system. Dulles concluded that as surely as the American empire would rise, Washington's prediction, the extant empires would fall. Dulles developed this outlook during the 1920s. The 1930s provided him with confirming evidence.

Indeed, barely thirty when he went to Versailles, and never more than a peripheral player during the negotiations, Dulles's experience profoundly affected his life story and his worldview. Although he remained an ardent Atlanticist convinced of the moral and political superiority of Western civilization, he never lost his bitterness toward Britain and France. Moreover, while he learned valuable lessons in diplomacy, he would not apply them for another quarter-century. That was because, disillusioned by what he saw and heard at Versailles, when Americans elected the Republican Warren G. Harding in 1920 on the anti-Wilsonian slogan of "Return to Normalcy," Dulles returned, or more accurately retreated, to Sullivan & Cromwell. And for the next two decades, the Great Depression notwithstanding, he lived the American dream by making lots and lots more money. Voted a full partner upon his return to New York in 1919, Dulles was the firm's managing partner by 1926. Overseeing a clientele that included J. P. Morgan & Company, Dillon, Read & Company, Brown Brothers & Harriman, Goldman Sachs, the American and Foreign Power Company, the International Nickel Company, the Overseas Securities Corporation, United Railways of Central America, and the United Fruit Company, among many others, Dulles orchestrated multimillion-dollar national and international deals as a matter of course. During the Hoover administration *Fortune* profiled him as one of nine (Dulles was first on the list) "20th century specimens of the Great American Attorney."[4]

The dream Dulles lived was that of most Americans during the Roaring Twenties. Few achieved it, but those who did not could compensate with bathtub gin or sublimate with the exploits of Babe Ruth and Al Capone. Yet this fixation on American-ness did not stop U.S. empire-building, nor did the passivity of Presidents Harding and Calvin Coolidge. Both, influenced by Secretary of Commerce Herbert Hoover, who succeeded to the presidency himself in 1929, encouraged business leaders, cultural producers, and others in the private sector to spread America's influence, interests, and ideals abroad. What they sought, and what they were wildly optimistic about acquiring, was an empire different from that envisioned by either Lodge or Wilson. It would not require the force of arms. It would not depend on international institutions. Generated by a process reminiscent of Seward's "political gravitation," it was an "Empire without Tears."[5]

Dulles was one of its architects. He put at the service of his Sullivan & Cromwell clients his first-rate legal mind, his already considerable international experience, and a global outlook nurtured from his days on his grandfather's knee. His wealth grew commensurately with theirs, and theirs grew exponentially as they acquired markets and secured investments throughout the world. Moreover, Dulles also served his clients by assisting in the formulation of first the Dawes Plan, the precursor to the Young Plan, the Young Plan itself, and finally the Polish Stabilization Plan, designed largely by his friend Jean Monnet. Remedying the structural flaws in Europe's economy, he recognized, was vital to the health of America's.

More than his concern for his client base and personal fortune drove the attention Dulles paid to the international order and America's position within it. If anything, he was more convinced than ever after Wilson's failures at Versailles and at home that global peace and civilization demanded U.S. leadership. In fact, it demanded U.S. dominance. Compared to the exciting domestic developments, he feared, an empire without tears, even a prosperous one that championed liberty (ironically, by the end of the 1920s many Americans associated liberty with the discredited Herbert Hoover), would insufficiently capture the public's imagination to prevent a retreat into parochialism if not isolationism. He enthusiastically joined with like-minded internationalists to establish the Council on Foreign Relations, and in 1922 published an article in the inaugural issue of its journal, *Foreign Affairs*. Over subsequent decades he published many more. Dulles also was an active participant in the Carnegie Endowment for International Peace (of which his grandfather was a founding member), the International Chamber of Commerce, the Foreign Policy Association, and other organizations dedicated to expanding America's worldwide influence.

As explained by the historian Emily Rosenberg, critics of Dulles's internationalism in the 1920s were the intellectual and philosophical heirs of the "anti-imperialists" who opposed America's global policies and priorities in the 1890s. In contrast to Lodge or for that matter John Watson Foster, Dulles did not apply the vocabulary of empire to the United States. These words he reserved for the Germans, the French, and other traditional empires that had subverted and perverted the Wilsonian vision. With the collapse of the global economy, ascendancy of Adolf Hitler and his National Socialist Party in Germany (a focal point of Sullivan & Cromwell's international practice), intensifying challenges to the Versailles settlements (ranging from Japan's conquest of Manchuria to Germany's remilitarization of the Rhineland to Italy's invasion of Ethiopia), Dulles's conceptual framework underwent a revision. Drawing on his sense of American exceptionalism, his religious convictions (albeit at this stage in his life Dulles rarely attended church), his familiarity with and writings on foreign relations, and his schooling in philosophy at Princeton and the Sorbonne, Dulles evolved an idiosyncratic conception of empires, liberties, and conflict (war in particular). His behavior was not always consistent with this conception. But the conception itself remained immutable.[6]

For Dulles the watershed came in 1937. This was the same year that Franklin D. Roosevelt began his second term and Hitler gathered his chief lieutenants in the Reich Chancellery to outline his program for *lebensraum*, the acquisition of greater "living space" for Germans. This juxtaposition would lead to a global conflagration over both empire and liberty. Dulles was insufficiently prescient to predict the eruption. Few could, or at least did. But probably to an extent greater than but a handful of Americans, he began early on to contemplate the stakes and implications. The catalyst was invitations he received to attend meetings sponsored by the League of Nations on the one hand and the Universal Christian Council for Life and Work (one of the organizations that would evolve into the World Council of Churches) on the other. The discussions inspired Dulles to think about the relations between peoples and polities in different ways, ways that led him to reach back to his religious foundations and study of philosophy. Dulles held throughout this life that the most effective strategy for working through a problem was to commit his ideas to paper. What he saw emerging in 1937 was a big problem. He decided to write a book.

The words poured out. Following his meetings in Europe, Dulles went on to Asia. War had broken out between Japan and China after the former invaded the latter in July. When mechanical troubles forced Dulles's return flight to lay over on Wake Island, he opted to journey the rest of the way by sea. Before he reached New York he completed the bulk of what in 1939 he published as *War, Peace, and Change*. Its concern was the global "cycle of recurrent violence." Its purpose was to provide a solution.[7]

Although Dulles did not write explicitly about either empire or liberty (save for "spiritual liberty"), the relationship between them was the book's subject. Dulles began with the Calvinist premise that selfishness "is a basic human instinct," and "the fact that human beings, all selfish, are in contact with each other inevitably brings dissatisfaction." This premise led to a second: the "conflict of selfish desires assumes, in its simple form, a struggle between those who primarily are satisfied and wish to retain that which they have and those who are dissatisfied and wish to acquire at the expense of others." In terms of global politics this struggle produced a state of perpetual tension between the haves, who by definition possessed preponderant power, and the have-nots, who at some point would seek to seize it. The haves would resist, resulting first in war, and then a redistribution of that power (and wealth). That result derived from the philosophical axiom that Dulles learned from Bergson: The "dynamic prevails over the static."[8]

This dichotomy between the powerful and the powerless, and between the haves and the have-nots, was inextricable from what Dulles called "the "boundary-barrier situation." This was the concept he used to describe the normative strategy employed by those with sufficient power to make the rules (the "group authority") to deny the wishes (i.e., to deny full liberty and opportunity) to those subject to the rules. Essentially this group authority maintains, Dulles explained, that it is helpless to accommodate certain demands because of established boundaries—limits. These boundaries can be territorial, commercial, legal, and more. Because the list of boundaries continues to grow, moreover, the tendency is for all sides to become increasingly "boundary-conscious." The concept of sovereignty, it followed logically for someone with Dulles's legal perspective, becomes a source of intensifying conflict. So long as one is bound to a single controlling authority, one cannot gain access to that which extends across the boundary to another.[9]

What is striking about Dulles's diagnosis is how dramatically his hierarchy of values differed from those associated with his eighteenth- and nineteenth-century predecessors. The differences would produce profound consequences. From Founding Fathers like Franklin through proud imperialists like Henry Cabot Lodge, the advocates of the American empire had focused on expanding economic opportunity, affording more room for the expansion of peoples and civilization, and of course, extending (or professing to extend) liberty to the subjugated. The aim of providing greater security was not ignored, yet it seemed either a secondary priority or at odds with the notions of exceptionalism and mission. The quest for security, however, particularly as defined as securing peace and avoiding (bloody) conflict, was the central theme of *War, Peace, and Change*. A decade after he published this book Dulles would become renowned for embarking on moral crusades and reducing statesmanship to a religious contest between good and evil. His most cogent expression of his outlook on international affairs, nevertheless, subordinates ideals to safety. "The particular form of security which society preponderantly wants is freedom from violent attack upon person and property."[10]

How different was Dulles's thinking from those who wrote or spoke about the intrinsic value of freedom per se. The premium that he placed on security against attack, particularly when juxtaposed with his identification of the "boundary-barrier situation," became the foundation of Dulles's advocacy of an American empire. Dulles's was not an Empire for Liberty, but an Empire for Security, an empire to confront an Empire against Liberty. The United States as the "group authority" had to make the rules and consistently extend the boundaries over which those rules applied. Further, because Dulles was convinced that "there cannot be any 'security' in a complete sense," his goal had to be boundaries so expansive and rules so inviolate that even the most dynamic state's effort to trespass would not pose a serious threat.[11]

Dulles interpreted the origins of World War II as largely confirming his prognosis. He identified Germany and Japan as the leading two "dynamic" powers. Dulles was quick to identify them as "great despotisms," and he detested their conduct. Their actions in China, Austria, and Czechoslovakia, as well that of the Italians in Ethiopia, he wrote in conventional American rhetoric, "is repugnant to civilized mankind." Yet Dulles refused to attribute their behavior to national character. The Germans and Japanese were people of "great energy," "industry," and "discipline," who manifested a commendable "willingness to sacrifice." The international system that allowed aging empires to make the rules was culpable. By seeking to hold back the tide of change, Britain and France refused to accommodate dynamic aspirations, just as they had more than a century before, when the United States had fought to establish its own dynamic empire. Dulles deplored Germany's and Japan's resort to violence, but it did not surprise him. Their aggression was "precisely that which we ought to have expected and been able to foresee."[12]

More surprising than the outbreak of a second global conflagration was the role Dulles played during it and how he emerged from it. Dedicated internationalist though he was, he initially counseled American noninvolvement. This was a clash of empires and empire wannabees, and the United States was better than any of them. But he expressed a willingness to reconsider his position "if any program could be evolved" that portended a fundamental adjustment of the relations among nations by showing "some promise of re-establishing a real era of peace rather than mere armistices." Having reconnected with his religious roots at the Oxford meeting of the Universal Christian Council for Life and Work in 1937, Dulles received the opportunity to develop such a program. In February 1941 he accepted an invitation from the Federal Council of Churches of Christ in America to chair a one-hundred-member Commission to Study the Bases of a Just and Durable Peace. Ten months later the Japanese attacked Pearl Harbor.[13]

The Federal Council directed the commission to educate Christians about the "moral, political, and economic foundations of an enduring peace" and prepare them "for assuming their appropriate responsibility for the establishment of such a peace." Dulles's ambitions were more expansive. His wanted to influence policymakers. Under his guidance the commission drafted "Six Pillars of Peace." Paralleling Wilson's Fourteen Points, the program's centerpiece was the establishment of a world organization that, in contrast to the now moribund League of Nations, would include as members the war's vanquished as well as victors, and of course the United States. These members would pledge allegiance to "pillars" that an enduring peace required: multilateral economic agreements that reflected liberal trade principles; treaties that were sufficiently elastic to accommodate changing conditions; guarantees of self-determination; mechanisms for controlling arms; and assurances of religious and intellectual freedom. Dulles presented the document personally to Franklin Roosevelt, who described it as "splendid" but did nothing with it. The president, Dulles fumed, lacked "the competence to deal with the problem of bringing this war to an acceptable end."[14]

Dulles spoke out of frustration. He understood that Roosevelt's competence was not the issue. The president's priority had to be to win the war. He was also constrained by politics, domestic as well as international. Dulles could not affect what took place on the battlefield, but as the public face of a large and influential religious constituency, he could influence politics. Embraced by Republican internationalists, Dulles by the time of the GOP convention in 1944 had become a principal advisor to party stalwarts, notably Senator Arthur Vandenberg of Michigan and Governor Thomas Dewey of New York. When Dewey received the party's nomination for president, he gave Dulles free reign over his statements on foreign policy. Although Dewey predictably lost, Dulles emerged from the campaign as a force in elite diplomatic circles. He now represented not only the Protestant Church but also the Republican Party. For this reason, following Roosevelt's death, the end of World War II, and the collapse of America's alliance with the Soviet Union, Dulles became vital to President Harry S. Truman's effort to evoke bipartisan support in a new, but this time cold, war. He attended conferences as a delegate, served as an ambassador-at-large, and advised the secretary of state, whether George Marshall or Dean Acheson.

Dulles's analysis of global politics evolved along with the transformation of international environment. Nevertheless, he held to his underlying diagnosis. In an ideal world states would behave according to the Christian precepts that he learned from his father and that guided his activities for the Federal Council of Churches. These precepts included liberty, broadly defined. Yet the lesson of two world wars, and all that happened in the years between them, was that the world was anything but ideal. States were made up of people, and people were selfish. Consequently, until, or unless, state leaders and followers universally accepted Christian precepts, peace, prosperity, and liberty demanded a vision and the capacity to implement it. Wilson's efforts at Versailles had failed, and the "Six Pillars of Peace" had been a nonstarter. In Dulles's view the British remained unreconstructed defenders of the status quo, or more precisely at the war's end, the status quo ante. In their effort to reclaim their past, they could count on French support—and vice versa. Conversely, the Soviets were dynamic and their leadership possessed "the cardinal virtue of being creative." As Dulles had once written, however, so had been the Nazis. Lesser powers were vulnerable to armed invasion, subversion, deception, or all three.[15]

Throughout the early Cold War Dulles's speeches and writings, both of which were prolific, drew on the lofty vocabulary of the church and America's Founding Fathers. He described his motivation as a "deep sense of mission." Much as in *War, Peace, and Change*, nevertheless, his emphasis was almost exclusively on security. Also much as in that book, his logic drove him to conclude that security required empire, an

American empire, although he never called it such. Indeed, he never defined it as such.[16]

Dulles's empire was not based on Henry Cabot Lodge–type territorial conquest, William Seward–type insular expansion, or any of the models of their predecessors. Nor would it rely on cultural, technological, or concomitant instruments like the interwar Empire without Tears. Dulles conceptualized geopolitical bipolarity, or in his words the division of "one world into incompatible halves," as the "boundary-barrier situation" that he had identified in *War, Peace, and Change*. This "paradigm" compelled the United States to serve as the "group authority" for the symbolically named "Free World," making the rules, insisting that they be followed, and guarding against all trespassers by exercising its power, its spiritual, ideological, economic, and, most important, military power. Dulles did not concern himself with the liberty of those subject to U.S. rules. He cared only that those within the "group authority" of the Kremlin had none of it, and they would deny it wherever their boundaries might spread. That absence of liberty in the Soviet empire was what mattered. His was an Empire for Liberty but not of Liberty.[17]

Dulles was not a theorist of empire. Further, more of a tactician than a strategist, his policies and programs developed piecemeal. Estimating at first that the Soviets were unlikely to accept great risks to cross Western boundaries, he considered U.S. leadership of collective security mechanisms such as the North Atlantic Treaty Alliance (NATO) and the European Recovery (Marshall) Program effective means of "containment." He was no less critical of Britain, France, and other European states. But he was content because the United States made the rules. Dulles determined that America's "group authority" had to expand, however, following the Communist success in China in 1949 and the North Korean invasion of South Korea the next year. In Asia, with the notable exception of Japan, where Dulles personally negotiated the treaty ending the U.S. occupation, America did not make the rules. There, moreover, the potential for Communists crossing boundaries, such as in Indochina, was exponentially greater. And what was true in Asia was true elsewhere in the less developed regions of the world—the Middle East, Africa, even Latin America, so close to home. America, Dulles warned in the midst of the Korean War, had to take whatever measures were necessary to "paralyze the slimy, octopus-like tentacles that reach out from Moscow to suck our blood."[18]

For this purpose containment was inadequate. America had to extend the sphere within which it made the rules. This required liberation, rolling back the Soviet empire and replacing it with an American one. In this way Dulles reinjected liberty into his vocabulary without the need to provide substance to its meaning. When General Dwight D. Eisenhower agreed to seek the Republican nomination for president in 1952, Dulles thought he had found a soul mate. Dulles had given up on the Truman administration, which in his judgment had allowed "a very definite shift in the balance in the world . . . in favor of Soviet Communism." He and Eisenhower were barely acquainted. Yet the World War II hero knew the value of seizing the initiative, and he was already experienced in liberation.[19]

In May 1952 Dulles flew to Paris to introduce himself to Eisenhower, who still commanded the NATO forces, and to lay before him his ideas. He prepared a memorandum that he soon revised for publication in *Life* magazine with the pointed title "A Policy of Boldness." The most effective means to contain the Soviets was to deter them from any mischief in the first place. To achieve that Dulles recommended, in words that would become famous, that the populations within the area enclosed by the U.S. "boundary" had to "develop the will and organize the means to retaliate instantly against open aggression by Red Armies, so that, if it occurred anywhere, we would strike back where it hurts, by means of our choosing." Yet an enduring solution required replacing Moscow's group authority with Washington's. Eisenhower worried that endorsing the concept of "massive retaliation" would serve as an excuse for atavistic isolationists to retreat behind a nuclear shield. This would result in a so-called Fortress America, precisely the opposite of what Dulles sought. The potential candidate seemed more attracted to the notion of liberation, although he would not commit himself to it.[20]

When Eisenhower launched his campaign, he did embrace liberation, or so it seemed. Although Dulles was the former general's (Eisenhower resigned from the army to run for political office) chief foreign policy advisor, his other assignments prevented him most of the time from traveling with the candidate. Chief among these was writing the foreign policy planks of the Republican platform. Liberation figured prominently, and Eisenhower signed on. When he accepted the nomination, he spoke in words that Dulles would have chosen. "I know something of the solemn responsibility of leading a crusade," Eisenhower told the delegates at the GOP convention. "I accept your summons. I will lead this crusade." Once elected, he selected Dulles as his secretary of state. Dulles was thrilled, that much more so because Eisenhower selected his brother, Allen Dulles, to direct the five-year-old Central Intelligence Agency (CIA). During the campaign Eisenhower had admonished Dulles always to qualify liberation as peaceful. Covert operations would thus be pivotal. The Dulles brothers perceived the CIA as the ideal instrument for expanding the U.S. boundaries—its empire.[21]

No secretary of state ever worked more closely or effectively with his president than did Dulles, and their mutual respect grew in proportion to their collaboration. Still, whereas Eisenhower's commitment to the North Atlantic Alliance was the raison d'être for his decision to seek the presidency, the negative impressions of the British and French that Dulles had formed as far back as Versailles and had articulated frequently ever since remained. If anything his despair had grown more intense. With the Cold War now the *idée fixe* of global politics, Dulles perceived everything through a bipolar lens. Consequently, he feared that as America pushed back the East to make more space for the West, its principal allies would prove more of a liability than an asset. Only a few months into the new administration, he presented his case to Eisenhower in a meeting at the White House. "In the world chess game, the Reds today have the better position," he began. Momentum had to shift, and that demanded "winning in one or more areas." Dulles left it to Eisenhower to interpret what "winning" meant, or what had to be won. He was unambiguous, however, about who must do the winning. The European leaders were "shattered 'old people'" who "want to spend their remaining days in peace and repose" in the hope that the "Soviets, like Ghenghes [*sic*] Khan, will get on their little Tartar ponies and ride back whence they came." Like Hitler and the Nazis, they would not. Their empire, like Hitler's, would endanger everyone everywhere.[22]

Exactly what Dulles hoped to achieve by this tirade cum lament is difficult to determine. He certainly did not want America to jettison its allies and face off against the Soviets by itself. Going it alone would overtax its resources (as it was, some 60 percent of federal expenditures, or more than 10 percent of America's gross national product, went toward defense), which even in the United States were not boundless. Like Eisenhower Dulles was a fiscal conservative. What is more, the potential need to balance guns and butter could sap America's dynamism. Dulles probably sought to encourage the administration to exercise more group authority, to lay down more rules and insist that the British and French obey them. He probably did not expect Eisenhower's response.

The president grilled Dulles with pointed questions, but he did not tell him he was wrong. Rather, he organized Operation Solarium (named after the room where the meeting occurred) to assess the available options. They ranged from containment to liberation. If Dulles were to receive the green light to pursue his vision of an American empire, this was his opportunity. What he received was a red light, or at least a deep yellow one. The Solarium exercise precipitated a comprehensive strategic review that by the end of the year produced Eisenhower's "New Look." While it allowed for liberation where the risk was low, the emphasis remained on containment. Further, U.S. relations with its allies would be characterized by cooperation, not coercion. America's group authority would be far from absolute.

Dulles did not get what he wanted, but he was satisfied with what he got. In part that was because the deliberations persuaded him to moderate his views. In greater part it was because even before the new strategy was in place, the U.S. empire began to replace the empires of its allies, if not that of the Soviets. Iran, or more precisely southern and eastern Iran, had been a British sphere of influence since London had reached an agreement with Russia to divide it between them in the twentieth century's first decade. While not perfect for either, the arrangement proved workable for both. Thrown together unexpectedly as allies in World War II, in late 1941 they cooperated in seating on the Peacock throne Mohammad Reza Shah Pahlavi in lieu of his pro-German father. When the Grand Alliance dissolved at the end of the war, so did Anglo-Soviet amity in Iran. With U.S. assistance in 1946 the British outmaneuvered Stalin. Because the Kremlin had withdrawn its troops, it could do nothing but watch as the British turned Iran virtually into their fiefdom. Exercising its influence primarily through the Anglo-Iranian (initially Anglo-Persian) Oil Company (AIOC), London paid rent and royalties to the shah and kept for itself practically all the company's earnings. Iranian nationalists demanded more. When Mohammad Mossadegh became prime minister after the assassination of his predecessor, he gave it to them. In May 1951 Mossadegh nationalized the AIOC.

The Eisenhower administration inherited a plan hatched by the British Secret Intelligence Service to oust Mossadegh. Truman had balked; Eisenhower did not. While Iran might not appear to fit the definition of a Soviet satellite, in Dulles's mind it came close enough. Mossadegh, he was convinced, was either in league with Iran's Communist Tudeh Party, or he was its unwitting tool. Hence Iran qualified as an area that the West should win. Or more accurately, it qualified as an area that the *United States* could win. Dulles, with his brother as his accomplice, was prepared to concert with the British to get rid of Mossadegh. They had multiple assets on the ground, whereas America had virtually none. But Dulles insisted that America would be in charge. It would make the rules. Further, Mossadegh's replacement had to be General Fazlollah Zahedi, a notorious Anglophobe. The result of Operation AJAX, consequently, would not only deny Iran to the Soviets but also produce the first shift from the British Empire to America's. In early August 1953 Eisenhower approved the plan. By the end of the month Mossadegh was in jail, Zahedi was prime minister, and the shah had become one of Washington's most valuable clients.

As an unintended consequence of Dulles's influence, the operation in Iran was a watershed in the growth of the American empire. Ironically given Dulles's religious background and his frequent references to spiritualism and the missionary impulse that had been historically integral to U.S. expansion, the compulsion to "uplift" less civilized peoples became a comparatively low priority. In this regard he differed from Eisenhower, who, again ironically, was more spiritual. But they agreed that the highest priority must be the security and the defense of the American way of life. Toward this end Dulles had advocated expanding America's group authority. In light of his geopolitical zero-sum calculus, this meant diminishing that of the Soviets by enveloping within Washington's patrolled boundaries all peoples and territory within Moscow's. The confluence of Operation Solarium and Operation AJAX resulted in a change in tactics. The U.S. empire would grow at the expense of its allies'. That growth would strengthen the Free World's existing boundaries even as it extended them to the nonaligned periphery. America's long-standing anticolonialism would produce an innovative imperium. It may not have extended liberty, but it stymied a system that by definition was antiliberty.

Indochina manifested this imperial New Look. Along with Algeria the linchpin of what remained of the French empire, Indochina's reclamation by Paris following the end of Japan's World War II occupation was central to remedying France's national identity crisis. Its nationalism collided with that of the Vietminh, which was heavily influenced by the Communism of its leader, Ho Chi Minh, and many of its members. The result was among the first of the postwar wars of national liberation. As the Cold War intensified, so did American assistance to the French. By the year Dulles took charge of the Department of State, America was footing the bill for about one-third of France's imperial project.

For Dulles the scenario was nightmarish from the start; he had little confidence in France's ability to protect the Free World's boundaries. Against the Germans in 1940 France had demonstrated a lack of military capabilities and national will. Dulles had attributed these shortcomings to France since World War I. It epitomized the static empires that produced the recurrent cycles of global violence that dynamic empires like Germany's and the Soviets' could exploit. The colonialism that France pursued was anathema to Dulles's principles and his prescriptions for global peace. Predictably, Dulles's responses to France's fall in 1940 had been to caution against rushing to its assistance. Subsequent events convinced him that he had been wrong.

Moreover, Dulles could no longer enjoy the luxury of commenting from the sidelines. He was responsible for safeguarding U.S. interests, and he assessed the threat to them as intolerable. At issue was not the liberty of the Indochinese to determine their future but the geostrategic reality. Indochina had proved invaluable to the Japanese as it launched its campaign to create a "Greater East Asia Co-Prosperity Sphere." Dulles was sure that it would prove equally valuable to the Soviets in their campaign for global dominion. As an immediate consequence of the failure to contain the Communist virus in Indochina, the security of Japan, the "workshop of Asia," which with the "fall" of China in 1949 was now the most valuable Western asset in the Far East, would become untenable. "The situation of the Japanese is hard enough with China being commie," Dulles commented. If Indochina and thus Southeast Asia also fell, "the Japs would be thinking how to get on the other side."[23]

There it was: sides and boundaries. And the reconfigurations would be massive and disastrous. France and Great Britain, whose empire would surely lose Malaya, a source of valuable rubber and tin, would suffer enough economic harm to undermine Europe's recovery. The political architecture in each of the continental countries west of the Iron Curtain was insufficiently solid to withstand the tremors. It was more than a year after he took office that Eisenhower expressed his famous domino analogy. Dulles was thinking in these terms much earlier and with much greater alarm. The fate of Indochina, he warned, was "more important than Korea because the consequences of loss there could not be localized, but would spread throughout Asia and Europe." Dulles knew what must be done. But he was not at all sure how to do it.[24]

Encouraging the French, on the one hand, to get on the right side of nationalism by promising to set the Indochinese free and, on the other, to take the fight more aggressively to the enemy did nothing to impede their deteriorating situation. By New Year's Day 1954 the Vietminh had trapped the French forces at Dienbienphu, in the remote northwest corner of Vietnam where it bordered Laos. By March their artillery had caused significant casualties and knocked out all avenues of resupply. France required American help if only to negotiate a settlement that would avoid surrender. Dulles's inclination to provide it was almost irresistible.

Yet he resisted. Dulles was willing to commit U.S. air and naval forces, but he would not place them at the service of the French empire. Nor was he prepared at this time to commit U.S. forces to serve an American empire. Dulles was not deterred by the concept. He always considered European imperial projects fundamentally different from America's. The United States could rely on capable indigenous elements to accept Washington's authority. This kind of indirect control would relieve the United States of much of the financial, military, and even ideological burden of empire, and through wise management would produce an empire stronger than those constructed ever before. Dulles had become an anticolonial imperialist, and he took Iran as his model. In Indochina, however, America had little indigenous support and by itself lacked the capability to exercise control over challenges to its authority. It was all but inevitable that it would confront the same kind of "boundary-barrier situation" as did France.

As a stopgap measure Dulles formulated a "United Action" plan. A coalition comprising the ANZUS-pact powers (Australia, New Zealand, and the United States), France, Great Britain, Thailand, the Philippines, and the Associated States of Indochina (Laos, Cambodia, and Vietnam's three components—Tonkin, Annam, and Cochin China) would collectively guarantee the security of each of its members. This coalition would finesse the conflict's appearing as either an imperial or a white man's war (which to many in the developing world were linked phenomena). Better yet, its establishment would achieve the French goal of providing the environment necessary for a negotiated settlement. It would deter the Communist Chinese and Soviets from providing material assistance to the Vietminh, who would exhaust themselves prior to exhausting the French forces. Dulles was not sanguine about the prospects of either assembling the coalition or, if he did, its having the desired effect. The odds grew longer almost immediately. Congress insisted that France agree to "internationalize" the war and Britain agree to participate in this internationalized effort before Americans committed themselves to provide any assistance. In addition, before Americans made any commitments of their own, the French had to commit themselves to Indochinese (primarily Vietnamese) independence.

Dulles had made scant progress by the beginning of May 1954. But the Vietminh had. On May 7 the French surrendered. Dulles received the news in Geneva, where he was attending the opening of a conference convened to determine the fate of Indochina (and settle the Korean War). He assumed that the colony would in one way or another be amputated from the French empire, but he was not prepared to propose its incorporation in America's. Yet Dulles barely considered the possibility of it emerging, whether as a whole or divided into its

components, independent (or at least viably independent). What remained, then, was the likelihood of Indochina's imprisonment within
the Soviet empire, or the Sino-Soviet empire. Imperial boundaries
would change, and that prospect scared him to death.

It showed. Looking every bit his sixty-six years, Dulles always appeared dour to the public. He routinely mispronounced "Communist"
(it sounded like "Comminist") as if it pained him even to utter the
word. At Geneva such traits were particularly pronounced. Projecting a demeanor characterized by one conference attendee as "almost
pathological rage and gloom," Dulles allowed the press to photograph
him childishly refusing to shake hands with Communist Chinese foreign minister Chou En-lai (Zhou Enlai). With equal churlishness he
objected to any seating arrangement that placed him in the vicinity
of a Communist delegate. When he did sit down he looked physically
distraught, his "mouth drawn down at the corners, and his eyes on the
ceiling, sucking his teeth." Dulles stayed at the conference only long
enough to deliver an opening harangue, returning to Washington immediately afterward.[25]

Unable to imagine the conference producing anything positive,
Dulles concluded that it was "in our interest" for negotiations to collapse. They did not. Confounding Dulles's predictions, the accord
reached, while perhaps not fitting his definition as positive, did not
include terms that Americans needed "to gag about." The Kremlin,
still in the process of regaining its footing after the death of Joseph
Stalin in March 1953, did not consider this real estate worth the risk
of a confrontation with the United States. And more than the Americans, the Communist Chinese appreciated the historic enmity between
their and the Vietnamese empire. Deprived of either's support, Ho Chi
Minh acquiesced to a Vietnam recognized as an independent polity but
divided administratively at the seventeenth parallel. Only the North
would be under Vietminh control, with the French (perhaps with the
assistance of others) securing the autonomy of the South until elections for a unified government were held in 1956. The remaining Indochinese colonies of Laos and Cambodia would receive independence
as well. Dulles enthusiastically supported the administration's consensus: America would not sign the final agreement, but it pledged not to
disturb any of the provisions.[26]

The United States not only disturbed but also violated the provisions. Dulles's contribution was pivotal. As if he could no longer escape the logic of his own decades-long thinking and writing, Dulles determined that the United States must replace France—and Great Britain—as the seat of a global, non-Communist empire. There was no alternative. The old imperial powers simply lacked the capabilities and the dynamism to manage what for centuries had been theirs, formally or informally. If left unsecured, these vulnerable areas would become easy prey for the Communists. It would be less costly, and less dangerous, if the United States embraced them now in contrast to having to liberate them later. America would succeed where the French and British had failed. They always had.

Developments in Vietnam demonstrated that this passage of empire would not be easy. Compared to what followed, the first steps were. Dulles orchestrated the construction of a collective security pact, the Southeast Asian Treaty Organization (SEATO), which enveloped France, Britain, and the other nations targeted in his United Action proposal. Separate protocols extended this protective umbrella to Laos, Cambodia, and the southern half of Vietnam, regardless of the proscriptions agreed to at Geneva. Dulles in fact would have preferred to exclude the French and British. Their participation was more likely to increase, or complicate, America's burden than relieve it. Tutored by Eisenhower, however, he compromised in order to maintain some semblance of harmony within the Alliance.

Events played out in a way that enabled Dulles to achieve objectives beyond his expectations. The catalyst was a native Vietnamese, which was extremely ironic given Dulles's ignorance of and disregard for anything indigenous to Vietnam. But Ngo Dinh Diem commanded attention. Invited by Emperor Bao Dai to form a government in the South, Diem was a proud and capable former bureaucrat under the French. Both his nationalist and anti-Communist credentials were impeccable. But his leadership skills were atrocious, which exacerbated the problem of his gaining the allegiance of Vietnam's Buddhist majority in the face of his own devout Catholicism. He was also inept politically, and thus was unable to allay suspicions of the French that he was a Francophobe, the suspicions of influential religious sects that he would not tolerate their autonomy, and the suspicions of organized

crime that he was too puritanical. If he had alternatives Dulles probably would not have selected Diem to bring order out of chaos in South
Vietnam. He could not identify any, and in his view, the "lack of political maturity on the part of the people themselves" made allowing the
Vietnamese the liberty to choose their leader a nonoption.[27]

Dulles's conclusion that America had to go with Diem drove his decision that the French had to go. They showed no inclination to step
aside, however, and Dulles was loath to push them. The tipping point
came in spring 1955, when the antagonism between Diem, the religious sects, and the Binh Xuyen, which controlled Saigon's police
forces and gambling operations, erupted into open warfare. Diem
blamed the French for provoking the crisis, and Dulles had no reason to challenge him. But General J. Lawton ("Lightning Joe") Collins,
whom Eisenhower had sent to Vietnam as his personal representative,
did. He advised the president to jettison Diem and replace him with
any one of several Vietnamese.

Dulles prepared to surrender to the inevitable. He did not have
to. With Diem receiving assistance from America's CIA, the tide of
battle shifted decisively in his favor. Dulles informed Collins that U.S.
support for Diem was unequivocal. He then flew to Paris to inform
French prime minister Edgar Faure the same thing. He added that if
the French insisted on removing Diem, they could no longer count on
American help in securing his successor. Faure relented. Within a year
he had ordered the withdrawal of French forces from Vietnam. The
boundaries of empire had changed again.

Dulles was content with this result. He appreciated the potential
costs of managing Vietnam—and its leadership. Indeed, in 1959 the
price began to escalate rapidly. But Dulles died that year. Had he lived,
he surely would not have regretted his or America's behavior. In his
opinion the United States could afford the cost, it must afford the cost,
and because America was America, that cost would be lower than
would be the case with any other country. Dulles would have preferred
that Vietnam evolve along lines congruent with American concepts of
liberty. But the contours of America's post–World War II empire did
not provide Washington with the requisite leverage to compel Diem to
mend his ways. Further, to Dulles Diem's hostility toward Communism
outweighed his hostility toward liberty.

Dulles never had or tried to make the time to consider the full implications of his actions. As soon as he decided he had put out one fire, he moved onto the next. And not long after the transition of Vietnam from France to the United States (which included America's support for Diem's refusal to participate in the elections scheduled for July 1956 to unify the country), Dulles encountered a crisis with implications that transcended even that with Vietnam. This time Dulles's goal was not for America to wrest the imperial role from either France or Britain. Instead, America wrested that role from both.

The crisis centered on the Suez Canal, the lifeline of the British Empire for almost a century. While the crisis exploded in October 1956, its proximate origins date to 1952, when a coterie of young army officers led by Gamal Abdul Nasser forced Egypt's very corrupt yet very pro-Western King Farouk to abdicate. Nasser was a pan-Arabist. He was likewise an Egyptian nationalist. Shortly after taking power, he demanded that the British evacuate its military bases surrounding the Suez Canal. Eisenhower and Dulles urged their British counterparts, Prime Minister Winston Churchill and Foreign Secretary Anthony Eden, to oblige. As a potent symbol of European imperialism, the bases inflamed Egyptian resentment toward the West at the very moment that the West desperately sought the region's allegiance—and just as desperately sought to deny it to the Soviets. A contested "boundary-barrier situation" again emerged.

The British reluctantly relented. Their gloom deepened when Nasser appeared unaffected. In 1955 he seemed to thumb his nose at the West by arranging to purchase arms from behind the Iron Curtain. Initially, Dulles contained his anger. He thought it still possible to win Nasser over, or at least keep him out of the Soviet camp. The key to success was money. America would offer some $400 million to finance building the Aswan Dam through a combination of outright grants, low-interest loans, and contributions from the World Bank. It would even persuade the British to pitch in. The appeal for Nasser would be irresistible, Dulles thought. Nasser perceived the dam as pivotal to Egypt's progress: it would be a source of electrical power, an instrument to control flooding along the Nile, a means to provide year-round irrigation, and, overarching everything, a testament to Egyptian modernization.

Nasser did not rise to the bait. He was not opposed to accepting the money. He made clear, though, that he would play no favorites and would be just as happy if the Soviets provided the financing. In July 1956 a furious Dulles called his bluff by rescinding America's offer. Rather than fold, Nasser nationalized the British-controlled Suez Canal Company, which owned and operated the canal. The tolls he collected would finance construction of the Aswan Dam, he announced. Dulles contained his urge to teach him a lesson. Strong-armed tactics could mean the loss of the "influence of the West in the Middle East and most of Africa . . . for a generation, if not a century." The Soviet Union would "reap the benefit." He conceived of a way to avoid this catastrophe. Dulles was confident that Nasser would be unable to keep the canal operating, and thus he would be unable to collect sufficient tolls. Sooner or later, he would come begging to the United States. Or he could avoid this humiliation by accepting Dulles's proposal of a Suez Canal User's Association (SCUA). It would be multilateral, comprised of all thirty-two countries that used the canal. SCUA would be empowered to collect tolls and ensure that a fair percentage of what it collected went to Egypt.[28]

Nasser did not trust the arrangement. The British were downright antagonistic toward it. Anthony Eden was now prime minister, and he considered the value of the Suez Canal as more than economic and strategic, although it was vitally important for both reasons. Suez was to Eden the final outpost of the British Empire and the legacy of its imperial glory. In his mind Nasser intended his behavior not so much to promote Egyptian modernization as British humiliation. To accept Dulles's "cock-eyed" proposal would signal the end of Britain's empire no less than Nasser's nationalization. London had to fight back, and for this purpose Eden reached out for help not to America but France. French ownership of stock in the Suez Canal Company was almost irrelevant. Of greater relevance was Paris's identification of itself as another beleaguered imperial power on Nasser's hit list. He was not responsible for the rebellion in Algeria, but he encouraged it. The French agreed to collude with the British. So did the Israelis, who feared that Nasser intended to use his recently purchased arms against the Jewish homeland.[29]

Operation Musketeer began on October 29. The plan was for Britain and France to follow up an Israeli seizure of the Sinai with a seizure of the canal. The result would be a permanent return to the status quo ante and Nasser's loss of credibility. At a minimum he would be ousted from power. If fortune shined on the operation, he would be killed. Fortune did not shine. Before a British and French armada could reach the canal, Nasser rendered it useless by scuttling enough Egyptian ships to block all transit.

Who was more livid, Dulles or Eisenhower, is unknowable. It makes no difference. It was bad enough that Britain, France, and Israel had concealed a poorly designed operation from the United States. It was worse because in playing the "part of the bully" by employing "crude and brutal" force, the three American allies deprived the Free World of claiming the moral high ground at the very moment when the real bully, the Soviets, crushed Hungarian freedom fighters. Dulles and Eisenhower were confident they could have exploited the incompatibility between the Soviet empire and liberty to win countless hearts and minds throughout the world. With the British and French (Israel's contribution reflected more localized dynamics) behaving in a manner reminiscent of the previous century's imperialist scramble, the concurrent interventions tracked too closely to draw a distinction.[30]

What Dulles could do was publicly denounce London and Paris, and in doing so distinguish between "their" empires and America's. "I doubt that any delegate ever spoke from this forum with as heavy a heart as I have brought here," Dulles told the United Nations General Assembly on November 1, 1956. He explained that Britain and France were two of America's "oldest, most trusted and reliable allies," and Washington viewed each with "deep friendship, admiration and respect." Nevertheless, because the objections of the administration and the American people to their effort to seize the Suez Canal involved "principles which far transcend the immediate issue," he was "impelled to make our point of view known to you and through you to the world." That point of view was that Nasser's regrettable and perhaps illegal conduct in nationalizing the Suez Canal did not excuse the imperial behavior of Britain and France. Using rhetoric reminiscent of Woodrow Wilson, he declared that the Age of Empires must end.[31]

Speaking the next day behind the closed doors to the National Security Council, Dulles clarified his point of view. "For many years now the United States has been walking a tightrope between the effort to maintain our old and valued relations with our British and French allies on the one hand, and on the other trying to assure ourselves of the friendship and understanding of the newly independent countries who have escaped from colonialism," he began. He then made explicit his judgment that this tightrope walk no longer could continue. "Unless we now assert and maintain" American leadership, he stated, we "will be looked upon as forever tied to British and French colonialist policies." Dulles did not say that he rejected empire. Rather, he rejected the British and French definition. Colonialism and colonies were not integral to an American empire, as shown in Iran and Vietnam. The basis for his empire was the notion of "group authority," which the United States could exercise informally through surrogates. This empire could serve as a bulwark against the expansion of that of the Soviets, and when given an opportunity, roll it back, while still maintaining the "friendship and understanding" of emerging nations within that group authority.[32]

Dulles later stated that had his November 1 speech to the UN been his "very last act on earth," he "would have liked it for [his] epitaph." It turned out to be neither (albeit the day following its delivery Dulles collapsed because of the cancer that in three years would kill him). But the speech did mark another way station in the evolution of his vision. Bowing to Washington's threat to allow the free fall of the value of the pound to continue as well as to the international pressure Dulles's speech galvanized, the British agreed to cease military operations. France had no choice but to follow suit. By the end of 1956 both began to withdraw their forces. Early the next year Congress passed the administration's Middle East Resolution, commonly known as the Eisenhower Doctrine. Its purpose was to protect under America's military and economic umbrella all Middle Eastern territory confronted by "overt armed aggression from any nation controlled by International Communism." The effect was to extend America's "group authority" to the Middle East. As the British Empire retreated east of Suez, America's took its place. Eviscerating the concept of an American Empire for Liberty, Dulles stated the obvious: "We must fill the vacuum of power which the British filled for a century—not merely the ability to act in an emergency but day in day out presence there."[33]

Dulles's successors would need to confront—in Vietnam, in the Middle East, almost everywhere—the very challenges to America's authority that he had predicted in *War, Peace, and Change*. Indeed, while the intensity of these challenges remained relatively low during his tenure (and lifetime), he did not doubt that they would grow. As a consequence, it was critical to his identification of American and "Free World" interests that the United States, and not the British, French, or any other traditional empire, face them. Only an American empire could counteract the Soviets'. So adamant was Dulles that the security and prosperity of the non-Communist "group" required American authority that he advocated extending the American empire to regions that were or had not been victimized by the British and French.

The prime example was Guatemala, the geopolitical linchpin of Central America and a vassal of the United States since the United Fruit Company had acquired paramount influence over its economy at the start of the twentieth century. A revolution in 1944 led by a loose coalition of intellectuals and junior army officers, however, set the country in a direction unexpected in either Washington or New Orleans (UFCO's headquarters). The revolutionary era's first president, Juan José Arévalo Bermej, promoted a philosophy he called "spiritual socialism." In practical terms it generated constitutional reforms, literacy and public health campaigns, rent controls, labor codes, and parallel initiatives designed to address long-standing political, social, and economic ills and lay the groundwork for development. His successor, former army colonel Jacobo Arbenz Guzmán, upped the ante. Most dramatically, Arbenz supported the legislature's enactment of Decree 900, the Agrarian Reform Bill that mandated the expropriation of a percentage of idle land and its rental to indigenous Guatemalans at affordable rates. The biggest loser was the largest landholder—the United Fruit Company. The company, known in Guatemala as the Octopus, got mad. It schemed to get even.

To Dulles, the American empire was never primarily about economics. He of course cared deeply about U.S. prosperity. He had been wildly successful while Sullivan & Cromwell's executive partner, and he perceived the United States as his most important client. As a

Wilsonian, moreover, he believed fervently in the power of international finance and commerce to heal global pathologies even as they spread wealth throughout America. Yet while he intended the group authority that he vested in the American empire to promote healthy liberal trade, stable currencies, and the like, he did not intend it to safeguard specific U.S. economic interests. They would prosper in a hospitable and secure environment. International Communism, the expansion of which Dulles considered the raison d'être of the Soviet empire, was incompatible with that environment. The American empire was the antidote.

Dulles was intimately familiar with UFCO's history in Guatemala. He had helped negotiate its contract with the government of Jorge Ubico y Castañeda in the 1930s that ensured the company's preferential treatment and political power. His reflexive opposition to Arbenz and Decree 900, nevertheless, can be attributed to UFCO's role as the plaintiff only insofar as it played the Communist card. The company's public relations campaign charged that agrarian reform and other planks in Arbenz's platform served the interests of the Kremlin, not the Guatemalan people. This was 1953 and 1954, the heyday of Joseph McCarthy. UFCO's syllogisms resonated throughout the United States. They certainly resonated with Dulles. "If the United Fruit matter were settled, if they gave a gold piece for every banana, the problem would remain just as it is today as far as the presence of communist infiltration in Guatemala is concerned," Dulles stressed. "That is the problem, not United Fruit." Dulles meant every word that he said.[34]

Dulles reflected the consensus in the administration. The only concerns related to possible fallout elsewhere in the hemisphere. Dulles did not share that concern. His point of reference was not the Good Neighbor Policy but the Monroe Doctrine. From the time that John Quincy Adams first developed its precepts, the Monroe Doctrine was favorable to America's empire and hostile to "alien" ones. Moreover, America's group authority in the hemisphere must remain inviolate. Thus, without trying to understand the Guatemalan heresy, Dulles determined that it must be eradicated. Eisenhower agreed, and it was. The president green-lighted the CIA's Operation PBSUCCESS. Launched on June 18, 1954, PBSUCCESS was an exercise in psychological warfare supported by bribes and assassinations. It worked. In less than two weeks Arbenz fled the country. UFCO's influence in Guatemala subsequently waned. Washington's remained. This was the end Dulles sought.

America's agent for counterrevolution in Guatemala was Carlos Castillo Armas, who headed a small band of dissidents and CIA-financed mercenaries with the inflated title of Army of Liberation. Dulles claimed that it liberated Guatemala from the Communists—or at least their surrogates. The result was to open a "new and glorious chapter" in the "great tradition of American States" and the history of freedom everywhere. In the event, it opened a sorry chapter in the history of Guatemala and the history of the United States. PBSUCCESS did not liberate Guatemala from the Communists or, for that matter, from the imperial control of the British or the French. It "liberated" Guatemala from its own people, and as a consequence made a mockery of the very word *liberty*. Castillo Armas was the first of a series presidents who, in the tradition of former caudillos, denied liberty to the vast majority of Guatemalans. Worse, they killed them.[35]

This denouement was not what Dulles hoped for. He intended the United States empire to counter the Soviets', which he defined as an empire against liberty. In the long-term perspective, it did. Nevertheless, the empire that Dulles was so instrumental in constructing was unequivocally not an empire of liberty. Whether wresting the imperial mantle from the British and French or building on the foundation laid by American decades earlier, what became the outposts of America's empire in Southeast Asia, in the Middle East, in Latin America, and elsewhere allowed for little liberty within its populations. As a consequence, Dulles bequeathed to his successors a "boundary-barrier situation" parallel to what in 1939 he described as the predicament of the French and the British. Dulles institutionalized the United States as a group authority unable to satisfy its "dynamic" members. He died in 1959, never able to resolve the dilemma that he helped to produce.

CHAPTER 6

Paul Wolfowitz and
the Lonely Empire

A NEW CHAPTER IN THE HISTORY of the American empire began the year Dulles died, although at the time no one perceived it as such. While policymakers and the attentive public fixed their eyes on the Berlin Crisis, which threatened to ignite the nuclear confrontation that everyone feared and some believed Dulles would welcome, almost unnoticed developments in Vietnam generated a challenge to American power fraught with implications for the present day.

Dulles succumbed to cancer on May 24, 1959. Three days later, Soviet premier Nikita Khrushchev allowed to expire his ultimatum that the Western powers either agree to withdraw from Berlin and make it a free, demilitarized city or, in six months, the Kremlin would abrogate the 1945 Potsdam Agreement and cede to East Germany unilateral authority for access to West Berlin. While the world's population breathed a sign of relief, cadres loyal to the Democratic Republic of Vietnam (North Vietnam) that had migrated south of the seventeenth parallel following the 1954 Geneva Accords began to implement Resolution 15 of the Politburo's Central Committee of the Vietnam Workers Party based in Hanoi. It called for the creation of an insurgent force in the south with the capability to wage a protracted struggle against Ngo Dinh Diem's regime in the Republic of Vietnam and its patron, the United States. By the end of the year these forces, fortified by cadres and supplies that journeyed down the soon-to-be-named Ho Chi Minh Trail, had instigated a series of "spontaneous uprisings" from central Vietnam south to the Mekong Delta.

Thus began "America's Longest War," a war that subverted Americans' identification with anti-imperialism. Many historians establish its beginning in 1965, when the administration of Lyndon Baines Johnson began to bomb North Vietnam and then committed increasing numbers of conventional U.S. troops to South Vietnam. Others trace the roots of America's participation in the conflict to 1945, when Harry Truman reversed Franklin Roosevelt's policy and acquiesced to the restoration of French control of its Indochinese colony, or 1950, when Truman recognized the French-created government of Bao Dai as a rival to that of Ho Chi Minh, or to 1955, when Eisenhower and Dulles decided to sink or swim with Ngo Dinh Diem.[1]

A more appropriate date is 1959. That year the Communist government in Hanoi gave up on its hope that it could unify Vietnam through political means. Its acceptance of the need for armed struggle led to America's direct military engagement. As the U.S. commitment intensified, so did domestic unrest. By the end of the 1960s the Cold War consensus that Dulles had worked so hard to forge and that provided essential public and congressional support for his brand of empire-building was under siege. This phenomenon was most manifest on college campuses throughout the country, where protests against the war fused with the campaigns for civil rights that gave way to proclamations of black power to produce "Years of Hope, Days of Rage." A prime example of this fusion was Cornell University. The photograph of gun-toting Black students, their leader sporting a bandoleer of ammunition, defiantly ending their occupation of Willard Straight Hall by marching past cheering members of the Students for a Democratic Society, seemed emblematic of the end of the American empire.[2]

Among the minority of Cornell students who remained distant from the turmoil associated with the Vietnam was the son of one of its distinguished faculty. Paul Wolfowitz, in the words of another Ithaca "townie" who graduated from Cornell in 1965, was "maybe the smartest person I've ever known." His whole family was smart. Born in Warsaw, Paul's father, Jacob (Jack), had immigrated to New York after World War I to escape Poland's rabid anti-Semitism. He earned the Ph.D. in mathematics from New York University, and soon gained recognition as one of the nation's leading experts in statistics. Jacob was teaching at Columbia when Paul was born in 1943, but moved to Cornell before his son was ten. Paul began to take classes at the university while still in high school. He aspired to attend Harvard but decided that he could not pass up the offer of a full scholarship to Cornell. The choice turned out to be more fateful than he imagined.[3]

Everyone who knew Paul assumed he would follow in his father's academic footsteps. At Cornell he majored in mathematics and chemistry, and he was outstanding at both. Yet Wolfowitz inherited from his father not only an aptitude for working with numbers, but also a profound engagement with history and politics, particularly the Holocaust and the Zionist cause. Jacob Wolfowitz escaped Poland before Hitler began his genocidal assault upon the Jews; many of his family members did not. The influence on young Paul was massive. While growing up he read what he conceded were "probably too many" books about the Holocaust, which he then coupled with books about Hiroshima. He lumped them together to produce what he labeled the "polar horrors." Having spent a year in Israel when he was fourteen, Wolfowitz entered Cornell predisposed to believe that there was great evil in the world. History taught that humankind must confront this evil or suffer horrific consequences.[4]

His studies at Cornell reinforced this predisposition, and the trajectory of Wolfowitz's intellectual development spiked during his sophomore year. His scholastic record qualified him for membership in the Telluride Association, and in 1962 he moved into Telluride House. Initially an association of high-performing electrical engineers, by the 1960s Telluride enveloped a select group of Cornell's best and brightest that spanned the spectrum of colleges and disciplines. For Wolfowitz, the experience became a family affair. His sister, two years older and a biology student, was Telluride's first female member. She was soon followed by Clare Selgin, an anthropology major who was two years younger than Wolfowitz and studied Indonesian dance. They would marry.

Because Cornell faculty lived at Telluride to advise the residents, Wolfowitz met Allan Bloom. A flamboyant, charismatic, "hedonistic and intensely intellectual" political theorist whose *Closing of the American Mind* became canonical reading for the American political Right in the late 1980s, Bloom was the model for the protagonist in Saul Bellow's 2000 novel *Ravelstein*. A Wolfowitz-based character, Paul Gorman, appears in the novel as well. Ravelstein predicts that with his "powerful mind" and "real grasp of great politics," young Gorman is a shoo-in for a prestigious cabinet position. Bellow exaggerates Wolfowitz's intellectual debt to his colleague at the University of Chicago. But Bloom did introduce Wolfowitz to the writings of Leo Strauss, Bloom's mentor.[5]

Strauss is best known for arguing that responsibility for the horrors of the twentieth century can be traced to modernity's rejection of classical values. This argument led him to endow the United States, because of the premium its political culture and ideology places on natural rights, with the potential to instruct the remainder of the world's nations about how to "escape from history" and proffer the "chance for modernity to be something more than merely modern." Strauss also stressed "the importance of a leader who was especially strong in his actions, firm in his beliefs, and willing to go against the grain to combat 'tyranny.'" The affinity between Straussianism and contemporary American neoconservatism is evident. It seems no less evident that through Bloom Wolfowitz became a Straussian. Hence his previous fixation on the Holocaust and what history teaches about evil merged with a nascent neoconservatism to produce an irresistible pull toward advocating an American empire that would redeem the world by, among other things, exporting its liberty.[6]

Yet Wolfowitz's path from Telluride to the Pentagon was not nearly this direct. He retained many of the relationships he forged through the association. Bloom, with whom Wolfowitz took but one course, was not one of them. Moreover, Strauss was highly suspicious of liberal democracy, and he wrote almost nothing about international affairs or U.S. foreign policy. More fundamentally, in contrast to Bloom's ambition and that of the so-called Leo-conservatives who, as Wolfowitz wrote, "Learned to Stop Worrying and Love the Pax Americana," one "searches in vain," Strauss's intellectual biographer points out, "for grand projects, reforms, or great political hopes in Strauss."[7]

What Bloom did was excite Wolfowitz to such an extent that to the surprise and chagrin of his father he turned down graduate study in biochemistry at MIT in favor of political science at the University of Chicago. He would follow his heart and study with Strauss. But almost immediately after matriculating in 1965, Wolfowitz's education underwent another twist. Although he took courses with Strauss, he chose as his advisor Albert Wohlstetter, a longtime policy analyst at the RAND (Research ANd Development) Corporation who had recently moved to Chicago. Wohlstetter was a native New Yorker; as an M.A. student he took a course with Jacob Wolfowitz at Columbia. An expert in nuclear theory and strategy who challenged the principles that underlay mutual assured destruction by preaching that America must cement its strategic superiority through technological innovation, his mathematical inclinations as well as his focus on the destructive power of the evil Soviet Union dovetailed with Wolfowitz's thinking. Wohlstetter influenced Stanley Kubrick's portrait of Dr. Strangelove. He also influenced Wolfowitz's growing conservatism.

Wolfowitz was a "lonely John F. Kennedy Democrat" when he attended high school in conservative Ithaca, New York, and as a nineteen-year-old undergraduate he had bussed to Washington to hear Martin Luther King announce, "I Have a Dream." Yet he was studying with Wohlstetter at the University of Chicago when in 1969 Cornell's black students took over Willard Straight Hall. And while Cornellians and college students across the nation were protesting against what they criticized as America's imperialistic war in Vietnam, Wolfowitz, who had been a founding member of Cornell's tiny Committee for Critical Support of the U.S. in Vietnam, was gaining entry into America's policymaking circles.[8]

In 1969 Wohlstetter recruited Wolfowitz, whose graduate studies entitled him to a deferment from the draft, to conduct research for the Committee to Maintain a Prudent Defense Policy, established by Dean Acheson and Paul Nitze to lobby for an anti-ballistic missile system. Wolfowitz, along with another Ph.D. student whom Wohlstetter recruited from Princeton, Richard Perle, produced a series of papers supporting funding for missile defense, which the Senate authorized at the end of the summer by a one-vote margin. Afterward, Wolfowitz returned to Chicago to write his dissertation. He wrote on water-desalinization in the Middle East, a process that produced plutonium as a by-product. He had collected material for the dissertation while in Israel conducting research for Wohlstetter, who feared that desalinization projects could lead to a covert nuclear weapons program. Wolfowitz's dissertation highlighted the danger that America would unwittingly assist rogue states to develop a nuclear capability and the inability of international inspectors to detect it. He had barely begun to write when he received an offer to teach at Yale. In 1970 Wolfowitz went off to New Haven; but he was hooked on Washington.

The impression Wolfowitz made on one of his students, Lewis "Scooter" Libby, who would gain renown as the chief of staff to Vice President Dick Cheney convicted of perjury for his role in making public the name of the CIA's Valerie Plame Wilson, was the most notable consequence of his teaching career at Yale. Otherwise, he focused on developments in Washington, somewhat enviously following the career of Perle, who rather than return to Princeton stayed to work for Washington senator Henry "Scoop" Jackson. That he did profoundly affected not only Wolfowitz but also the American empire. To the dismay of both young defense intellectuals, President Richard M. Nixon used their victory in the fight over the ABM system as a chip to negotiate, as part of the 1972 SALT I agreement with the Soviets, a ban on such systems. As a sop to the hawkish Jackson, Nixon concurrently replaced the head of the U.S. Arms Control and Disarmament Agency (ACDA) with the hawkish Fred Iklé. Iklé invited Wolfowitz to join his staff.

Wolfowitz remained with the ACDA until the end of the Gerald Ford administration. During these four years Nixon suffered the disgrace of Watergate and resignation, the United States exited ignominiously from Vietnam, Cambodia's Khmer Rouge embarrassed the United States by seizing and then releasing the crew of the USS *Mayaguez*, and the Soviet Union appeared to mock détente by supporting Cuban inroads into Angola. To some Americans, moreover, the nuclear superiority that the United States had enjoyed since the onset of the Cold War, and which Dulles exploited to expand U.S. influence while limiting if not pushing back that of the Soviets, seemed to evaporate. Among those who alleged that the U.S. empire was in retreat and its security was in jeopardy were Henry Jackson and Paul Nitze.

The juxtaposition of Nixon's fall from grace and the unraveling of Henry Kissinger's strategy of détente afforded Wolfowitz the opportunity to climb the ladder of what came to be called the neoconservative Right. Although through his employment with the ACDA Wolfowitz "worked" in the Nixon and Gerald Ford administrations, he, in James Mann's apt words, "viewed himself as Kissinger's opposite, his adversary in the realm of ideas." He detested Kissinger's effort to remove morality from American foreign policy, and he perceived détente as violating the lessons of the Holocaust by postulating that good and evil could coexist. Wolfowitz liked to say that the Poles had the perfect phrase for what this bankrupt point of view produced: "the stability of the graveyard."[9]

Wolfowitz likewise subscribed to Wohlstetter's thesis that Kissinger's effort to establish a global balance of power based on strategic parity between the United States and the Soviet Union recklessly endangered American security because the Kremlin lacked the moral scruples to be trusted and possessed the technological capacity to cause incalculable damage when it cheated. This last critique overlapped Wolfowitz's growing contempt for the CIA. Doubtless influenced again by Wohlstetter, Wolfowitz came to conclude that "intellectual dishonesty" pervaded the U.S. intelligence community, a phenomenon that he traced to an "analytical style . . . intrinsically linked to the academic tradition of liberalism."[10]

In the wake of Watergate and America's collapse in Vietnam, the CIA came under withering attack during congressional hearings. Wohlstetter, Nitze, and others exploited its weakened condition to pile on. They charged that a succession of National Intelligence Estimates (NIEs) provided misleading support for Kissinger's détente by severely underestimating Soviet capabilities and intentions. They also began to rally around California's governor Ronald Reagan as a sympathetic would-be candidate for the presidency. In response a beleaguered President Ford fired CIA director William Colby and replaced him with former Texas congressman George H. W. Bush. Almost immediately after moving into Langley, Bush established a team of analysts to produce another estimate of the Soviet threat to compete with the CIA's most recent assessment. He appointed the Russian historian and rabid anti-Communist Richard Pipes to chair this "Team B." Pipes asked Henry Jackson's aide Richard Perle whom he would recommend to conduct research. Perle suggested Wolfowitz. Pipes borrowed Wolfowitz from the ACDA. As a summer intern to assist him, Wolfowitz hired a "brother" from Cornell's Telluride, Frances Fukuyama.

Team B produced an estimate of the Soviet threat that was much more foreboding than the CIA analysts' current one. The CIA failed to take into account in its assessments the Soviet's terrifying technological advances in weaponry, it charged, and it downplayed the Kremlin's quest for global hegemony. In what would become for Wolfowitz a standard critique, Team B indicted the Agency's analysts for relying so heavily on satellite imagery and signals intelligence that it overlooked what the Soviet leaders said—and their proxies did. By the time Team B submitted its report in 1976 Ford was too preoccupied with the campaign to do anything with it. His defeat by Georgia Democrat Jimmy Carter all but assured the report would be shelved. From Wolfowitz's perspective the exercise, nonetheless, taught an invaluable lesson. The consensus among scholars and experts is that Team B's judgments were mostly off the mark. Yet Wolfowitz claimed, "The B-Team demonstrated that it was possible to construct a sharply different view of Soviet motivation from the consensus view of the analysts, and one that provided a much closer fit to the Soviets' observed behavior."[11]

Simply by approving the establishment of Team B, Ford and Bush further undermined the credibility of America's intelligence community and amplified suspicions about the viability of détente. Détente remained U.S. policy during the initial Carter years, but with Kissinger joining Nixon on the sidelines, it could not survive the Soviet invasion of Afghanistan in 1979. Neither could the Carter presidency, particularly because the Afghan crisis followed so closely the crisis produced by the abduction of American hostages in Iran. The grief that befell Jimmy Carter proved a boon to Ronald Reagan. He captured the White House promising to restore American pride, American power, and the American Empire for Liberty.

How successful Reagan was remains highly contested. What can be said for sure is that by labeling the Soviet Union the "Evil Empire," and providing an environment in which Wolfowitz and his intellectual and strategic allies could thrive, his presidency provided a platform in the twenty-first century for the Second New American Empire. As an astute student of empire argues, the Reagan era "reenergized conservatives and neoconservatives," thereby reviving the zero-sum perspective on global politics. According to this frame of reference, the opponent of the Evil Empire was by definition the Righteous Empire. The defeat of one could only mean the triumph of the other.[12]

Wolfowitz began building toward this end while Carter was president. Unlike many Republicans, he remained in government after Ford's departure. Although he was much more comfortable with the hawks that populated Team B, Wolfowitz sympathized with Carter's emphasis on human rights. By this time he had developed an "almost missionary sense" of the U.S. "ability to build a better world." Moreover, attributing responsibility for the Holocaust and Hitler's reign of terror to the cowardice and absence of a sense of moral obligation of the many, he was inspired by political leaders whom he perceived as equating statesmanship with individual acts of courage. So moved was Wolfowitz by Anwar Sadat's 1977 visit to Jerusalem, for example, that he taught himself Arabic in order to "appreciate the valor of Sadat's speech in the original."[13]

Wolfowitz's messianic impulses intensified over the next decades. Concurrently, he developed new forebodings about America's security that likewise intensified. Under Carter Wolfowitz held the obscure post of deputy assistant secretary of defense for regional planning. His mandate was to study those areas that in the aggregate were misnamed the Third World where U.S. interests appeared vulnerable. Foreshadowing the evolution of his thinking, Wolfowitz confounded his superiors by identifying the Persian Gulf region in general and Iraq in particular as a potential grave danger. Because the West lacked a credible deterrent in the area, because at stake were vital oil reserves, and because the Arab-Israeli conflict presented a ready platform for mischief-making, the likelihood of a Soviet thrust southward into the Middle East, Wolfowitz warned, was significantly greater than a Soviet move against the NATO countries in Western Europe.

What is more, even absent a Soviet gambit, U.S. interests would remain threatened by the possible emergence of a regional hegemon, and Wolfowitz pointed to Iraq as the most probable candidate. Not until 1979 did Saddam Hussein Abd al-Majid al-Tikriti ascend to the presidency of Iraq. Notwithstanding Saddam's prominent role a decade earlier in the coup that brought the Baath Party to power in Iraq and his subsequent service as vice president, Wolfowitz had yet to conclude that he was evil incarnate. Still, that Iraq promoted Arab radicalism, was committed to Israel's destruction, and received a steady stream of Soviet arms was sufficient cause for concern. Wolfowitz recommended that as a hedge against Baghdad's regional designs, America begin immediately to augment its military capabilities to the point when it could protect Kuwait, Saudi Arabia, and other possible Iraqi targets.

Wolfowitz's alarm fell mostly on deaf ears during the first half of Carter's administration. But in 1979 the surprise overthrow of Iran's shah, coupled with the seizure of the U.S. embassy and the Soviet invasion of Afghanistan, made officials in Washington more receptive to Wolfowitz's premonitions. These events also served as a catalyst for bringing to Washington Ronald Reagan. Reagan generated an atmosphere in which strategically placed advisors and like-minded journalists and intellectuals could launch a conservative insurgency that first challenged, then chipped away at, and eventually discarded fundamental tenets of America's post–World War II global posture, policies, and strategy.

Still a minor actor in 1979 and 1980, Wolfowitz began a steady rise to prominence. He boasted that he defied categorization because he was a "principled realist" or a "pragmatic idealist." He borrowed from the programs and precepts of both Lodge and Wilson. His conceptual lineage, nevertheless, can be best traced to Dulles—but not to the Dulles that emerged as secretary of state to Eisenhower in the 1950s and pursued a defensive empire intended to contain the Soviets. Wolfo-witz's model was the moralistic and moralizing nuclear saber-rattling Dulles lampooned in Herblock cartoons. This Dulles talked the talk of an American Empire for Liberty. Wolfowitz intended to walk the walk.[14]

Wolfowitz remained below the public's radar screen under Reagan even as his star grew in radiance. Moving from the Pentagon back to Foggy Bottom, for the first two years he directed the State Depart-ment's Policy Planning Staff (PPS), as had Paul Nitze in 1950 when he wrote NSC-68, the seminal Cold War document that called for greater dynamism in the pursuit of rolling back the Soviet empire. At this point he was, in the words of two Republican Party foreign policy experts, "more of a mainstream official than the activist ideologue he was later to become." Nevertheless, his behavior demonstrated that he was sep-arating himself from the Washington mainstream, earning a "reputa-tion as a foreign policy iconoclast, a mild-mannered intellectual with a steely ideological core."[15]

Wolfowitz brought with him to the PPS young staffers predisposed to think the way he did, such as Libby; Fukuyama; Zalmay Khalilzad, another Wohlstetter student at Chicago who would serve George W. Bush as ambassador to Afghanistan and Iraq and U.S. representative to the United Nations; and Dennis Ross, who was more of a centrist than the others but had worked with Wolfowitz in the Pentagon on the Persian Gulf project and shared his profound concerns about the Mid-dle East. The PPS recommended policy changes from the Carter years. Most prominent were the recommendations that America provide greater support for Israel and less for China. Wolfowitz considered these revisions strategically sound. Equally important, they would sig-nal the world that America would seek both to reinforce and to spread liberty and democracy.

Wolfowitz was making global democratization his trademark. Shortly after taking over the State Department from Alexander Haig, George Schultz appointed Wolfowitz assistant secretary for Far East-ern affairs. While he served in that position, in 1986 the escalating popular uproar that followed the assassination of Benigno Aquino in the Philippines forced its longtime despotic president, Ferdinand Marcos, to hold national elections. The election, Wolfowitz assumed, would demonstrate that Marcos retained widespread support. In the event, however, Marcos defeated Aquino's widow, Corazon (Cory), only by engaging in blatant fraud and thuggery. The ensuing anti-Marcos "People Power" movement precipitated the defection of pivotal elements of the Filipino military. Reversing his earlier views, Wolfowitz was instrumental in convincing a skeptical Reagan to endorse Aquino as president, leaving Marcos with no choice other than to accept safe haven in Hawaii. From then on Wolfowitz would cite these developments as evidence that the United States not only could assist nations in their transition to democracy, but also that this transition would generate a groundswell of popular support. The United States could spread the American dream by exporting democracy. Greater liberty would inexorably follow.

As a reward for Wolfowitz's contribution to what Schultz perceived as the administration's model success in the Philippines, in 1986 the secretary of state offered his Jewish assistant the U.S. ambassadorship to Muslim Indonesia. Wolfowitz's motivations for accepting were personal. Indonesia had been at the center of his wife Clare's scholarly universe since she had gone there as a high school exchange student, and its importance to her grew after it became the focus of her anthropological studies. Soon after his arrival in Jakarta, moreover, Wolfowitz himself "went native." Over the next three years he learned the language; he studied the culture; he toured the neighborhoods. He even won a cooking contest.

Suharto's autocratic control of Indonesia remained unassailable at the time. Nevertheless, Wolfowitz, albeit gingerly, admonished the dictatorial president to promote greater "openness in the political sphere." He also befriended Abdurrahman Wahid, an avowed proponent of democracy who headed one of Indonesia's largest Muslim parties. Suharto remained in power for almost another decade. But his resignation in 1998 and Wahid's election as president a year later confirmed for Wolfowitz that the United States was indeed engaged in the project of replacing evil with good, and that its ideals and values appealed to Jews, Protestants, and Muslims alike. With the Cold War still driving global politics, the United States was but one of two competing empires when Reagan's presidency came to an end. Wolfowitz, though, was already imagining the world enjoying the beneficence of only one, an American Empire for Liberty.[16]

Wolfowitz had always been a follower: of his father, of Bloom, of Wohlstetter, some might say even of Perle. Now, without intending to do so, he was assuming leadership of a political and intellectual movement committed to turning his vision into a reality: neoconservatism. Although its roots traced to disaffected socialists and Trotskyists in the 1930s and 1940 and Cold War liberals repelled by the radicalism and cultural relativism of the 1960s, neoconservatism as a force in U.S. politics and a springboard for what some call America's "liberal imperialism" or "democratic imperial[ism]" took off in the late 1970s and early 1980s. Not unlike 1950s McCarthyites, adherents saw themselves as "lonely prophets standing in the breach between implacable foes on the one hand and weak-kneed liberals (and paper-pushing bureaucrats) on the other."[17]

In terms of voting patterns, Reagan converted to the Republican Party a plethora of socially progressive public officials and intellectuals, many but not all of whom proudly wore the label of Scoop Jackson Democrats. Even before the 1972 election, these liberals, "mugged by reality," to borrow Irving Kristol's popular aphorism, began to distance themselves from what they perceived as the George McGovern brand of isolationism and, more generally, the Democratic Party's tolerance of Soviet Communism and naive attitude toward defense.[18]

Reagan also galvanized Republicans who had condemned the Kissinger policy of détente. That Kissinger had any confidence that the Soviets could be trusted was bad enough. Worse, détente endowed the Kremlin with sufficient legitimacy to make possible a negotiated peace with the Evil Empire. Worse still, Kissinger's strategy acknowledged limits to American power. As a consequence, rather than seek to make the world a better place for everyone by extending U.S. influence and authority, America should seek only to halt its decline and avoid the pitfalls that Paul Kennedy popularly labeled "imperial overstretch."[19]

The neoconservatives (and their hard-line anti-Soviet allies) would have none of this, and they were sure that Reagan wouldn't either. Reflecting the essence of America's attitude toward the world from the days of Franklin and Adams and extending through Seward, Lodge, and Dulles (and acutely sensitive to Kissinger's Europeanism), neoconservatives resolutely held to the premise of American exceptionalism. Exceptionalism encompassed a wide spectrum of U.S. attributes, but chief among them was its righteousness. In contrast, much of the world—not just the Soviets—were evil, ruled by the "children of darkness," in Reinhold Niebuhr's words, who "prey on the naiveté of their often soft-headed opponents."[20]

This dichotomy between the good America and the evil "other" leaves little space for compromise; hence neoconservatives were wary of negotiations and multilateral institutions. In fact, what amounts to a Manichaean outlook on global politics drove them to discount the international systems' inherent nuances that confounded U.S. politicians and pundits in the aftermath of the Vietnam War. As one critic writes, neoconservative thought is "not so much the product of a particular set of precepts or perceptions about the world and humanity as it is the product of a particular intellectual temperament. It is a temperament that favors pugnacity, bold thinking, and grand, encompassing visions of the world and the future. It is a temperament that shuns complexity, tactical adjustment, and the role of patience in geopolitical maneuverings."[21]

While accurate up to a point, this characterization overlooks principles that provide coherence to an otherwise inchoate philosophy. Some of these apply to domestic politics. Most neoconservatives are, or initially were, favorably disposed toward the welfare state, believe free markets make for free people, and identify family and religion as the two basic pillars of a good society. But what links them together most fundamentally is their "set of precepts about the world and humanity" that this critic shunts to the side. At the top of the list is a belief that America's missionary impulses and its national interest are identical. "It is the national interest of a world power, as this is defined by a sense of national destiny, that American foreign policy is all about," writes Irving Kristol, neoconservatism's godfather. Neoconservatives, his son William later added, identified the United States with the "politics of liberty."[22]

Consequently, there should be no tension between a human rights agenda and the imperatives of geopolitics, and the internal character of a regime matters. For these reasons, because an international land-scape pockmarked with governments and nations hostile to United States values is inimical to the pursuit of its national objectives and aspirations, America has a duty to its own as much as the world's population to make the world safe for democracy and liberty. It must mold the international environment to benefit the United States, and in doing so abandon the practice of Kennan, Kissinger, and other real-ists (and for that matter Dulles) of distinguishing between vital and secondary interests. For neoconservatives, then, the U.S. must also abandon its atavistic aversion to using force. American must not hesi-tate to place its power in the service of democracy, liberty, and other ingredients of U.S. exceptionalism (among which were its religious and family values). If that necessitates behaving unilaterally, so be it.

The Reagan doctrine that called for promoting "freedom fighters" encouraged the neoconservatives to believe they had a comrade in the White House, a president who was an "ideological determinist" and would pursue their expansive agenda. In the end many were disap-pointed. As Mark Gerson writes in his ode to neoconservatism, the "problem with Reagan concerns not what he thought and said, but what he did—or more accurately, what he did not do." His reluctance to confront Polish prime minister Wojciech Witold Jaruzelski's govern-ment's crackdown again Solidarity, the anti-Communist trade union, for example, let alone his deal making with the Soviets over missiles, "demonstrated striking foreign policy weaknesses."[23]

Wolfowitz had worries about Reagan from the start. Among the neo-conservatives' most public faces was Jeane Kirkpatrick, whose semi-nal publication "Dictatorships and Double Standards" so impressed Reagan that he adopted her argument as policy and invited her to join his cabinet as America's ambassador to the UN. The so-called Kirkpat-rick Doctrine called for the United States to support anti-Communist regimes and organizations, no matter how authoritarian and antidem-ocratic their character. There would be hell to pay, she cautioned, if America turned its back on the shah of Iran, Nicaragua's *caudillo*, and others of their dictatorial ilk, including Ferdinand Marcos. Wolfowitz embraced the doctrine's anti-Communism. Yet he became progres-sively more outspoken in asserting that the United States should be prodemocracy. The fall of Marcos provided Wolfowitz with evidence that the United States could, Kirkpatrick Doctrine to the contrary, oppose all forms of authoritarianism, Communist and non-Communist.[24]

In short, for Wolfowitz Kirkpatrick was insufficiently Wilsonian. Indeed, his tenure under Reagan was marked by sharp differences with superiors who thought him an "idealistic crank." For reasons now steeped in irony, among those with whom he clashed was Donald Rumsfeld. Rumsfeld in 1983 traveled to Iraq as Reagan's envoy to Saddam Hussein in order to assure the Iraqi president of U.S. support in his war with Iran and gain his cooperation on matters throughout the Middle East. In a two-and-a-half-hour meeting with Tariq Aziz that covered multiple issues, Saddam's deputy prime minister and foreign minister stressed that Americans and Iraqis "shared many common interests" and expressed his pleasure that Rumsfeld's courtship had "removed whatever obstacles remained in the way of resuming diplomatic relations." Rumsfeld concurred; Wolfowitz could not have disagreed more. Their interests diverged, and a huge obstacle remained: Saddam Hussein was a tyrant who disdained liberty.[25]

While an index of his worldview and fraught with implications for the future, Wolfowitz's row with Rumsfeld and many others in the Reagan administration turned out to be inconsequential for what the neoconservative Charles Krauthammer dubbed America's post–Cold War "unipolar moment." Around him coalesced a number of second-tier officials, such as Perle and Elliot Abrams, who avidly subscribed to his point of view. But Wolfowitz was the intellectual heavyweight as well as the most strategically well placed. Further, his fealty to Wohlstetter, combined with his perception that as the avatar of liberty and democracy the United States was locked in mortal combat with global tyrants, made him attractive to more politically ambitious and less intellectually engaged Republicans. These were more hardheaded realists who saw the world as a Darwinian struggle for survival. What defined the fittest was not values or ideology but power—and the willingness to build on and exploit that power. Rumsfeld was one of these realists who believed in the efficacy of brute force. They concluded that Wolfowitz's activism complemented theirs. Rumsfeld and his protégé Dick Cheney followed in the footsteps of Bloom, Wohlstetter, Nitze, Iklé, Schultz, and others in recognizing Wolfowitz's abilities and taking him under their wing.[26]

In particular, they cleared for Wolfowitz a path into the administration of George H. W. Bush. Rumsfeld had been a rival of Bush since the two were ambitious congressmen together in the 1960s. As Gerald Ford's first chief of staff, Rumsfeld had arranged in Machiavellian style to exile Bush to Beijing to head the U.S. Liaison Office (America had yet to establish formal diplomatic relations). He then saddled Bush with the directorship of the CIA in the agency's post–William Colby, post–Church Committee days. It had been Colby who had revealed the CIA's darkest secrets (the "Family Jewels") to Senator's Frank Church's oversight committee. Rumsfeld's premise was that removing Bush from the national scene, situating him in the crosshairs of the GOP's rabid pro–Nationalist China's constituencies, and identifying him with America's disreputable intelligence service would doom his presidential aspirations.

Rumsfeld's efforts failed; as a result he was persona non grata to the elder Bush. His influence nevertheless loomed large through Cheney. Rumsfeld had all but made Cheney's career. As Nixon's director of the Office of Economic Opportunity, he had taken on the young man from Wyoming as an intern, and under Ford, appointed him deputy assistant to the president. Then, in the so-called Halloween Massacre, Rumsfeld in 1975 orchestrated Ford's selection of Cheney to succeed him as chief of staff after he replaced James Schlesinger as secretary of defense. Cheney subsequently won election to Congress for five terms; during six of those years he chaired the Republican National Committee. Hence when Bush became president it was Cheney's turn to run the Pentagon. For his undersecretary of defense for policy, he chose Wolfowitz.

Cheney, let alone Wolfowitz, had no idea how momentous that choice would be. The Cold War remained the prevailing weltanschauung throughout America and the world when Bush took office. Cheney in particular held adamantly to the belief that Mikhail Gorbachev's leadership of the Kremlin did not mitigate the Evil Empire's aggressive designs. He interpreted Gorbachev's "New Thinking" as "theatrics at best or deception at worst," a tactic intended to lull the United States into a false sense of security. But in November 1989 began the transformation of the Berlin Wall into thousands of souvenir items. By the time the process ended two years later, the Soviet Union was no more. The United States was the last empire standing.[27]

How the American empire would behave was anyone's guess. Events in the Middle East provided the initial evidence, and it was very ambiguous. Wolfowitz was at the center of those events. Developments in the Middle East from the Iraqi incursion into Kuwait in 1990 through the Gulf War of 1991 constituted poetic justice in the sense that Wolfowitz's fixation on the Middle East constitutes a central and unifying theme of his life. His father was a resolute Zionist, his sister moved to Israel after her marriage, his former wife is an expert on Muslim Indonesia, and following his separation he dated a British national with a part-Syrian, part-Saudi mother who grew up practicing Islam in Tunisia and Saudi Arabia. He knew both Hebrew and Arabic, and during the 1970s he raised a warning flag about potential threats to the United States in the Persian Gulf region even as he vigorously criticized those officials in both the Carter and Reagan administrations who advocated doing business with Yasser Arafat and the Palestinian Liberation Organization. Saddam Hussein's invasion of Kuwait brought into play practically every issue about which Wolfowitz was most passionate.

In delivering his State of the Union Address in January 1991, President Bush, paraphrasing Woodrow Wilson, identified the end of the Cold War as an opportunity to create a "new world order, where diverse nations are drawn together in common cause to achieve the universal aspirations of mankind: peace and security, freedom, and the rule of law." Saddam Hussein's decision to order some 100,000 troops, armed with weapons once provided by the Soviet Union, to cross the boundary dividing Iraq from Kuwait started a process that turned this New World Order into America's Second New Empire. Wolfowitz was a leading architect of this metamorphosis and its conceptual fountainhead.[28]

From that fateful day in August 1990 when Saddam gobbled up Kuwait's oil fields through the commencement of the allied ground campaign some seven months later (the air assault began a month before) to the cease-fire that went into effect less than one hundred hours after that, Wolfowitz appeared as a bit player, ceding starring roles to Bush, Joint Chiefs of Staff chairman Colin Powell, field commander General H. Norman Schwartzkopf, and of course Cheney. Saddam had a laundry list of explanations for his behavior. Western imperialists were responsible for Kuwait's separation from Iraq (ancient Mesopotamia) in the first place, he lectured. It was for centuries a district in the Iraqi province of Basra until the World War I victors amputated it in the course of dismantling the Ottoman Empire. The Iraqis had protested ever since; Saddam was righting a historical wrong by remedying the grievous injury done to Iraq. Deprived of Kuwait, Iraq lacked access to the sea to sell its oil, and what oil it could sell had to be at deflated price due to Kuwait's unconscionably high production.

Iraq desperately needed the revenue in order to pay off the debt, approaching $100 billion, it had incurred during its lengthy war with Iran—a war that, Rumsfeld had made clear when serving as Reagan's envoy, America wanted Iraq to win. In fact, it was because of what he considered the tacit alliance formed between Iraq and the United States earlier in the decade that Saddam assumed that the United States would not interfere with his irredentism. Only eight days before his troops launched the invasion, April Glaspie, Bush's ambassador to Iraq, had told him personally: "We have no opinion on your Arab-Arab conflicts, such as your dispute with Kuwait. . . . I have direct instructions from President Bush to improve our relations with Iraq. We have considerable sympathy for your quest for higher oil prices, the immediate cause of your confrontation with Kuwait."[29]

Yet Bush decided that he must resist Saddam's aggression. He was sympathetic to Iraq's needs, and he knew the history of Iraq's relationship to both Kuwait and the United States. Nevertheless, a synthesis of his own conflicted views and those of his advisors drove him to draw a line in the sand. Saddam's invasion put at risk the security of the global oil supply. By controlling more than half of the world's known reserves, Saddam could determine when, to whom, and at what price it would flow. Further, the United States could hardly take the lead in ushering in a new, Wilsonian world order if it left unchallenged such a blatant resort to force, violation of international law, and disregard for sovereignty and territorial integrity. Over the last half-century Americans had defeated two enemies of liberty: Hitler's Germany and Stalin's Soviet Union. Again the United States must defend the Free World.

Wolfowitz cheered from the sidelines; there is no evidence that he influenced the president. Still, Bush's reasoning perfectly matched what Wolfowitz had been saying since the Carter era. Moreover, if Wolfowitz had any reservations about Bush's choice to seek sanctions from the

United Nations and assemble a coalition in its name to oppose Saddam, he did not express them. He probably did not feel strongly about the issue one way or another. Wolfowitz was not as suspicious of multilateral institutions as were many conservatives and neoconservatives. He simply did not think they much mattered. If America could rally an assemblage of countries to follow its lead, he saw no reason not to. The key was U.S. leadership. And in the event, Bush received remarkable support from a broad spectrum of nations. These countries did not necessarily identify America as the natural leader of a new world order, and they certainly did not expect the new world order to mutate until it became indistinguishable from an American empire. They did, however, concur that Saddam was a ruthless tyrant who, once in control of half the world's oil, would pose a clear and present danger to the strong as well as the weak. He had to be stopped.

Initially every American move seemed a good one. A coalition of close to fifty nations from around the globe signed onto first a boycott of, and then a military operation against, Iraq. With the exception of Iran and Jordan, this coalition enveloped the Arab Middle East. Schwartzkopf headed a force of more than a half-million troops, and nations like Japan that did not send troops sent money to pay for them. Already pummeled for a month by the bombing campaign that preceded the ground attack, Desert Storm, Iraq's resistance crumbled. Saddam's promised "Mother of All Battles" never happened. His effort to induce the Arab nations to defect by goading Israel into retaliating against the Scud missiles he fired on its cities failed. U.S. smart weapons such as the Tomahawk and Patriot missiles, while performing below Wohlstetter's predictions and the U.S. military's claims, penetrated Saddam's bunkers and on occasion even destroyed his Scuds. Shell-shocked and demoralized, by the thousands Saddam's army either surrendered or fled. On February 26, Desert Storm's forty-second day, Saddam announced that he would withdraw all Iraqi forces from Kuwait. On February 27 Bush called an end to ground operations.

For Wolfowitz, therein lay the rub. Bush's decision to halt military operations short of occupying Baghdad, which reflected a consensus in his administration, had a revolutionary impact on Wolfowitz. He kept his own counsel at first. His boss, Secretary of Defense Cheney, agreed with Bush. As Cheney told his *Frontline* interviewer after ending his tenure at the Pentagon, "The idea of going into Baghdad, for example, or trying to topple the regime wasn't anything I was enthusiastic about." Saddam was "just one more irritant, but there's a long list of irritants in that part of the world." Wolfowitz regarded Saddam as much worse than an irritant. The euphemistically titled president's instruction to his surviving forces to slaughter thousands of Shi'ites in Iraq's south and thousands of Kurds in its north to secure his Sunni regime in the wake of his defeat and retreat from Kuwait confirmed his bona fides as a tyrant. Tyrants had to be destroyed. But the United States lacked the will. Some "U.S. officials" and "military commanders," Wolfowitz wrote for the *National Interest*, concluded that a "rapid disengagement" would allow America "to avoid getting stuck with postwar objectives that would prevent us from ever disengaging." Wolfowitz assessed this conclusion as calculating, mistaken, and unconscionable.[30]

Although his judgments had been moving in this direction for years, the display of Saddam's ruthlessness after Bush called a halt to the military operation cemented Wolfowitz's conviction that the United States must remain engaged, and by engaged he meant militarily engaged, until it had ridded the world of all those tyrants who held in contempt the values and liberties that the United States stood for. Monsters cannot be contained. Saddam's ethnic cleansing reinforced the lesson that Wolfowitz took from the Holocaust: despots of "the order of evil" of Hitler, Stalin, and Saddam "tend not to keep evil at home, they tend to export it in various ways and eventually it bites us." They had to be defanged before they could bite. Wolfowitz became a convert to preemption.[31]

Wolfowitz's worldview from this time on, writes Andrew Bacevich, who has followed him attentively for decades, more "than [that of] any of the other *dramatic personae* in contemporary Washington," represented the product of "an extraordinary certainty in the righteousness of American actions married to an extraordinary confidence in the efficacy of American arms." Wolfowitz began a campaign to actualize America's mythic mission. He would harness America's unassailable moral purposes to its unassailable military might. Reinhold Niebuhr had it all wrong; John Foster Dulles had been right, before the weight of office crushed his crusading spirit.[32]

Wolfowitz's perspective drove the initial draft of Bush's 1992 Defense Planning Guidance (DPG) document. Integral to the Defense Department's annual review, the DPG is a cornerstone for future planning and budgeting. In light of what Wolfowitz perceived as the catastrophic consequences of the precipitous drawdown of U.S. forces in Iraq, he seized on this first post–Cold War DPG as an opportunity to articulate principles that would lay the foundation for his definition of an Empire for Liberty. In charge of the project, he entrusted the drafting largely to those who shared his views. Chief among these were his former student Scooter Libby and his fellow Telluride alumnus Zalmay Khalilzad; Khalilzad did most of the writing. Input also came from Perle and Wohlstetter. Critics of U.S. global ambitions in the twenty-first century derided the DPG's diagnoses and prescriptions by labeling it the "Wolfowitz Doctrine." That label is misleading. Although Wolfowitz was its driving force, it was a collective effort. Because the collective sought to reconcile some of the internal contradictions that bedeviled his thinking, he personally did not evaluate it as fully satisfactory.[33]

According to the DPG draft, the central feature of the post–Cold War era, and thus the linchpin for any new world order, was U.S. primacy. The United States did not arrive at this pinnacle by default. Rather, America was destined to win the Cold War and the hearts and minds of populations worldwide because of its exceptional character, values, and power, all of which served the cause of liberty. Nevertheless, there remained hostile global forces. Saddam commanded one, but he was not alone. And others would emerge in the future.

The DPG recommended that the United States take full advantage of its current preeminence to ensure that this status continued—indefinitely if not in perpetuity. Toward this end it should pursue a two-track strategy. To the extent possible, America should "sufficiently account for the interests of the advanced industrial nations to discourage them from challenging our leadership or seeking to overturn the established political and economic order." In other words, the United States must support constructive policies and programs that co-opted potential opposition and generated a tidal wave of support for American leadership.[34]

The second track addressed those few nations, defined as rogue nations governed by despotic regimes, that identified their interests as inimical to those of America and rejected its design for a new world order. As an antidote, America had to institutionalize "the mechanism for deterring potential competitors from even aspiring to a larger regional or global role." This mechanism was the unequivocal and ever-increasing military superiority required to transform the unipolar moment into a unipolar era. America could guarantee its preeminence, according to Wolfowitz's subsequent summary, "by demonstrating that [its] friends will be protected and taken care of, that [its] enemies will be punished, and that those who refuse to support [it] will live to regret having done so."[35]

A widely read critique of contemporary U.S. foreign policy interprets the draft DPG as a "blueprint for permanent American global hegemony." More accurately, it was a blueprint for the Second New America Empire. But the draft left open the question of whether that empire would be an Empire for Liberty, and that troubled Wolfowitz. In an effort to synthesize the disparate views of neoconservatives and traditional conservatives while ensuring that the document appealed to Secretary of Defense Cheney, the primary drafter, Khalilzad, had focused a lot on power and only a little on ideology. Toward this end he took a page out of Henry Cabot Lodge's book on Wilson and the Versailles Treaty. The draft portrayed the world as inherently dangerous notwithstanding the demise of Communism, adhered to the premise that nations act in their own self-self interest, and rejected the prospect that either economic interdependence or multilateral institutions would mitigate the anarchy of the global system. For this reason military supremacy trumped everything. "You've discovered a new rationale for our role in the world," Cheney congratulated Khalilzad.[36]

Only in the most general sense did the draft DPG highlight the salience of the equation between the United States and liberty, the salutary effect America's commitment to spreading liberty and democracy would have on global peace and security, and, because of the universal appeal of liberty, America's ability to export it to all continents and regions. Cheney did not think this slight significant. In the tradition of most managers of U.S. foreign and security policy, he was uneasy about interjecting ideology as a variable in the strategic equation. Wolfowitz saw things differently. He bridged the divide between neoconservatives and traditional conservatives. Unlike previous empires that rose and fell, America, Wolfowitz resolutely believed, could retain its predominance because of the synergy between its interests, power, and principles. That synergy explained why other nations would embrace its Empire for Liberty. The DPG had to pay more than lip service to it.

Bush did not subscribe to Wolfowitz's vision, and he was at odds with neoconservatives throughout his tenure. Bush had been around politics his entire life, however, and as Reagan's second in command he had been struck by how effectively that president's rhetoric electrified the nation. Bush recognized that he lacked Reagan's gift of oratory. Moreover, he was uncomfortable with the lofty vocabulary of liberty and democracy. He could go as far as his 1991 State of the Union, but no farther. Yet Bush feared that the draft's references to U.S. primacy (not simply leadership), its concern for potential rivals, its disregard of multilateral institutions, and parallel language associated with the power politics of realpolitik would alienate the U.S. electorate as much as traditional allies. He insisted that Wolfowitz's shop rewrite the DPG.

Libby did much of the rewriting. The end result retained the basic thrust of the initial draft but couched it in "far more diplomatic language." No longer was there great emphasis on "the perpetuation of a one-superpower world." It did not matter. By the time of its completion Bill Clinton, adopting the mantra, "It's the economy, stupid," had defeated Bush in the 1992 election, paving the way for Democrats to take charge of America's international relations. Committed to globalization and interdependence, and according to some allergic to using military force, Clinton's philosophy appeared the polar opposite of that expressed in the DPG, whichever draft. Wolfowitz had stayed in government after Carter's election. He thought he could make a difference. He did not feel that way about Clinton. In 1993 he accepted the deanship of Johns Hopkins's Paul H. Nitze School of Advanced International Study (SAIS), named after one of his former mentors.[37]

The most enduring legacy of the process of drafting the DPG is that it provided a conceptual framework for unifying the pessimistic Cheney-type "apostles of brute force" and the optimistic Wolfowitz-type proselytizers of liberty. Both perceived that mankind's hope lay solely with the United States. Yet while Cheney believed that America had to save the world from itself, Wolfowitz preached that America had the capability to remake the world. The drafting and the revising of the DPG forged a common bond between them. These so-called hegemonists allied over the need to project and exercise power, to proceed unilaterally, and to exterminate the evil-doers. Notwithstanding continual dissent, since 1821 John Quincy Adams's declaration that America "does not go abroad in search of monsters to destroy" had constrained the American empire. During the two Clinton administrations Republican (and a growing number of Democratic) conservatives and neoconservatives came to agree that the international environment, increasingly characterized by civil wars, ethnic conflict, and terrorist outrages, demanded that America reverse Adams's dictum. Americans must destroy monsters. They did not agree, however, on what would come after the destruction.[38]

Agreement seemed unnecessary. While dean of SAIS Wolfowitz became a charter member of the Project for a New American Century (PNAC). Robert Kagan and William Kristol, both descended from neoconservative royalty, founded the PNAC in 1997 to preserve and reinforce "America's benevolent global hegemony" as the architecture for the "new global order." By that year a critical mass of veterans of the Reagan and Bush administrations, along with others from across the political spectrum who worried that the United States was insufficiently promoting and defending its global interests, had given up on Clinton's foreign policy. Some had initially applauded the administration's stress on enlarging the sphere of democracy. But the administration's "inattention to the realities of power politics," its "undue emphasis on commercial considerations to the detriment of national security concerns," and its "exaggerated faith in the peace-inducing properties of trade and multilateral institutions" turned their lukewarm support into resolute opposition. As Fukuyama writes in explaining his attraction to and then alienation from neoconservatism, Kagan and Kristol idealized Lodge and Teddy Roosevelt. They excoriated Clinton for failing to pursue a policy of "national greatness," thereby opening the door for a resurgence of Democratic McGovernism and Republican isolationism.[39]

As for those never willing to give Clinton the benefit of the doubt, the humiliation America suffered in Somalia and Haiti and his indecisiveness in Bosnia and Kosovo, compounded in each case by his cooperation with the UN and hesitation to use force, cemented their hostility.

Nowhere was this more manifest than in the Middle East. There, ranted Clinton's critics, efforts to broker a peace between Israel and the Palestinians on the basis of their moral equivalence and a "land for peace" formula jeopardized the security of liberty and democracy's best hope in the region. Toleration of Saddam Hussein and Islamist extremists jeopardized America's security. "The history of this century should have taught us to embrace the cause of American leadership," read the PNAC's statement of principles. "We need to accept responsibility for America's unique role in preserving and extending an international order friendly to our security, our prosperity, and our principles." The Clinton administration was failing America and the world. Those committed to the PNAC "aim to change this," its website announced. "We aim to make the case and rally support for American global leadership."[40]

The PNAC did not do much, but it represented a lot. It became the umbrella organization under which individuals who agreed about little other than a shared ambition to shape the world to correspond to an American design could rally to the cause of Washington's "global leadership." Wolfowitz, Libby, and Khalilzad, each a contributor to the draft DPG, all appeared on its website as original signers of its statement of principles. So did Cheney, Rumsfeld, Iklé, and other "assertive nationalists" more concerned with power than principle. Wolfowitz cared less about the distinctions between the signatories than their utility in destroying monsters. Destroying monsters was the prerequisite for establishing an American empire, and an American empire was the prerequisite for an Empire for Liberty.[41]

Wolfowitz's highest priority was to rid the world of Saddam Hussein. Publicly calling for his overthrow would send the right signals—that America would not tolerate those who rejected U.S. values and primacy. In this regard the George H. W. Bush administration as well as the Clinton administration, had acted irresponsibly. Opposition to Saddam and frustration over continued American impotence would unite crusaders for liberty, proponents of a more muscular global posture, and political opportunists. Accordingly, Wolfowitz campaigned tirelessly for the forcible ouster of Saddam. He wrote articles and op-ed pieces and testified to Congress about the moral perversity and strategic stupidity of allowing the Iraqi tyrant to remain in power. He also enthusiastically endorsed the PNAC's open letter urging Clinton "to enunciate a new strategy that . . . should aim, above all, at the removal of Saddam Hussein's regime from power." The signatories in addition to Wolfowitz included Rumsfeld, former director of Central Intelligence James Woolsey, Richard Armitage, Wolfowitz's counterpart at State when Marcos ended his rule in the Philippines, and a representative sampling of the PNAC's leading neoconservatives. They vowed that they were "ready to offer our full support in this difficult but necessary endeavor."[42]

They were really not. What they were ready to do was support any candidate in 2000 that championed regime change in Iraq and pursued a "Project for the New American Century," which meant an imperial project. Ironically, they found their candidate in George H. W. Bush's son, George W. Bush. During his presidential campaign Bush scored points against the Democrat Al Gore by asserting that because the United States "stands alone in the world right now in terms of power," it must be "humble" so that other nations will "welcome" its promotion of liberty.[43]

Once he was elected, Bush's behavior was anything but humble. Advised during the transition by the so-called Vulcans, a coterie of second-tier veterans of the Reagan and George H. W. Bush administrations, the second President Bush adopted the principles laid out in the 1992 DPG draft that his father and Clinton had rejected. Bush agreed that American primacy must remain unchallenged and unchallengeable, that concepts such as collective security and multilateral cooperation jeopardized securing U.S. goals, and that U.S. values held universal appeal. Yet while these values appealed universally, only America possessed the capacity fully to embrace and project them. For this reason the United States was exceptional. Also for this reason opponents of those values—liberty and freedom above all—would target the United States for destruction. Consequently, in the name of global liberty and democracy promotion, America had to destroy them first. Since 1945 the United States had relied on its economic dominance and control of multilateral institutions to bend other nations to its will, producing what a British journalist called America's "secret empire." For the Vulcans, the empire should not be secret, and the international environment in the twenty-first century demanded that it be built by American power.[44]

The most influential Vulcan (with the possible exception of Condoleeza Rice, who managed them), Wolfowitz wanted to be secretary of defense. He was notorious for his disorganization and administrative ineptness, however, so Bush nominated him to serve under the masterful bureaucrat Donald Rumsfeld. Wolfowitz would be deputy secretary of defense. He seemed an excellent choice. No one could question his credentials. Further, he looked as well as acted the part of an authentic public intellectual who thrived on complexity and cared only about getting things right. "Lanky, jug-eared, tousle haired, he seemed a man without vanity, capable of casually wetting a pocket comb with saliva, or of shedding his shoes before visiting a Turkish mosque, thereby revealing a homely hole in his sock."[45]

Wolfowitz made clear that his thinking had not changed now that he was no longer a backbencher. During his confirmation hearing he testified that the "whole region would be a safer place, Iraq would be a much more successful country, and the American national interest would benefit greatly if there were a change of regime in Iraq." The Senate confirmed him unanimously, and he took office on March 2, 2001. Second in command to Rumsfeld in his third stint in the Pentagon, Wolfowitz's influence extended beyond his formal title. As a true believer in assertive nationalism and "the number-one theoretician" of the administration's "neoconservative phalanx," no one had been more instrumental in developing the conceptual framework for Bush's global posture, and no one was more attuned to or sympathetic to the president's agenda. Almost sixty, his jet black hair turning to gray yet still projecting "the air of a promising brainy student being groomed for great things," Wolfowitz "was still an underling." Nevertheless, writes the astute journalist James Mann, he was "the most influential underling in Washington."[46]

Echoing the comments of the managers of Bush's foreign policy, Wolfowitz told Sam Tanenhaus in a *Vanity Fair* interview that "September 11th changed a lot of things and changed the way we need to approach the world." For some that was the case. They came into office intending to focus their efforts on building a defense against missile attacks, restructuring America's military and global force posture, and avoiding any behavior that resembled state building. But for Wolfowitz, the terrorist attacks on the World Trade Center and Pentagon were akin to a self-fulfilling prophesy. They confirmed a worldview that had been evolving since he spent his youth learning about the Holocaust and his early adulthood studying with Leo Strauss and Albert Wohlstetter. The attacks reinforced Wolfowitz's conviction that American peace and security required that it bring to fruition Jefferson's vision of an Empire for Liberty, with the operative word being *for*. To ensure liberty for all, America must destroy liberty's enemies. This maxim, which before long suffused the Bush Doctrine and his administration's 2002 Statement of National Security, had been Wolfowitz's core belief for years. For years as well, Wolfowitz had identified Saddam Hussein as liberty's number one enemy. It was only logical, therefore, that only four days after September 11 Wolfowitz counseled Bush, as he entitled one of his articles, to "Bring Saddam Down." Many who served Bush can be called architects of the Iraq War. Nevertheless, Wolfowitz was, to cite a *New Yorker* profile, its "most passionate and compelling advocate."[47]

Bush tabled Wolfowitz's advice while he directed that America open the first front of the soon-to-be-called Global War on Terror (GWOT) in Afghanistan. Iraq, said the president, would "keep for another day." By the end of 2001 preparations for that day were under way. Wolfowitz was among the most vociferous in indicting Saddam Hussein both for being in bed with Usama bin Laden and his Al Qaeda network of terrorists and for retaining a hidden stash of Weapons of Mass Destruction (WMD) even as he surreptitiously developed a nuclear capability. With arrogance produced by the combination of his intellectual accomplishments, decades-long record of success in challenging conventional wisdom, and certainty that he had right on his side, Wolfowitz dismissed any doubts about Saddam's guilt, whether they arose from within or outside of America's intelligence community.[48]

On March 19, 2003, the Bush administration, ignoring domestic demonstrations and international protests, launched Operation Iraqi Freedom (named Operation Iraqi Liberation until a staffer brought attention to the acronym, OIL). Six months later Wolfowitz reflected on the official explanation for Bush's decision. For "reasons that have a lot to do with the U.S. government bureaucracy," he conceded, the administration "settled on the one issue that everyone could agree on[,] which was weapons of mass destruction." Subsequently Wolfowitz elaborated, but only slightly. He explained that whereas within the intelligence community Saddam's possession of WMD "has never been in controversy," among the analysts "there's been a lot of arguing back and forth about how much Iraq is involved in terrorism."[49]

Wolfowitz left out other motives for advocating intervention, ranging from securing access to the region's oil to buttressing Israel and reducing regional tensions to accelerating the transformation of the U.S. military to avenging the attempted assassination of George H. W. Bush. Wolfowitz was perhaps the sole major administration figure who considered each one of these considerations a legitimate and sufficient *casus belli*. His ambition, nevertheless, extended even beyond them. Rumsfeld wanted to transform the U.S. military. Wolfowitz, identifying with what the iconic neoconservative Norman Podhoretz labeled a "new species of imperial mission for America," wanted to transform the Middle East and then the world. By invading Iraq the America would provide a "global public good."[50]

Wolfowitz's hubris led to what may turn out to be the greatest strategic blunder in U.S. history, a blunder that could prove fatal to the American empire. It did prove fatal to Wolfowitz's ability to promote that empire, although indirectly and unexpectedly. At first it appeared that the U.S. invasion would achieve its objectives at a smaller cost than even its most optimistic proponents predicted. As Wolfowitz and his allies anticipated, with the exception of the United Kingdom, America's primary allies refused to endorse a preemptive attack. Thus notwithstanding Bush's claim that America led a "coalition of the willing," it essentially intervened unilaterally. In less than two months Baghdad fell, and Saddam and his lieutenants fled into hiding. On May 1, 2003, a Navy S-3B Viking, with "George W. Bush Commander-in-Chief" inscribed on the cockpit, landed on the deck of the carrier USS *Abraham Lincoln*. Out climbed the president wearing a green flight suit and clutching a white helmet. In a brief speech to the troops televised worldwide, Bush declared victory in "this battle . . . fought for the cause of liberty and for the peace of the world." In the background stretched a banner with the words "Mission Accomplished" blazoned on it.[51]

Those words came to haunt the president. The mission was to find and destroy Saddam's WMD. There were none. The mission was to cripple Al Qaeda by cutting off its connection to Iraq. There were no connections. As the U.S. Occupation foundered, Bush's reputation and effectiveness went into a free fall. In terms of Wolfowitz's mission, the outcome was worse. He immediately realized that the fiasco would undermine the administration's capability to take preemptive military action in the future even as it emboldened its enemies. Ultimately Americans captured Saddam; judging him guilty of crimes against humanity, Iraqis executed him. But he was such a pitiful sight that he hardly served as a model tyrant.

The outcome in Iraq was so catastrophic for Wolfowitz because its liberation and liberalization were to serve as the cornerstone of a new Middle East that would provide a shining example of the potential of an American empire, much as the Philippines had provided an example fifteen years earlier. Bush had vowed not to engage in nation building. Although among the minority in the administration sympathetic to nation building in the cause of democracy building, Wolfowitz assured the president and the American people that nation building would not be necessary. The Iraqis "view us as their hoped-for liberator. They know that America will not come as a conqueror," he said the week prior to the invasion. "Our plan . . . is to remain as long as necessary, and not one day more." That would not be long, because the Iraqis "are driven by the dream of a just and democratic society in Iraq." With minor U.S. tutelage and financial assistance, indigenous leaders would guide Iraq's "political and economic reconstruction," embracing democracy and establishing liberal institutions. Oil revenues would pay the cost.[52]

Wolfowitz saw no need to plan for an "occupation," even one that turned out as well as that of Germany and Japan following World War II. He likewise saw no need to plan for many troops to remain in Iraq. With regime change achieved, they, and his attention, could shift to other areas in need of liberation and liberalization, especially Iran and North Korea, the last two-thirds of what in his 2002 State of the Union Bush had labeled the Axis of Evil.

Developments shattered Wolfowitz's prediction, along with it his global strategy and its ideological underpinnings. By the time of Saddam's hanging on December 30, 2006, Iraq had become an American nightmare, and an even greater one for the Iraqis. Iraq's museums had been looted, its economy devastated, and its fragile ethnic balance splintered. In the run-up to the U.S. invasion Wolfowitz had described evaluations of the ethnic tension within Iraq as "exaggerated." In the invasion's aftermath that tension erupted into a civil war, euphemistically described as "sectarian violence." Complementing this civil war was a guerilla war, an insurgency fought by Shi'ites and Sunnis who hate each other but hate the American occupiers more. The number of Americans killed since the invasion has eclipsed 4,000, with all but a couple hundred of these lives lost since Bush declared "Mission Accomplished." The Iraqi death total is exponentially greater. Because the vast majority have been civilians, the number cannot even be estimated.[53]

This mayhem and carnage did not prevent Iraq from holding elections in 2005. An unexpectedly high turnout ratified a constitution that sanctioned subsequent elections for a government committed to forging national unity. While Wolfowitz and others claimed progress, post-Saddam Iraq spiraled toward disaster. Headed by the Shi'ite prime minister Nouri al-Maliki, the new government appeared no more capable than the preceding interim one of providing security or reconciliation. As Maliki's coalition partners defected in droves, terrorist death squads took thousands of lives each month, mostly Iraqis but many Americans as well. Wolfowitz envisioned Operation Iraqi Freedom turning Baghdad into the Manila of the 1980s. Instead it turned into 1980s Beirut.

By the last years of Bush's presidency a combination of the war-weariness that consumed Iraq, the decision of many Sunni insurgents to turn their guns against Al Qaeda in Iraq (the so-called Sunni Awakening), a surge in the number of U.S. troops, and a better pacification strategy orchestrated by American General David Petraeus moderated the violence. For Wolfowitz the improvement in conditions, whether sustainable or transient, came too late. His identification with the postinvasion calamity made him a political liability for Bush.

The president cut Wolfowitz loose from the administration but provided him another platform to pursue his Empire for Liberty by appointing him president of the World Bank. Wolfowitz knew next to nothing about international banking and finance. But he did know that the World Bank was about more than banking and finance. Like himself, it "represented a peculiar blend of idealism and Realpolitik."

Established along with the International Monetary Fund at the 1944 Bretton Woods Conference as an institutional means to promote economic reconstruction and development and otherwise manage the global marketplace, from its inception the World Bank reflected American power and purposes. It would use dollars (loans) rather than bullets to establish an international system that played by American rules, aspired to American standards, and shared American values. Although its initial focus was on the industrial nations of Europe and Asia, over the years it concentrated increasingly on fighting poverty and assisting the economic growth of the developing regions of the world. The premise, driven more by theory than practice, was that the synergy between these two aims would enhance international liberty.[54]

As the nation that emerged from World War II with the globe's greatest industrial production, volume of exports, and capital accumulation, America was the World Bank's largest shareholder. It provided the bank with a home just down the street from the White House, and it nominated the president. The Board of Governors approval was but a formality. Wolfowitz was the tenth, and with the exception of the Eugene Meyer (the wealthy *Washington Post* publisher who in 1946 presided over the bank only long enough to get it off the ground), his tenure was the shortest. He did not intend for it to be. Neither did George Bush.

Wolfowitz and the World Bank made for a fitful match from the start. Yet some observers held out hope for his success. They banked on his intelligence, energy, social conscience, and crusading spirit to compensate for his financial inexperience, and perhaps even his managerial ineptitude. Moreover, the legacy of Iraq also gave him a special incentive. Similar to Robert McNamara after Vietnam, one journalist wrote, the World Bank could afford Wolfowitz "refuge to wring the blood from his hands." It likewise provided him with the means. Unable to use the force of arms to remake nations in America's image, he would use loans, or the denial of loans. Wolfowitz dedicated his presidency of the World Bank to rooting out corruption. He attacked corrupt officials and corrupt regimes with the same zeal and single-mindedness that he did tyrants and tyrannical regimes. In the words of one commentator, Wolfowitz genuinely believed "that an idealistic faith in freedom could sweep aside" them all.[55]

On one level Wolfowitz's goals were universally appealing. "When Paul Wolfowitz speaks publicly these days, he is usually making good sense," editorialized his severe critic, the *New York Times*, about his anticorruption campaign. And what he said did make sense. Widespread corruption throughout the developing world was undermining efforts both to relieve poverty and promote development. Wolfowitz said it best. The "bank's mission was to send children to school, to help mothers be healthier, to provide jobs for poor people — not to have resources siphoned off into the hands of the corrupt and greedy."[56]

The problem lay not so much with the message as the messenger. Wolfowitz was damaged goods when he took over the World Bank. Notwithstanding its domination by the United States throughout its history, the bank was quintessentially multilateral. Its membership had grown from 44 to 185 nations, each one represented on the Board of Governors. Wolfowitz brought to his first meeting his reputation for arrogance, self-righteousness, ideological inflexibility, contempt for the conventional wisdom and the professionals responsible for it, and of course the unilateralism associated with the Bush administration. Worst of all, the world press portrayed him as "a global symbol of U.S. imperialism," "an instrument of U.S. power and U.S. priorities."[57]

Colleagues and associates at the bank viewed Wolfowitz with grave suspicion. His "zeal on corruption" reminded many officials there "of what they say was his messianic but unrealistic faith" that he could force liberty and democracy on Iraq. They argued that cutting off loans to corrupt regimes would not help populations living in poverty. Further, because corruption was so pervasive, observers were skeptical of Wolfowitz's targeting criteria. Even as he denied assistance to states like Cambodia, Congo, Ethiopia, Bangladesh, and even India, for example, he extended or expanded it to others—nations high on the Bush's list of strategic assets, such as Pakistan, Lebanon, and Afghanistan. Most controversial was his "emphasis on increasing the World Bank footprint in Iraq," despite the consensus among the World Bank staff that Iraq was too dangerous, too unstable, and owing to its oil reserves, too rich to qualify for a loan. That he ignored their expertise and placed implementation of his policies in the hands of a small group of officials that he brought with him to the bank exacerbated mistrust in his leadership. The perception inside the bank, commented one close observer, was that Wolfowitz's "real agenda remains hidden, and that it reflects priorities from the Bush Administration."[58]

How Wolfowitz's tenure at the World Bank ended is steeped in irony, and in tragedy. In this sense the end was appropriate for someone who represents the most recent iteration of America's Empire for Liberty. Wolfowitz came to grief because of his relationship with Shaha Riza, whom he became involved with after separating from his wife. Born in Tunisia and raised in Saudi Arabia, Riza's Middle Eastern background was for Wolfowitz a source of immediate attraction. So were her attributes and attitudes. Riza studied international relations at Oxford, gained recognition as a vocal proponent of democracy and women's rights in the Islamic world, and earned respect at the World Bank as a leading expert on the Middle East and North Africa. The problem was that although a seven-year veteran of the bank in 2005, Riza could not remain there once Wolfowitz took office. As president he was her supervisor.

By arranging for Riza's transfer to the State Department, Wolfowitz fed the perception that he retained inappropriate personal ties with the administration. That State assigned Riza to work with Dick Cheney's daughter, Elizabeth, to create a government-funded foundation committed to the promotion of democracy in the Middle East compounded Wolfowitz's mistake. So did Riza's compensation package; although her salary was still tax exempt because she was paid through the World Bank, she received a raise of almost 50 percent, bringing the total to over $190,000.

World Bank officials and the press jumped on Wolfowitz's intervention as evidence of impropriety. He had made the battle against corruption his signature issue, but he certainly appeared corrupt himself. Still, were Wolfowitz not so intimately tied to the Bush administration, and were he not in so many ways the personification of the twenty-first century's "Ugly American," he probably would have suffered at most a reprimand. As his longtime friend Richard Perle put it, those in and out of the World Bank targeted Wolfowitz because "they didn't like what they think he did when he was deputy secretary." In the event, on March 17, 2007, after a committee established by the board to investigate his behavior charged him with violating the Bank's ethical and governance guidelines, Wolfowitz resigned. He conceded missteps yet insisted that he had "acted ethically and in good faith in what I believed were the best interests of the institution." But circumstances dictated that it was "in the best interests of those whom this institution serves for [its] mission to be carried forward under new leadership."[59]

Appointed a visiting scholar at the American Enterprise Institute, Wolfowitz's public career is on hold. So is America's Empire for Liberty.

POSTSCRIPT

....

The Dark Side

THE SIX MEN whose story this book tells believed fervently in the America that they helped to build, shape, and expand.[1] The America they believed in was the America that Thomas Jefferson and his colleagues wrote about in the Declaration of Independence and risked their lives to create against seemingly insuperable odds. At the core of this America was the sanctity of the inalienable rights of all men, chief among which was liberty. Franklin, Adams, Seward, Lodge, Dulles, and Wolfowitz were not unique. In each of their lifetimes, which collectively span America's history, there were other policymakers, opinion makers, decision makers, some of whom held greater power, who believed what these six believed and whose stories likewise fit the grand narrative of the American empire.

In this regard, the subjects of this book, with their diverse backgrounds and dissimilar career paths, both represent and reflect values and ideals that have endured within the American identity since the era of the Founding Fathers. Certainly they were smarter than most, more articulate than most, and more ambitious than most. In the end, all were more privileged than most. Yet the language they spoke and the policies and programs they promoted were "mainstream Americana." Liberty meant different things to different people at different times. Nevertheless, in the popular imagination across generations, America is the land of liberty. Americans acquired territory, fought wars, and overthrew foreign governments for the purpose of preserving and promoting liberty. The evidence presented in this book reveals that this was not always the purpose. But Franklin, Adams, Seward, Lodge, Dulles, and Wolfowitz believed it was. And so did most Americans. They were not tricked into accepting this purpose. They believed that America stood for liberty and stood against empire. They believed that America was exceptional. When "ground truth" diverged from these beliefs, they rationalized the discrepancy by arguing that long-term benefits sometimes required compromises, or they dismissed incongruities as anomalies, as aberrations. Rhetoric trumped reality.

In many respects America, highlighted by the centrality of liberty to its political culture, is exceptional. For that reason the role that Americans' sense of exceptionalism has played in subverting the concept of Empire for Liberty is all the more tragic. Both the architects and supporters of the growth of the American empire held that by expanding U.S. territory, influence, and control Americans brought greater liberty to others even as they protected and increased their own. But therein lay an inherent contradiction. If Americans were exceptional, only they could fully appreciate liberty's blessings, constructively contribute to and participate in liberal institutions of government, and recognize that with liberty came responsibility. Non-Americans, whether because of race, religion, "national character," or similar attributes, could not. Hence American campaigns to spread liberty inexorably generated conflict with peoples who were insufficiently "exceptional." They had to be conquered, subjugated, or worse. An American Empire *for* Liberty became something of an oxymoron.

Until the Global War on Terror, most Americans did not see this tension between America's empire and its commitment to liberty. Most Americans were inner-directed, and focused on pursuing their own lives, livelihoods, and liberties. Unless directly affected, they paid scant attention to external affairs, defined as external to their particular and often parochial circumstances and interests. When called to take up arms, they did so on the premise that it was for a good cause. They were fighting the enemies of liberty—whether British imperialists, southern slaveholders, northern opponents of states' rights, German militarists, Italian fascists, or Communist totalitarians. Not only was America protecting its own liberties, but it was also defending the principle of self-determination and liberating captive peoples.

Periodically dissenters challenged this premise; the eras of the Mexican War, the Philippine war, and most notably, the Vietnam War are exemplars. Yet in the aftermath of these conflicts, the protest movements disbanded, a process often accelerated by revelations about the oppressive policies and programs of the adversaries—true enemies of liberty. As for America, it voluntarily granted independence to the

Filipinos. Its soldiers marched down an Avenue des Champs-Élysées lined with cheering throngs of French men, women, and children, and then it liberated the concentration camps. It helped write a new, democratic constitution for Japan. It opened its universities to thousands of Vietnamese who fled the Communist regime. There were no walls in America to keep citizens from escaping to freedom, as in Berlin. The United States did not maintain gulags.

Americans overwhelmingly interpreted their government's response to the terrorist attacks on the World Trade Center and the Pentagon according to their beliefs about the American empire (it was not one) and liberty (America was its bastion). Indeed, with few exceptions they accepted on faith the George W. Bush administration's explanation for the barbarous deed: Al Qaeda, which hated liberty, killed Americans because they loved it. They rejoiced when America wielded its military might to oust the Taliban, not only because Afghanistan harbored Usama bin Laden, but also because the Taliban's contempt for liberty was equal to that of Al Qaeda. They rejected democracy, they suppressed free thought, and they treated women like chattel. The invasion of Iraq was almost as popular. Saddam Hussein had weapons of mass destruction. More fundamentally, he was a tyrant who had turned those weapons on his own people. This was not a war for empire. This was a war for liberty. And for most Americans, certainly those who fought, it was.

The resistance Americans encountered in Iraq following the defeat of Saddam Hussein and his army, especially the casualties they suffered at the hands of those whom they had purportedly come to liberate, turned many of these same Americans, in fact a majority of Americans, against the war. Some came to agree with critics worldwide who charged America with imperialism. Books with "American Empire" in their title flew off the shelves. But if the Global War on Terrorism turns out to cause Americans to rethink who they are, to revisit their history, and to revise their beliefs about America's global mission, it will not be primarily because of their sacrifices on the battlefield, sobering as they are. It will be because of the challenges the GWOT has presented not so much to international conventions as to their core values—their devotion to liberty above all. The GWOT has forced Americans to confront who they are.

For many Americans, the GWOT is no longer about eradicating Al Qaeda, the Taliban, and their allies, real and imagined. Nor is it about promoting liberty, though Bush used that word forty-nine times in his second inaugural address. The GWOT is about Abu Ghraib prison and extraordinary rendition. American unquestionably recoil when they learn that their countrymen committed atrocities. They were horrified by the massacre of women and children in the village of My Lai, Vietnam. But Vietnam was a dirty war without fronts, and battle-weary young soldiers can act irrationally when placed in horrific environments. Abu Ghraib was different. It was a prison. The enemy was in jail. Yet their American captors subjected their prisoners to "sadistic, blatant, and wanton criminal abuses." Photographs were taken of smiling soldiers, cigarettes dangling from their mouths, pointing to Iraqis whom they had bound hand and foot, forced to strip naked, piled on one another; they placed hoods over their heads. These Americans manifestly took great delight in denying liberty to their prisoners— even the liberty to retain some semblance of dignity. They were the tyrants; they were the barbarians.[2]

The reports of detention, torture, and rendition may have affected Americans' self-image even more. Culpability for the abuses at Abu Ghraib seemed not to reach linearly high up the chain of command. As with the My Lai massacre, the guilty parties were few in number. Even if authorized by the Department of Defense to apply the "enhanced" interrogation techniques in which they were trained, they were exceptions, according to official reports. But detention, torture, and rendition were systemic, orchestrated by the Central Intelligence Agency with the Bush administration's explicit approval. The CIA held their prisoners in secret (a "hidden global internment network" of "black sites") and subjected them to methods of interrogation such as waterboarding (the near-drowning ploy that Vice President Cheney brushed aside as a "dunk in the water") that were so tortuous that they were prohibited by the Army Field Manual. In cases known as "extraordinary rendition," moreover, the CIA "outsourced" its interrogations. It arranged for the transfer of captured suspects to countries with reputations for torturing prisoners—frequently political prisoners.[3]

Such practices severely test the American narrative. So do practices closer to home. The Bush administration established military tribunals in Guantánamo Bay, Cuba (U.S. territory) that, by declaring suspected terrorists "enemy combatants," abrogated their civil liberties by denying them due process. They could be prosecuted on the basis of secret evidence and unnamed witnesses. Even on America's home soil, Bush claimed that foreign nationals legally residing in the United States could be declared enemy combatants and indefinitely held in military prisons without formal charges. America's system of justice is the bedrock of its defense of liberty. Even though the Bush administration's efforts suffered defeat after defeat in American courts, the efforts alone called into question whether America was so exceptional after all. So did the sanctioning of warrantless "wiretapping." The Bush presidency's terrorist surveillance program authorized the National Security Agency to monitor and intercept telephone, email, Internet, and other communications that involved any party that the NSA considered a foreign threat. It did not matter if the communication began or ended on U.S. soil.

One can only speculate about the lasting effect of such behavior. But with thousands of American troops still in Iraq, conditions in Afghanistan deteriorating precipitously and consuming Pakistan, crises brewing or erupting throughout much of the globe, anti-Americanism as rampant among allies as enemies, and as of this writing the U.S. economy at the brink of depression, Americans may finally have lost their appetite for expansion—and empire.

Moreover, U.S. behavior at home as well as abroad has undermined Americans' self-identity by casting doubt on whether the United States truly is the avatar of liberty. In his thirteen-minute televised farewell address to the American public in January 2009, George W. Bush used the words *liberty* and *freedom* nine times. "In the 21st century, security and prosperity at home depend on the expansion of liberty abroad," he proclaimed, echoing what over the previous two centuries became a familiar theme to the U.S. public. "If America does not lead the cause of freedom, that cause will not be led."[4]

Yet by this time Bush's approval ratings had sunk to the lowest in U.S. history, and three months before the American people had elected as their president an African American whose father was Kenyan and whose first schooling was in Indonesia. Barack Obama made "change" the central theme of his campaign. Proclaiming that Americans "reject as false the choice between our safety and our ideals," Obama used his inaugural address to repudiate virtually every program, pillar, and value associated with the Bush administration. Then on his first day in office, in the hyperbolic words of the *Washington Post*, Obama "declared an end to the 'war on terror'" by announcing his intention to close the U.S. prison at Guantánamo and nullify the legal opinions and orders that sanctioned "secret prisons, renditions, and harsh interrogations." Shortly after completing his first one hundred days in office, the president, confronted with the criticism that he was jeopardizing America's security, returned to the theme. "I believe with every fiber of my being that in the long run we also cannot keep this country safe unless we enlist the power of our most fundamental values," he proclaimed. Because of these values, he explained, the United States repeatedly was able to "enlist free nations and free peoples everywhere in the common cause and common effort of liberty."[5]

Obama has made clear he objects to the instruments, not the purposes, of Bush's "war." He unequivocally has not prescribed less American engagement with the world. Indeed, even as Obama proposed measures to extricate U.S. forces from Iraq, he mandated an increased deployment to Afghanistan. Further, his continued sanctioning of military tribunals for detainees and other parallel measures has disappointed organizations such as the American Civil Liberties Union. Still, Obama called the 2008 election "one of the defining moments" in history.[6] For Americans, judging by their manifest receptivity to his message, that definition may well incorporate less empire and more liberty.

NOTES

....

Introduction: Contending with the American Empire

1. Arthur M. Schlesinger Jr., "The American Empire? Not So Fast," *World Policy Journal* 22 (Spring 2004), available at http://www.worldpolicy.org/journal/articles/wpj05-sp/schlesinger.html (accessed March 9, 2006); Washington letter to Marquis de Lafayette, August 15, 1786, http://teachingamericanhistory.org/library/index.asp?document=321 (accessed May 31, 2009).

2. Anders Stephanson, "A Most Interesting Empire," in *The New American Empire*, ed. Lloyd C. Gardner and Marilyn Young (New York: New Press, 2005), 256.

3. Niall Ferguson, *Colossus: The Price of America's Empire* (New York: Penguin, 2004). Ferguson likewise quotes Bush's first secretary of state, Colin Powell: "We have never been imperialists" (7).

4. Highlighting the span of Williams's decades of influential scholarship are *The Tragedy of American Diplomacy* (New York: Delta Books, 1959), *The Roots of the American Empire: A Study of the Growth and Shaping of a Social Consciousness in a Marketplace Society* (New York: Random House, 1969); and *Empire as a Way of Life: An Essay on the Causes and Character of America's Present Predicament Along with a Few Thoughts on an Alternative* (New York: Oxford University Press, 1980); Lloyd C. Gardner, Walter LaFeber, and Thomas McCormick, *The Creation of the American Empire: U.S. Diplomatic History* (Chicago: Rand McNally, 1973).

5. Samuel Flagg Bemis, *A Diplomatic History of the United States* (New York: Holt, 1936), 468; transcript, "World Sees 'Imperialism' in America's Reach, Strength," National Public Radio, *All Things Considered*, November 2, 2006, http://www.npr.org/templates/story/story.php?storyId=6423000 (accessed November 3, 2006); David A. Lake, "Escape from the State of Nature: Authority and Hierarchy in World Politics," *International Security* 32 (2007): 49.

6. Charles S. Maier, "An American Empire? The Problems of Frontiers and Peace in Twenty-first Century World Politics," in Gardner and Young, *The New American Empire*, xi.

7. Robert W. Merry, *Sands of Empire: Missionary Zeal, American Foreign Policy, and the Hazards of Global Ambition* (New York: Simon and Schuster, 2005), 218.

8. Niall Ferguson, "Empires with Expiration Dates," *Foreign Policy*, September–October 2006, 50.

9. Andrew Bacevich, *American Empire: The Realities and Consequences of U.S. Diplomacy* (Cambridge: Harvard University Press, 2002); Victoria De Grazia, *Irresistible Empire: America's Advance through Twentieth-Century Europe*

(Cambridge: Belknap Press of Harvard University Press, 2005); David Harvey, *The New Imperialism* (New York: Oxford University Press, 2003); Chalmers Johnson, *The Sorrows of Empire: Militarism, Secrecy, and the End of the Republic* (New York: Metropolitan Books, 2004); John B. Judis, *The Folly of Empire: What George W. Bush Could Learn from Theodore Roosevelt and Woodrow Wilson* (New York: Scribner, 2004); Michael Mann, *Incoherent Empire* (London: Verso, 2003); Merry, *Sands of Empire*; William E. Odom and Robert Dujarric, *America's Inadvertent Empire* (New Haven: Yale University Press, 2005); Charles S. Maier, *Among Empires: American Ascendancy and Its Predecessors* (Cambridge: Harvard University Press, 2006); Walter Nugent, *Habits of Empire: A History of American Expansion* (New York: Knopf, 2008); Lake, "Escape from State of Nature," 48.

10. In addition to all the above save for the study by Odom and Robert Dujarric, which is mixed, see especially on the political right, Clyde Prestowitz, *Rogue Nation: American Unilateralism and the Failure of Good Intentions* (New York: Basic Books, 2003); on the left, Ann Norton, *Leo Strauss and the Politics of American Empire* (New Haven: Yale University Press, 2004).

11. Deepak Lal, "In Defense of Empires," in *The Imperial Tense: Prospects and Problems of American Empire*, ed. Andrew J. Bacevich (Chicago: Ivan R. Dee, 2003): 29–46; Ferguson, *Colossus*, 2; Michael Ignatieff, *Empire Lite: Nation-Building in Bosnia, Kosovo, and Afghanistan* (London: Vintage, 2003), 10–11.

12. Niall Ferguson, "The Next War of the World," *Foreign Affairs*, September–October 2006, 71.

13. Max Boot, *The Savage Wars of Peace: Small Wars and the Rise of American Power* (New York: Basic Books, 2002); John Lewis Gaddis, *Surprise, Security, and the American Experience* (Cambridge: Harvard University Press, 2004).

14. Robert Jervis, *American Foreign Policy in a New Era* (New York: Routledge, 2004), 79; Geir Lundestad, "The American 'Empire' 1945–1960," in *The American "Empire" and Other Studies of US Foreign Policy in a Comparative Perspective* (New York: Oxford University Press, 1990), 38–62; Michael H. Hunt, *The American Ascendancy: How the United States Gained and Wielded Global Dominance* (Chapel Hill: University of North Carolina Press, 2007), 311; Barack Obama's Address to the Muslim World in Cairo, June 4, 2009, http://www.nytimes.com/2009/06/04/us/politics/04obama.text .html?_r=1&scp=3&sq=Obama%20Address%20to%20the%20Muslim%20 World&st=cse (accessed June 4, 2009).

15. Odd Arne Westad, *Global Cold War: Third World Interventions and the Making of Our Times* (New York: Cambridge University Press, 2005), 10.

16. Thomas Jefferson to George Rogers Clark, December 25, 1780, in *Papers of Thomas Jefferson*, ed. Julian P. Boyd (Princeton: Princeton University Press, 1951), 4:237–38; Jefferson to James Madison, April 27, 1809, in *The Writings of Thomas Jefferson*, ed. Andrew A. Lipscomb and Albert Ellery Bergh (Washington, D.C.: Issued under the auspices of the Thomas Jefferson Memorial Association of the United States, 1903–4), 12:277; Robert W. Tucker and David C. Hendrickson, *Empire of Liberty: The Statecraft of Thomas Jefferson* (New York: Oxford University Press, 1992).

17. Ted Widmer, *Ark of the Liberties: America and the World* (New York: Hill and Wang, 2008), 54.

18. Eric Hobsbawn, *On Empire: America, War, and Global Supremacy* (New York: Pantheon, 2008), xiv.

19. Michael W. Doyle, *Empires* (Ithaca, N.Y.: Cornell University Press, 1986), 30–31, 93–97.

20. Stephen Howe, *Empire: A Very Short Introduction* (New York: Oxford University Press, 2002), 15–60, 30, 57–58; Richard Van Alstyne, *The Rising American Empire* (New York: Oxford University Press, 1960), 2; Dominic Lieven, *Empire: The Russian Empire and Its Rivals* (New Haven: Yale University Press, 2001), xiv; Stephen Peter Rosen, "Imperial Choices," in Bacevich, *The Imperial Tense*, 211, 214–15.

21. Arthur M. Schlesinger Jr., *The Cycles of American History* (Boston: Houghton Mifflin, 1986), 5, 138–39.

22. The concept is identified with John A. Gallagher and Ronald E. Robinson, "The Imperialism of Free Trade," published in the *Economic History Review* in 1953. On the article, their subsequent scholarship, and the implications for understanding empire, see *Imperialism*, ed. Wm. Roger Louis (New York: New Viewpoints, 1976).

23. Carl Parrini, "Theories of Imperialism," in *Redefining the Past: Essays in Diplomatic History in Honor of William Appleman Williams*, ed. Lloyd C. Gardner (Corvallis: Oregon State University Press, 1986), 65–66. See also Frank Ninkovich, *The United States and Imperialism* (Malden, Mass.: Blackwell, 2001), 5–6; Marilyn B. Young, "Imperial Language," in Gardner and Young, *The New American Empire*, 32; Van Alstyne, *Rising American Empire*, 6–7. For the classic theoretical frameworks that have influenced the literature on imperialism since the beginning of the twentieth century, see Joseph A. Schumpeter, *Imperialism [and] Social Classes: Two Essays* (1919; Cleveland: World Books, 1955); J. A. Hobson, *Imperialism* (1902; Ann Arbor: University of Michigan Press, 1965); V. I. Lenin, *Imperialism: The Highest Stage of Capitalism* (1917; New York: International Publishing, 1959).

24. Howe, *Empire*, 57–58.

25. William Langer, *The Diplomacy of Imperialism: 1890–1902* (New York: Knopf, 1935); Wm. Roger Louis, "Introduction," in Louis, *Imperialism*, 2–4; Susan Reynolds, "Empires: A Problem of Contemporary History," *Historical Research* 79 (2006): 158.

26. Schlesinger, *Cycles of History*, 141–43.

27. Drawing on "poststructural" or "deconstructionalist" theories often associated with French philosophers Jacques Derrida and Michel Foucault and labeled postmodernism, in the last two decades of the twentieth century many scholars attributed the construction and maintenance of empires to impersonal "discourses" that governed personal behavior, not traditionally identified sources of power. See Ninkovich, *United States and Imperialism*, 245; and, for an illustrative collection of essays, *Cultures of United States Imperialism*, ed. Amy Kaplan and Donald Pease (Durham, N.C.: Duke University Press, 1994).

28. Lal, "In Defense of Empires," 30–31; Charles Maier, "Imperial Limits," in Kaplan and Pease, *Cultures of Imperialism*, 204–5. Initially in the "Significance

of the Frontier in American History," a paper presented at the meeting of the American Historical Association in Chicago in 1893, and then in subsequent publications, Frederick Jackson Turner famously argued that America's national character was forged on the "crucible of the frontier." Turner's subsequent book, *The Frontier in American History* (New York: Henry Holt, 1920) is available in full at http://xroads.virginia.edu/~HYPER/TURNER/ (accessed March 20, 2006).

29. Ferguson, *Colossus*, 209–12.

30. David C. Hendrickson, *Peace Pact: The Lost World of the American Founding* (Lawrence: University of Kansas Press, 2000).

31. Alexander DeConde, *This Affair of Louisiana* (Baton Rouge: Louisiana State University Press, 1976), 244; Gerald Stourzh, *Benjamin Franklin and American Foreign Policy*, 2nd ed. (Chicago: University of Chicago Press, 1969), 59.

32. William Appleman Williams, *The Contours of American History* (Cleveland: World Publishing, 1961), 214.

33. Walter LaFeber, *The New Empire: An Interpretation of American Expansion, 1860–1898*, 35th anniversary ed. (Ithaca, N.Y.: Cornell University Press, 1998), 24.

34. Ernest N. Paolino, *The Foundations of the American Empire: William Henry Seward and U.S. Foreign Policy* (Ithaca, N.Y.: Cornell University Press, 1973), 13–14.

35. Daniel Webster, Second Reply to Hayne, January 26–27, 1830, http://www.dartmouth.edu/~dwebster/speeches/hayne-speech.html (accessed June 1, 2009).

36. Warren Cohen, *Empire without Tears: America's Foreign Relations, 1921–1933* (Philadelphia: Temple University Press, 1987); Emily Rosenberg, *Spreading the American Dream: American Economic and Cultural Expansion, 1890–1945* (New York: Hill and Wang, 1982); Frank Costigliola, *Awkward Dominion: American Political, Economic, and Cultural Relations with Europe, 1919–1933* (Ithaca, N.Y.: Cornell University Press, 1985).

37. John Foster Dulles, *War, Peace, and Change* (New York: Doubleday, 1939).

38. Geir Lundestad, "Empire by Invitation? The United States and Western Europe, 1945–1952," *Journal of Peace Research* 23 (1986): 263–77.

39. Stephen Howe, "The Concept of Empire: Revival, Reappraisal, or Rehabilitation," unpublished paper, 8 (author's possession).

Chapter 1: Benjamin Franklin

1. Samuel Flagg Bemis, *The Diplomacy of the American Revolution* (Bloomington: Indiana University Press, 1967), 49.

2. Ibid.

3. All fifteen of Franklin's "Silence Dogood" letters are available at http://www.historycarper.com/resources/twobf1/contents.htm (accessed April 10, 2006).

4. I borrow this idea from David Waldstreicher, *Runaway America: Benjamin Franklin, Slavery, and the American Revolution* (New York: Hill and Wang, 2004).

5. Stourzh, *Benjamin Franklin*, 3.

6. Robert Kagan, *Dangerous Nation: America's Foreign Policy from Its Earliest Days to the Dawn of the Twentieth Century* (New York: Vintage, 2007), 24; Carl Van Doren, *Benjamin Franklin* (New York: Viking Press, 1938), 261.

7. Stourzh, *Benjamin Franklin*, 44; Craig Whitford, "Ben Franklin on Stamps," at http://www.historybuff.com/library/refbfranklin.html (accessed April 12, 2006); Van Doren, *Benjamin Franklin*, 138–41, 210–13. In 1847 America's first postage stamp featured Franklin.

8. Fred Anderson and Andrew Clayton, *Dominion of War: Empire and Liberty in North America* (New York: Viking Penguin, 2005), 44–45.

9. Richard Drinnon, *Facing West: The Metaphysics of Indian-Hating and Empire-Building* (Norman: University of Oklahoma Press, 1997), 99–100; Stourzh, *Benjamin Franklin*, 40–49, 60–61.

10. H. W. Brands, *First American: The Life and Times of Benjamin Franklin* (New York: Doubleday, 2000), 244.

11. Stourzh, *Benjamin Franklin*, 19–20; *The Autobiography of Benjamin Franklin*, ed. Louis P. Masur (Boston: Bedford Books, 1993), 88–89; Anders Stephanson, *Manifest Destiny: American Expansion and the Empire of Right* (New York: Hill and Wang, 1995), 10–11.

12. Van Doren, *Benjamin Franklin*, 215–18.

13. Benjamin Franklin, *Observations Concerning the Increase of Mankind, Peopling of Countries, etc.*, at http://bc.barnard.columbia.edu/~lgordis/earlyAC/documents/observations.html (accessed April 13, 2006).

14. Ibid.

15. Ibid.

16. Ibid.

17. Quoted in Stourzh, *Benjamin Franklin*, 50–51.

18. Anderson and Clayton, *Dominion of War*, 113–18.

19. An image of the woodcut is available at http://www.foundingfathers.info/stories/gadsden.html.

20. Stourzh, *Benjamin Franklin*, 54; Edmund S. Morgan, *Benjamin Franklin* (New Haven: Yale University Press, 2002), 80–92.

21. *Autobiography of Benjamin Franklin*, 126–27.

22. George Washington to Mary Washington, July 18, 1955, at http://www.nationalcenter.org/Braddock'sDefeat.html (accessed April 19, 2006).

23. Anderson and Clayton, *Dominion of War*, 56; Kagan, *Dangerous Nation*, 24; Van Alstyne, *Rising American Empire*, 26.

24. Stourzh, *Benjamin Franklin*, 81.

25. Ibid., 74.

26. Ibid., 79, 76.

27. Ibid., 78.

28. Van Doren, *Benjamin Franklin*, 289; Stourzh, *Benjamin Franklin*, 77, 81.

29. Brands, *First American*, 334.

30. Ibid., 347.

31. Van Doren, *Benjamin Franklin*, 321–22.

32. Stourzh, *Benjamin Franklin*, 100.

33. Van Doren, *Benjamin Franklin*, 332.

34. Ibid., 352. Van Doren reproduces virtually the entire "transcript" of the questions and Franklin's responses on pp. 336–52.

35. Morgan, *Benjamin Franklin*, 162–63.

36. Felix Gilbert, *To the Farewell Address: Ideas of Early American Foreign Policy* (Princeton: Princeton University Press, 1961), 34.

37. Hutchinson to Richard Jackson, August 30, 1765, at http://www.history home.co.uk/c-eight/america/bosriot.htm (accessed April 25, 2006).

38. http://www.americanrevwar.homestead.com/files/TEAPARTY.HTM (accessed May 31, 2009).

39. Van Doren, *Benjamin Franklin*, 387–88.

40. Ibid., 450.

41. Brands, *First American*, 453.

42. Walter Isaacson, *Benjamin Franklin: An American Life* (New York: Simon and Schuster, 2003), 72.

43. Franklin, "Rules for Reducing a Great Empire to a Small One," at http://aibi.gospelcom.net/politics/DOCS/Rules%20For%20Reducing.pdf (accessed February 1, 2006).

44. Van Doren, *Benjamin Franklin*, 461–78.

45. Ibid., 475.

46. Stourzh, *Benjamin Franklin*, 111.

47. Sheila L. Kemp, *Benjamin and William Franklin: Father and Son, Patriot and Loyalist* (Boston: Bedford Books, 1994), 119; Julian P. Boyd, *Anglo-American Union: Joseph Galloway's Plans to Preserve the British Empire, 1774–1778* (Philadelphia: University of Pennsylvania Press, 1941), 6.

48. Bemis, *Diplomacy of the American Revolution*, 49.

49. Walter LaFeber, *The American Age: U.S. Foreign Policy at Home and Abroad, 1750 to the Present*, 2nd ed. (New York: Norton, 1994), 20; Gilbert, *To the Farewell Address*, 34, 44–54.

50. Yale's Avalon Project has made available online both the Treaty of Amity and Friendship and the Treaty of Alliance at http://www.yale.edu/lawweb/avalon/diplomacy/france/fr1788-1.htm and http://www.yale.edu/lawweb/avalon/diplomacy/france/fr1788-2.htm, respectively (accessed May 2, 2006).

51. Van Alstyne, *Rising American Empire*, 56–57.

52. Stourzh, *Benjamin Franklin*, 208; Bemis, *Diplomacy of the American Revolution*, 197.

53. The Paris Peace Treaty of September 30, 1783, at http://www.yale.edu/lawweb/avalon/diplomacy/britain/paris.htm (accessed May 3, 2006).

54. Van Alstyne, *Rising American Empire*, 9.

55. Jefferson to George Rogers Clark, December 25, 1780, in Boyd, *Papers of Thomas Jefferson*, 4:237–38, at http://www.monticello.org/library/reference/famquote.html (accessed January 27, 2006).

56. Robert W. Tucker and David C. Hendrickson, *The Imperial Temptation: The New World Order and America's Purpose* (New York: Council on Foreign Relations Press, 1992), 167.

57. Brands, *First American*, 221.

58. Anderson and Clayton, *Dominion of War*, 187–91; James Chace, "In Search of Absolute Security," in Bacevich, *The Imperial Tense*, 121.

Chapter 2: John Quincy Adams and America's Tortured Empire

1. *John Quincy Adams and American Continental Empire: Letters, Papers, and Speeches,* ed. Walter LaFeber (Chicago: Quadrangle Books, 1965), 13–14; James E. Lewis Jr., *John Quincy Adams: Policymaker for the Union* (Wilmington, Del.: Scholarly Resources, 2001), 3.

2. Samuel Flagg Bemis, *John Quincy Adams and the Foundations of American Foreign Policy* (New York: Knopf, 1949), 4–6.

3. Ibid., 14, 21.

4. LaFeber, *John Quincy Adams,* 15.

5. Kagan, *Dangerous Nation,* 127.

6. Gilbert, *To the Farewell Address,* 145.

7. Bemis, *Adams and the Foundations,* 96–102.

8. LaFeber, *American Age,* 63; Stephanson, *Manifest Destiny,* 18. Berkeley's original words were "Westward the Star of Empire takes its sway."

9. James E. Lewis Jr., *The Louisiana Purchase: Jefferson's Noble Bargain?* (Chapel Hill: University of North Carolina Press, 2006); Jefferson to James Madison, April 27, 1809, in Lipscomb and Bergh, *Writings of Thomas Jefferson,* 12:277; Thomas Jefferson, Notes on the State of Virginia, 1787, Query XIX, at http://m-berry.com/scanned%20Documents/Jeffersonian%20Agrarianism.pdf (accessed October 28, 2008).

10. LaFeber, *John Quincy Adams,* 17–18, 23; Lewis, *John Quincy Adams,* 51; Stephanson, *Manifest Destiny,* 59–60.

11. Lewis, *John Quincy Adams,* 14–16; Bemis, *Adams and the Foundations,* 118–21.

12. Lewis, *John Quincy Adams,* 16.

13. Ibid., 24.

14. Bemis, *Adams and the Foundations,* 182.

15. LaFeber, *John Quincy Adams,* 17–18; Bemis, *Adams and the Foundations,* 136–49.

16. Jefferson to Madison, April 27, 1809.

17. Bemis, *Adams and the Foundations,* 121–22.

18. LaFeber, *John Quincy Adams,* 17.

19. Bemis, *Adams and the Foundations,* 167–72.

20. Ibid., 301. See also James G. Cusick, *The Other War of 1812: The Patriot War and the American Invasion of Spanish East Florida* (Gainesville: University of Florida Press, 2003).

21. Lewis, *John Quincy Adams,* 27.

22. Jefferson letter to William Duane (August 4, 1812), *The Jefferson Cyclopedia,* 124, http://books.google.com/books?id=2D0gAAAAIAAJ&pg=PA124&lpg=PA124&dq=Jefferson+mere+matter+of+marching&source=bl&ots=goy4RWLzqv&sig=rHgPHrNERuva22MddjK6ysu3He4&hl=en&ei=Y5MlSsXPDIusMonU4bQF&sa=X&oi=book_result&ct=result&resnum=2 (accessed June 2, 2009).

23. Bemis, *Adams and the Foundations,* 185–86; Lewis, *John Quincy Adams,* 27–28.

24. Bemis, *Adams and the Foundations,* 191.

25. Ibid., 125–26.

26. Ibid., 218.

27. George C. Herring, *From Colony to Superpower: U.S. Foreign Relations since 1776* (New York: Oxford, 2008), 239.

28. Bemis, *Adams and the Foundations*, 253.

29. Lewis, *John Quincy Adams*, 78; LaFeber, *John Quincy Adams*, 49–51, 56–57.

30. Convention of 1818 between the United States and Great Britain, October 20, 1818, http://www.yale.edu/lawweb/avalon/diplomacy/britain/conv1818 .htm (accessed May 24, 2006); Lewis, *John Quincy Adams*, 49.

31. Anderson and Clayton, *The Dominion of War*, 233; Lewis, *John Quincy Adams*, 47.

32. Bemis, Adams, *Adams and the Foundations*, 313–24; Lewis, *John Quincy Adams*, 54.

33. LaFeber, *John Quincy Adams*, 72–74.

34. LaFeber, *American Age*, 78.

35. LaFeber, *John Quincy Adams*, 72–74.

36. Ibid., 74–77; Anderson and Clayton, *Dominion of War*, xviii–xix; Drinnon, *Facing West*, 109–11.

37. Bemis, *Adams and the Foundations*, 327.

38. LaFeber, *John Quincy Adams*, 82–85.

39. Ibid., 36–37; Bemis, *Adams and the Foundations*, 338–40.

40. LaFeber, *John Quincy Adams*, 88–89; Van Alstyne, *Rising American Empire*, 95.

41. Lewis, *John Quincy Adams*, 127–28; LaFeber, *John Quincy Adams*, 86–87.

42. Bemis, *Adams and the Foundations*, 341–42.

43. LaFeber, *John Quincy Adams*, 45.

44. Ibid., 98–99, 36–37.

45. Bemis, *Adams and the Foundations*, 386–87.

46. LaFeber, *John Quincy Adams*, 70–72, 129–31; Ninkovich, *United States and Imperialism*, 94; Bemis, *Adams and the Foundations*, 384–85; Lewis, *John Quincy Adams*, 90.

47. Bemis, *Adams and the Foundations*, 366–68, 407.

48. LaFeber, *John Quincy Adams*, 141–43.

49. Ibid.

50. Samuel Flagg Bemis, *John Quincy Adams and the Union* (New York: Knopf, 1956), 155; Bemis, *Adams and the Foundations*, 208.

51. Stephanson, *Manifest Destiny*, 40; Anderson and Clayton, *Dominion of War*, 245; Lewis, *John Quincy Adams*, 130.

52. Stephanson, *Manifest Destiny*, 60–61; Lewis, *John Quincy Adams*, 134–35.

53. Bemis, *Adams and the Union*, 334–40; Mead, *Special Providence*, 44.

54. LaFeber, *John Quincy Adams*, 146; Thomas R. Hietala, *Manifest Design: Anxious Aggrandizement in Late Jacksonian America* (Ithaca, N.Y.: Cornell University Press, 1985), 52.

55. "John Quincy Adams: Gag Rule Controversy, Petition Purporting to Come from Slaves," http://www.wfu.edu/~zulick/340/gagrule2.html (accessed June 3, 2009).

Chapter 3: William Henry Seward
Reimagines the American Empire

1. Stephanson, *Manifest Destiny*, 59; Kagan, *Dangerous Nation*, 281.
2. Glyndon G. Van Deusen, *William Henry Seward* (New York: Oxford University Press, 1967), 106–7; Widmer, *Ark of the Liberties*, 140.
3. Paolino, *Foundations of American Empire*, 81.
4. Van Deusen, *William Henry Seward*, 64–67.
5. Ibid.
6. Ibid., 103–4.
7. Ibid.; Thornton Kirkland Lothrop, *William Henry Seward* (Boston: Houghton, Mifflin, 1899), 45–46; Paolino, *Foundations of American Empire*, 11–13.
8. Van Deusen, *William Henry Seward*, 104–5.
9. William H. Seward, *Elements of Empire in America* (New York: C. Shepard, 1844), 6–9.
10. Van Deusen, *William Henry Seward*, 104–5.
11. Nugent, *Habits of Empire*, 243, 251.
12. William Seward Speech to the U.S. Senate, March 11, 1850, http://www.archive.org/stream/speechofhonwhsew00sewarich/speechofhonwhsew00sewarich_djvu.txt (accessed June 2, 2009).
13. Ibid.
14. Van Deusen, *William Henry Seward*, 200–206; Paolino, *Foundations of American Empire*, 3–4.
15. Van Deusen, *William Henry Seward*, 139–40.
16. Reginald Horsman, *Race and Manifest Destiny: The Origins of American Racial Anglo-Saxonism* (Cambridge: Harvard University Press, 1981), 184.
17. Van Deusen, *William Henry Seward*, 203.
18. Seward speech to the U.S. Senate, March 11, 1850.
19. Ibid.
20. Paolino, *Foundations of American Empire*, 26–27.
21. Ibid.; Van Deusen, *William Henry Seward*, 208.
22. Van Deusen, *William Henry Seward*, 208–9; Paolino, *Foundations of American Empire*, 7.
23. Paolino, *Foundations of American Empire*, 7; Van Deusen, *William Henry Seward*, 147–48; Walter LaFeber, *The Cambridge History of American Foreign Relations*, vol. 2, *The American Search for Opportunity, 1865–1913* (New York: Cambridge University Press, 1993), 8–9; Drinnon, *Facing West*, 271.
24. Van Deusen, *William Henry Seward*, 147–48; Paolino, *Foundations of American Empire*, 36.
25. William H. Seward's "Irrepressible Conflict" Speech, October 25, 1858, http://www.nyhistory.com/central/conflict.htm (accessed June 2, 2006).
26. Ibid.
27. Van Deusen, *William Henry Seward*, 247–48.
28. Ibid., 281–82; Lothrop, *William Henry Seward*, 254–70.
29. Norman B. Ferris, *Desperate Diplomacy: William H. Seward's Foreign Policy, 1861* (Knoxville: University of Tennessee Press, 1976), 154; Van Deusen, *William Henry Seward*, 365.

30. Stephanson, *Manifest Destiny*, 18.

31. Van Deusen, *William Henry Seward*, 511–12.

32. LaFeber, *American Search for Opportunity*, 1–3.

33. Van Deusen, *William Henry Seward*, 378.

34. Van Alstyne, *Rising American Empire*, 176–77; Stephanson, *Manifest Destiny*, 62.

35. Paolino, *Foundations of American Empire*, 11–13; LaFeber, *New Empire*, 28; LaFeber, *American Search for Opportunity*, 9.

36. LaFeber, *New Empire*, 408–9; Paolino, *Foundations of American Empire*, 107.

37. Paolino, *Foundations of American Empire*, 45–75.

38. Van Deusen, *William Henry Seward*, 537–48.

39. Paolino, *Foundations of American Empire*, 34–35.

40. Ibid., 127.

41. Van Deusen, *William Henry Seward*, 549; Drinnon, *Facing West*, 270–75.

Chapter 4: Henry Cabot Lodge and the New American Empire

1. Drinnon, *Facing West*, 257, 270–75.

2. John A. Garraty, *Henry Cabot Lodge: A Biography* (New York: Knopf, 1953), 123–28; Warren Zimmerman, *First Great Triumph: How Five Americans Made Their Country a World Power* (New York: Farrar, Straus and Giroux, 2002), 149.

3. William C. Widenor, *Henry Cabot Lodge and the Search for an American Foreign Policy* (Berkeley and Los Angeles: University of California Press, 1983), 28–35, 18–19; Garraty, *Henry Cabot Lodge*, 12–13.

4. Widenor, *Henry Cabot Lodge*, 71; Henry Cabot Lodge, *Alexander Hamilton* (Boston: Houghton, Mifflin, 1883), 11; Zimmerman, *First Great Triumph*, 166; Widenor, *Henry Cabot Lodge*, 4–8 (author's emphasis).

5. Garraty, *Henry Cabot Lodge*, 79.

6. Ibid., 98.

7. Widenor, *Henry Cabot Lodge*, 69.

8. Zimmerman, *First Great Triumph*, 187.

9. Widenor, *Henry Cabot Lodge*, 36–41, 141–44.

10. Zimmerman, *First Great Triumph*, 184–86.

11. Widenor, *Henry Cabot Lodge*, 67–68.

12. Sylvester K. Stevens, *American Expansion in Hawaii, 1842–1898* (Harrisburg: Archives Publishing, 1945), 4; Julius Pratt, *Expansionists of 1898: The Acquisition of Hawaii and the Spanish Islands* (Baltimore: Johns Hopkins University Press, 1936), 34.

13. LaFeber, *New Empire*, 153; Merze Tate, *The United States and the Hawaiian Kingdom: A Political History* (New Haven: Yale University Press, 1965), 210.

14. The U.S. government quoted the queen's abdication letter when it officially apologized to the Native Hawaiians one hundred years later. United States Public Law 103-50, 103rd Congress, Joint Resolution 19, November 23, 1993, http://www.hawaii-nation.org/publawall.html (accessed November 22, 2006).

15. Stephen Kinzer, *Overthrow: America's Century of Regime Change from Hawaii to Iraq* (New York: Times Books, 2006), 32.

16. Julius W. Pratt, "The 'Large' Policy of 1898," *Mississippi Valley Historical Review* 19 (1932): 231; Henry Cabot Lodge, "Our Blundering Foreign Policy," *Forum 19* (1895): 9; Widenor, *Henry Cabot Lodge*, 81; Garraty, *Henry Cabot Lodge*, 149–53.

17. Garraty, *Henry Cabot Lodge*, 149–53; Zimmerman, *First Great Triumph*, 149–52.

18. Lodge, "Our Blundering Foreign Policy," 16; Zimmerman, *First Great Triumph*, 152; Schlesinger, *Cycles of History*, 143–51; Pratt, "Large Policy," 232.

19. Zimmerman, *First Great Triumph*, 100.

20. LaFeber, *New Empire*, 262.

21. Henry Cabot Lodge, "England, Venezuela, and the Monroe Doctrine," *North American Review* 160 (June 1895): 651–59; Schlesinger, *Cycles of History*, 138–39; LaFeber, *New Empire*, 262; Widenor, *Henry Cabot Lodge*, 76.

22. Widenor, *Henry Cabot Lodge*, 81–83; Garraty, *Henry Cabot Lodge*, 155–63; Ernest R. May, *Imperial Democracy: The Emergence of America as a Great Power* (New York: Harcourt Brace, 1961), 370.

23. Ninkovich, *United States and Imperialism*, 16, 30; Widenor, *Henry Cabot Lodge*, 86.

24. Zimmerman, *First Great Triumph*, 175.

25. Garraty, *Henry Cabot Lodge*, 189–90; Henry Cabot Lodge, For Cuban Intervention, Congressional Record, 54 Cong., 1 Sess., pp. 1971–72, http://www.mtholyoke.edu/acad/intrel/lodge1.htm (accessed June 14, 2006); Kaplan, *Dangerous Nation*, 410.

26. Zimmerman, *First Great Triumph*, 262.

27. Russell Mead, *Special Providence: American Foreign Policy and How It Changed the World* (New York: Routledge, 2002), 108–9. Mead argues that normatively Lodge was not "gratuitously imperialistic." That was true only after the war in the Philippines.

28. John A. Gable, "Credit 'Splendid Little War' to John Hay," *New York Times*, July 9, 1991; Garraty, *Henry Cabot Lodge*, 189–90.

29. Widenor, *Henry Cabot Lodge*, 108 and 108 n. 207; Ninkovich, *United States and Imperialism*, 24–28.

30. Widenor, *Henry Cabot Lodge*, 111–14.

31. Garraty, *Henry Cabot Lodge*, 197–98.

32. Robert L. Beisner, *Twelve against Empire: The Anti-Imperialists, 1898–1900* (Chicago: University of Chicago Press, 1985), xxvi.

33. Zimmerman, *First Great Triumph*, 386, 415.

34. Henry Cabot Lodge, "The Philippines: A Speech before the U.S. Senate," March 7, 1900, in Henry Cabot Lodge, *Speeches and Addresses, 1894–1909* (Boston: Houghton Mifflin, 1909), 317–73.

35. Ibid.

36. Widenor, *Henry Cabot Lodge*, 117–18; Lodge, "The Philippine Islands: A Speech."

37. Paul A. Kramer, "Race-Making and Colonial Violence in the U.S. Empire: The Philippine-American War as Race War," *Diplomatic History* 30 (2006): 169–210.

38. Henry Cabot Lodge, "The Restriction of Immigration," http://us.history.wisc.edu/hist102/pdocs/lodge_immigration.pdf (accessed November 6, 2006).

39. Emma Lazarus, "The New Colossus," http://www.libertystatepark.com/emma.htm (accessed December 15, 2008); Peter Kolchin, "Whiteness Studies: The New History of Race in America," *Journal of American History* 89 (June 2002), http://www.historycooperative.org/journals/jah/89.1/kolchin.html (accessed June 3, 2009); Frederick Jackson Turner, "The Significance of the Frontier in American History," July 12, 1893, http://xroads.virginia.edu/~Hyper/TURNER/chapter1.html (accessed March 7, 2007).

40. Henry Cabot Lodge, Corollary to the Monroe Doctrine, http://academic.brooklyn.cuny.edu/history/johnson/lodgemd.htm (accessed March 7, 2007).

41. Garraty, *Henry Cabot Lodge*, 312.

42. Ibid., 294–97.

43. Widenor, *Henry Cabot Lodge*, 198–99.

44. Woodrow Wilson Speech to Congress, April 2, 1917, http://www.firstworldwar.com/source/usawardeclaration.htm (accessed March 9, 2007).

45. Woodrow Wilson's Fourteen Points, January 8, 1918, http://avalon.law.yale.edu/20th_century/wilson14.asp (accessed June 3, 2009).

46. Garraty, *Henry Cabot Lodge*, 344; The Covenant of the League of Nations (including amendments adopted to December 1914, http://avalon.law.yale.edu/20th_century/leagcov.asp (accessed March 9, 2007).

47. Merry, *Sands of Empire*, 83–84; Henry Cabot Lodge on the League of Nations, August 12, 1919, http://www.firstworldwar.com/source/lodge_leagueofnations.htm (accessed November 10, 2008).

Chapter 5: John Foster Dulles and the Conflicted Empire

1. Avery Dulles, S.J, "John Foster Dulles: His Religious and Political Heritage," *The Flora Levy Lecture in the Humanities* 14, ed. Maurice W. duQuesnay and Albert W. Fields (Lafayette: University of Southwestern Louisiana, 1994), 4.

2. Ronald W. Pruessen, *John Foster Dulles: The Road to Power* (New York: Free Press, 1982), 32.

3. Philip Mason Burnett, *Reparations at the Paris Peace Conference: From the Standpoint of the American Delegation*, 2 vols. (New York: Columbia University Press, 1940), 1:600–4.

4. "N.Y. Corporation Lawyers," *Fortune*, January 1931, 61–67.

5. Cohen, *Empire without Tears*.

6. Emily Rosenberg, *Financial Missionaries to the World: The Politics and Culture of Dollar Diplomacy, 1900–1930* (Durham, N.C.: Duke University Press, 2003), 150.

7. Dulles, *War, Peace, and Change*, ix.

8. Ibid., 6–8, 138–39.

9. Ibid., 123–25.

10. Ibid., 31.

11. Ibid., 30–31.

12. Ibid., ix, 81–82, 144–51.

13. Dulles to William E. Borah, April 3, 1939, "Borah, William E.—1939," John Foster Dulles Papers, Princeton University (hereafter, DP-Princeton).

14. Mark G. Toulouse, *The Transformation of John Foster Dulles: From Prophet of Realism to Priest of Nationalism* (Macon, Ga.: Mercer University Press, 1985),

58; Memorandum of conference with the president, March 26, 1943, "Federal Council of the Churches of Christ in America—Commission to Study the Bases of a Just and Durable Peace—1943," DP-Princeton; Pruessen, *John Foster Dulles*, 227.

15. Dulles to Arthur Hays Sulzberger, October 21, 1943, "Sulzberger, Arthur Hays—1943," DP-Princeton.

16. Kinzer, *Overthrow*, 115.

17. John Foster Dulles, "Thoughts on Soviet Foreign Policy," *Life*, June 3, 1946, 112ff.

18. Department of State Press Release, May 29, 1951, "Soviet Union and the Communist Party--1951," DP-Princeton.

19. John Foster Dulles, *War or Peace* (New York: Macmillan, 1950), 63.

20. Dulles, "Foreign Policy Memorandum," April 11, 1952, "Dulles, John Foster, 1952," Allen W. Dulles Papers, Princeton University.

21. Herbert S. Parmet, *Eisenhower and the American Crusades* (New York: Macmillan, 1972), 101.

22. Memorandum of conversation, [probably by Cutler], "Solarium Project," May 8, 1953, lot 66D148, SS-NSC files, RG 59, National Archives II, College Park, Md.

23. Richard H. Immerman, "Between the Unattainable and the Unacceptable: Eisenhower and Dienbienphu," in *Reevaluating Eisenhower: American Foreign Policy in the 1950s*, ed. Richard A. Melanson and David Mayers (Urbana: University of Illinois Press, 1987), 121.

24. Memorandum of conversation, March 24, 1953, *Foreign Relations of the United States, 1952–54* (Washington, D.C.: GPO, 1982), 13:419.

25. George C. Herring, "'A Good Stout Effort': John Foster Dulles and the Indochina Crisis, 1954–1955," in *John Foster Dulles and the Diplomacy of the Cold War*, ed. Richard H. Immerman (Princeton: Princeton University Press, 1990), 220.

26. Richard H. Immerman, "The United States and the Geneva Conference of 1954: A New Look," *Diplomatic History* 14 (1990): 60; Herring, "Good Stout Effort," 223.

27. Hunt, *American Ascendancy*, 217.

28. Dwight D. Eisenhower, *Waging Peace, 1956–1961* (Garden City, N.Y.: Doubleday, 1965), 36.

29. Wm. Roger Louis, "Dulles, Suez, and the British," in Immerman, *Dulles and Cold War*, 148.

30. Chester J. Pach Jr. and Elmo Richardson, *The Presidency of Dwight D. Eisenhower*, rev. ed. (Lawrence: University of Kansas Press, 1991), 133; Donald Neff, *Warriors at Suez: Eisenhower Takes America into the Middle East* (New York: Simon and Schuster, 1981), 475.

31. John Foster Dulles statement in the UN General Assembly, November 1, 1956, *Department of State Bulletin* 35 (July–December 1956): 751–55.

32. Louis, "Dulles, Suez, and the British," 153.

33. Townsend Hoopes, *The Devil and John Foster Dulles* (Boston: Little, Brown, 1973), 337; *Public Papers of the Presidents of the United States: Dwight D. Eisenhower, 1957* (Washington, D.C.: GPO, 1958), 6–17; Hunt, *American Ascendancy*, 219.

34. Richard H. Immerman, *The CIA in Guatemala: The Foreign Policy of Intervention* (Austin: University of Texas Press), 82.

35. Ibid., 179.

Chapter 6: Paul Wolfowitz and the Lonely Empire

1. George C. Herring, *America's Longest War: The United States in Vietnam, 1950–1975*, 4th ed. (New York: McGraw Hill, 2001).

2. Todd Gitlin, *The Sixties: Years of Hope, Days of Rage* (New York: Bantam, 1993).

3. David Dudley, "Paul's Choice," *Cornell Alumni Magazine Online*, July–August 2004, http://cornellalumnimagazine.com/Archive/2004Julaug/features/Feature.html (accessed July 2, 2007).

4. Peter J. Boyer, "The Believer: Paul Wolfowitz Defends His War," *New Yorker*, November 1, 2004, http://www.newyorker.com/archive/2004/11/01/041101fa_fact (accessed April 10, 2007).

5. Allan Bloom, *Closing of the American Mind* (New York: Simon and Schuster, 1987); Saul Bellow, *Ravelstein* (New York: Viking, 2000); James Fallows, "The Unilateralist: A Conversation with Paul Wolfowitz," *Atlantic Monthly*, March 2002, http://www.theatlantic.com/doc/200203/fallows (accessed May 9, 2007).

6. Norton, *Leo Strauss*, 118–23; James Mann, *Rise of the Vulcans: The History of Bush's War Cabinet* (New York: Viking, 2004), 26–28.

7. Paul Wolfowitz, "Statesmanship in the New Century," in *Present Dangers: Crisis and Opportunity in American Foreign and Defense Policy*, ed. Robert Kagan and William Kristol (San Francisco: Encounter Books, 2000); Daniel Tanguay, *Leo Strauss: An Intellectual Biography*, trans. Christopher Nadon (New Haven: Yale University Press, 2007), 86.

8. Bill Keller, "The Sunshine Warrior," *New York Times*, September 22, 2002, http://select.nytimes.com/search/restricted/article?res=F30D13FE3C540C718 EDDA00894DA404482 (accessed June 27, 2007); Dudley, "Paul's Choice." Increasingly isolated at Cornell because of his support for the Vietnam War, Jack Wolfowitz in 1970 left for the University of Illinois.

9. Mann, *Rise of the Vulcans*, 26–28; Boyer, "The Believer."

10. James Risen, *State of War: The Secret History of the CIA and the Bush Administration* (New York: Free Press, 2006), 71–73; Mann, *Rise of the Vulcans*, 76.

11. Mann, *Rise of the Vulcans*, 73–75.

12. Maier, *Among Empires*, 246.

13. Keller, "The Sunshine Warrior."

14. Sam Tanenhaus, "The Right: Down, but Maybe Not Out," *New York Times*, May 20, 2007; John M. Owen IV, "Democracy, Realistically," *National Interest* 83 (2006): 35; Lloyd Gardner, "Present at the Culmination," in Gardner and Young, *The New American Empire*, 22–23.

15. Stefan Halper and Jonathan Clarke, *America Alone: The Neo-Conservatives and the Global Order* (New York: Cambridge University Press, 2005), 173; Karen DeYoung, "For Washington Insider, Job Was an Uneasy Fit," *Washington Post*, May 18, 2007.

16. Alan Sipress and Ellen Nakashima, "Jakarta Tenure Offers Glimpse of Wolfowitz," *Washington Post*, March 28, 2005.

17. Halper and Clarke, *America Alone*, 18–19; Ivo H. Daalder and James M. Lindsay, *America Unbound: The Bush Revolution in Foreign Policy* (Washington, D.C.: Brookings, 2003), 46–47; Jacob Heilbrunn, *They Knew They Were Right: The Rise of the Neocons* (New York: Doubleday, 2008), 137.

18. Gary North, "An Introduction to Neoconservatism," http://www.lewrockwell.com/north/north180.html (accessed August 9, 2007); quotations by Irving Kristol, *Conservativeforum.org*, http://www.conservativeforum.org/authquot.asp?ID=36 (accessed September 7, 2007).

19. Paul Kennedy, *The Rise and Fall of the Great Powers: Economic Change and Military Conflict, 1500–2000* (New York: Random House, 1987).

20. Reinhold Niebuhr, *Children of Light and the Children of Darkness: A Vindication of Democracy and a Critique of Its Traditional Defenders* (New York: Scribner's, 1945); Mark Gerson, *The Neoconservative Vision: From the Cold War to the Culture Wars* (Lanham, Md.: Madison Books, 1997), 17.

21. Merry, *Sands of Empire*, 172–73.

22. Irving Kristol, *Reflections of a Neoconservative: Looking Back, Looking Ahead* (New York: Basic Books, 1983), xiii; Heilbrunn, *They Knew They Were Right*, 212.

23. Gerson, *Neoconservative Vision*, 250–51.

24. Jeanne J. Kirkpatrick, *Dictatorships and Double Standards: Rationalism and Reason in Politics* (New York: Simon and Schuster, 1982) (originally published in the November 1979 issue of *Commentary*).

25. David Milne, "Intellectualism in US Diplomacy," *International Journal* 62 (2007): 646; U.S. Department of State Circular Telegram, "Rumsfeld Mission: December 20 Meeting with Iraqi President Saddam Hussein," December 21, 1983, http://www.gwu.edu/~nsarchiv/NSAEBB/NSAEBB82/iraq31.pdf (accessed April 28, 2007); U.S. Embassy London to Secretary of State, "Rumsfeld One-on-One Meeting with Iraqi Deputy Prime Minister and Foreign Minister Tariq Aziz," December 21, 1983, http://www.gwu.edu/~nsarchiv/NSAEBB/NSAEBB82/iraq32.pdf (accessed August 2, 2007).

26. Charles Krauthammer, "The Unipolar Moment," *Foreign Affairs* 70 (1990): 23–33.

27. Vladislav Zubok, *A Failed Empire: The Soviet Union in the Cold War from Stalin to Gorbachev* (Chapel Hill: University of North Carolina Press, 2007), 324.

28. George H. W. Bush's State of the Union Address, January 29, 1991, http://www.thisnation.com/library/sotu/1991gb.html (accessed August 3, 2007).

29. Excerpts from Iraqi Document on Meeting with U.S. Envoy, http://www.chss.montclair.edu/english/furr/glaspie.html (accessed August 6, 2007). Although the focus is on U.S.-Iranian friendship, these words do not appear in the transcript made available at the George H. W. Bush Library and Margaret Thatcher Foundation: http://www.margaretthatcher.org/document/0DFD0DDB2BA34EF59F2570CE7EEE03C8.pdf (accessed June 5, 2009).

30. Thomas E. Ricks, *Fiasco: The American Military Adventure in Iraq* (New York: Penguin, 2006), 6–7.

31. Ibid., 16–17.

32. Andrew J. Bacevich, "Trigger Man," *American Conservative*, June 6, 2005, http://www.amconmag.com/2005a/2005_06_06/article1.html (accessed August 6, 2007).

33. Jon Basil Utley, "Answering the 'Wolfowitz (Bush) Doctrine' on American Empire," *AntiWar.Com*, August 24, 2001, http://antiwar.com/utley/?articleid=1628 (accessed April 28, 2006).

34. Bacevich, *American Empire*, 43–46.

35. Ibid.; Keller, "The Sunshine Warrior."

36. Bacevich, *American Empire*, 43–46; 1992 Draft Defense Planning Guidance," *Right Web Profile* (Silver City, N.M.: International Relations Center, October 25, 2006), http://www.rightweb.irc-online.org/profile/1992_Draft_Defense_Planning_Guidance (accessed July 3, 2007).

37. Patrick Tyler, "Pentagon Drops Goal of Blocking New Superpowers," *New York Times*, May 23, 1992.

38. Stanley Hoffman, "The Foreign Policy the US Needs," *New York Review of Books*, August 10, 2006, http://www.nybooks.com/articles/19217 (accessed August 19, 2006); Daalder and Lindsay, *America Unbound*, 40–45.

39. William Kristol and Robert Kagan, "Introduction: National Interest and Global Responsibility," *Present Dangers*, 7; Aaron L. Friedberg, "Asian Allies: True Strategic Partners," in Kristol and Kagan, *Present Dangers*, 197; Francis Fukuyama, *America at the Crossroads: Democracy, Power, and the Neoconservative Legacy* (New Haven: Yale University Press, 2006), 42–43.

40. Project for the New American Century Statement of Principles, June 3, 1997, http://www.newamericancentury.org/statementofprinciples.htm (accessed August 12, 2007).

41. Daalder and Lindsay, *America Unbound*, 46–47.

42. Bacevich, *American Empire*, 205–6; Elliott Abrams, Richard L. Armitage, et al., Open Letter to Clinton, January 26, 1998, http://www.newamericancentury.org/iraqclintonletter.htm (accessed August 12, 2007).

43. NewsHour with Jim Leherer Transcript, Presidential Debate, October 12, 2000, http://www.pbs.org/newshour/bb/politics/july-dec00/for-policy_10-12.html (accessed August 14, 2007).

44. Daalder and Lindsay, *America Unbound*, 197.

45. Karl E. Meyer and Shareen Blair Brysac, *Kingmakers: The Invention of the Modern Middle East* (New York: Norton, 2008), 385.

46. Ricks, *Fiasco*, 27; Lloyd C. Gardner, "Present at the Culmination," in Gardner and Young, *The New American Empire*, 22–23; Fallows, "The Unilateralist"; Mann, *Rise of the Vulcans*, 22.

47. Boyer, "The Believer"; Mann, *Rise of the Vulcans*, 235–38; Deputy Secretary Wolfowitz, interview by Sam Tannenhaus [sic], *Vanity Fair*, May 9, 2003 (updated May 29, 2003), http://www.defenselink.mil/transcripts/2003/tr20030509-depsecdef0223.html (accessed February 3, 2006).

48. Daalder and Lindsay, *America Unbound*, 103–5.

49. Paul Wolfowitz, interview by Tanenhaus, May 9, 2003; Deputy Secretary Wolfowitz, interview by Karen DeYoung, *Washington Post*, May 28, 2003.

50. Fukuyama, *America at the Crossroads*, 95; Andrew J. Bacevich, *The New American Militarism: How Americans Are Seduced by War* (New York: Oxford, 2005), 95.

51. Transcript of President Bush's speech from the flight deck of the USS *Lincoln*, May 1, 2003, http://www.cnn.com/2003/US/05/01/bush.transcript/ (accessed August 18, 2007).

52. Remarks as delivered by Deputy Secretary of Defense Paul Wolfowitz, Omni Shoreham Hotel, Washington, D.C., Tuesday, March 11, 2003, http://find articles.com/p/articles/mi_m0PAH/is_2003_March_11/ai_104438393 (accessed August 15, 2007).

53. Ricks, *Fiasco*, 95–96.

54. John Cassidy, "The Next Crusade: Paul Wolfowitz and the World Bank," *New Yorker*, April 9, 2007, http://www.newyorker.com/reporting/2007/04/09/070409fa_fact_cassidy/ (accessed April 11, 2007).

55. Ibid.; Sebastian Mallaby, "Blinkered By His Big Ideas," *Washington Post*, April 23, 2006.

56. "Mr. Wolfowitz and the Bank," *New York Times*, January 2, 1007; Steven R. Weisman, "Wolfowitz Corruption Drive Rattles World Bank, *New York Times*, September 14, 2006.

57. Cassidy, "The Next Crusade."

58. Weisman, "Wolfowitz Corruption"; DeYoung, "For Washington Insider;" Cassidy, "The Next Crusade."

59. Statements of Executive Directors and President Wolfowitz, May 17, 2007, http://web.worldbank.org/WBSITE/EXTERNAL/NEWS/0,,contentMDK:21339650~menuPK:34463~pagePK:34370~piPK:34424~theSitePK:4607,00.html (accessed August 20, 2007); Alan Weisman, *Prince of Darkness: Richard Perle: The Kingdom, the Power, and the End of Empire in America* (New York: Union Square Press, 2007), 233.

Postscript

1. For the subtitle of this postscript I borrow from Jane Mayer, *The Dark Side: The Inside Story of How the War on Terror Turned into a War on American Ideals* (New York: Doubleday, 2009). In an interview following the September 11 attacks, Vice President Dick Cheney said of America's response, "We will also have to work, though, sort of the dark side." Afterward, inside the White House "Dark Side" became Cheney's nickname. Barton Gellman, *Angler: The Cheney Vice Presidency* (New York: Penguin, 2008), 160–61.

2. Widmer, *Ark of the Liberties*, 321; Seymour M. Hersh, "Torture at Abu Ghraib," *New Yorker*, May 10, 2004, http://www.newyorker.com/archive/2004/05/10/040510fa_fact (accessed November 22, 2008).

3. Mark Danner, "US Torture: Voices from the Black Sites," *New York Review of Books*, April 9, 2009, http://www.nybooks.com/articles/22530?email (accessed April 28, 2009); Mark Mazzetti and Scott Shane, "After Sharp Words on C.I.A., Obama Faces a Delicate Task," *New York Times*, December 2, 2008; Report, U.S. Senate Armed Services Committee Inquiry into the Treatment of Detainees in U.S. Custody, Executive Summary, November 20, 2008, http://documents.nytimes.com/report-by-the-senate-armed-services-committee-on-detainee-treatment#p=1 (accessed April 22, 2009).

4. Transcript of President Bush's Last Televised Address, January 16, 2009, *New York Times*, January 16. 2009.

5. Barack Obama's Inaugural Address, January 20, 2009, *New York Times*, January 21, 2009; Dana Priest, "Bush's 'War' on Terror Comes to a Sudden End," *Washington Post*, January 23, 2009; President Obama's Speech on National Security, *New York Times*, May 21, 2009, http://www.nytimes.com/2009/05/21/us/politics/21obama.text.html?ref=politics (accessed May 22, 2009).

6. Barack Obama's Acceptance Speech, August 28, 2008, *New York Times*, August 29, 2008.

IMAGE SOURCES

Chapter 1. Benjamin Franklin. An engraving by H. B. Hall from the original picture in Passel painted from life by J.A. Duplessis in 1783, which was in the possession of John Bigelow Esq. in 1896 (United States Library of Congress Prints and Photographs Division)

Chapter 2. John Quincy Adams. From a daguerreotype taken in 1848 by Southworth & Hawes shortly before Adams's death

Chapter 3. William Henry Seward. 3-D image by Pete Zoppi, who used several 3-D computer graphics programs—including Maya, Mudbox, Mental Ray, and Photoshop—to create this image (original portrait circa 1860)

Chapter 4. Henry Cabot Lodge. Half-length portrait (United States Library of Congress Prints and Photographs Division)

Chapter 5. John Foster Dulles. Dec. 31, 1943 (Nina Leen, Time Life Pictures)

Chapter 6. Paul Wolfowitz. U.S. Secretary of Defense Paul Wolfowitz at press conference in Manila, June 3, 2002 (Department of Defense)

abolitionism, 95, 102
Abrams, Elliot, 211
Abu Ghraib prison, 235
Academy of Philadelphia, 24–25
ACDA. *See* U.S. Arms Control and Disarmament Agency
Acheson, Dean, 201
Adams, Abigail Smith, 60
Adams, Charles Francis, 99, 105, 118, 120, 127, 129
Adams, Charles Francis, Jr., 151
Adams, Henry, 60, 131–34
Adams, John, 50–53, 56, 60–62, 64–65, 66
Adams, John Quincy: accomplishments and times of, 60; American empire, vision of and efforts toward building, 79, 81, 86, 91, 120; birth and early years of, 61–62; choice of for this volume, 16, 232; as congressman, 93–97; early diplomatic career of, 62–64; Franklin and, 61, 79; Jackson and, 81–84; Jefferson, relations with, 62, 66; Jefferson's Embargo Act, support for, 70–72; Jefferson's expansionism, support for, 65–69; Latin America and the Monroe Doctrine, 87–92, 194; liberty and territorial expansion, tension between, 69, 79, 86–88, 91–92, 94–97, 111; McKinley's reversal of, 148; Mexican War, opposition to, 97, 99; as minister plenipotenitiary to Britain, 79; as minister plenipotentiary to Russia, 72–76; negotiations with the British and the Treaty of Ghent, 75–78; presidency of, 92–93; searching abroad for monsters to destroy, dictum against, 220; as secretary of state, 79–92; Seward and, 99–100, 102, 104, 127; slavery, position on, 80, 87, 91–92, 94–96; Transcontinental Treaty, negotiations with

Spain leading to, 16, 83–86; in the U.S. Senate, 66–72; war with Britain, concerns regarding, 74
Adams, Samuel, 45, 47, 60
Afghanistan, 224, 237
Alaska, 124–25
Alaska-Siberia telegraph line (Collins' Overland Telegraph), 124
Albany Plan, 32–33
Albany Regency, 100
Alexander I (czar of Russia), 72, 75–76, 89–90
Alien and Sedition Acts, 65
Alliance, Treaty of (France and America), 52–53
All-Mexico movement, 111
Al Qaeda, 224, 234–35
Ambrister, Robert, 82
American Civil Liberties Union, 237
American Empire: the "Adams-Seward-Hay" empire, 129; Britain-France conflict and, 60, 63–68; the Central Intelligence Agency as instrument for, 180; colonialism of Britain and France, distinguished from, 192; contemporary challenges to Americans' beliefs regarding, 233–37; debate over the existence of, 1–4; Dulles's vision(s) of, 170, 172–75, 177–79, 192–95; economic opportunity *vs.* security as goal of, 174–75; as "Empire without Tears," 171–72; the Franklin/Adams vision of Manifest Destiny and, 68, 71, 85, 91, 93, 120, 123 (*see also* Adams, John Quincy); Franklin's choice of over British, 49; Franklin's vision of, 26–30, 32–33, 79; fundamental questions regarding, 4; as "homogenizing," 13; imperialism and claims for liberty as goal of, 135; the Jefferson-Madison vision of, 72; liberty as a constant in the

American Empire (*continued*)
    narrative of, 5, 232–33 (*see also*
    liberty); Lodge's imperialist vision
    of, 135, 140–54; the Louisiana
    Purchase, 67–70; multilateral *vs.*
    unilateral internationalists, tension
    between visions of, 160–61, 164; "of"
    or "for" liberty, distinction between,
    5; peculiarities of, 13–14; power of,
    12; Reagan's vision of in opposition
    to the Evil Empire, 204; Seward's vi-
    sion of, 99, 103–14, 120–21; Wilson's
    vision of, 158; Wolfowitz's vision of,
    217–20. *See also* Manifest Destiny
American Enterprise Institute, 231
American exceptionalism: Adams's
    belief in, 87; Bush's belief in, 222;
    Dulles's belief in, 172; Foster's
    belief in, 166; Franklin's claim of,
    28; the Global War on Terrorism as
    challenge to claims of, 236; liberty
    and, dilemma of, 233; Lodge's belief
    in, 161; neoconservatives' belief in,
    209–10
American Philosophical Society, 24
Amity and Commerce, Treaty of, 52
Anderson, Fred, 84
Anglo-Iranian Oil Company, 182
anti-imperialists, 150–51
Anti-Mason Party, 100
"A Policy of Boldness" (Dulles), 179
Aquino, Benigno, 207
Aquino, Corazon, 207
Arafat, Yasser, 213
Arbenz Guzmán, Jacobo, 193–95
Arbuthnot, Alexander, 82
Arévalo Bermej, Juan José, 193
Armitage, Richard, 222
Arthur, Chester, 133
Aswan Dam, 189–90
Augustus, Gaius Julius Caesar (em-
    peror of Rome), 7
Autobiography (Franklin), 27
Axis of Evil, 226
Aziz, Tariq, 211

Bache, Benjamin Franklin, 61
Bagot, Charles, 79
balance of power, first explicit refer-
    ence to the concept of, 21
Bancroft, George, 130

Bao Dai (emperor of Vietnam), 187, 197
Baruch, Bernard, 167, 169
Bayard, James, 76
Bell, John, 116
Bellow, Saul, 199
Bemis, Samuel Flagg, 2, 6, 77, 91
Benton, Thomas Hart, 133
Bergson, Henri, 167, 174
Berkeley, Bishop George, 65, 120
Berlin Crisis, 197
"Big Sister Policy," 136
bin Laden, Usama, 224, 234
Birney, James, 104
Blaine, James G., 133, 135–39, 144, 164
Bloom, Allan, 199–200, 211
Bonaparte, Napoleon. *See* Napoleon
    Bonaparte (emperor of France)
Boone, Daniel, 33
Booth, John Wilkes, 120
Boston Massacre, 44
Boston Tea Party, 44–45
"boundary-barrier situation" (Dulles),
    174–75, 178, 185, 189
Braddock, Edward, 33–34
Breckinridge, John, 116
Britain: Adams as secretary of state,
    diplomacy with, 79–81; the Ameri-
    can colonists, deteriorating relations
    with, 40–49; Dulles's view of, 177;
    France, eighteenth-century struggle
    for dominance with, 21–22, 26,
    30–31, 33–38; Franklin's diplomatic
    efforts aimed at, 34–49, 53–56;
    Franklin's view of colonial expan-
    sion and, 26–30; French interven-
    tion in Mexico, nonsupport of, 119;
    Iran, 181–82; Latin America, inter-
    est in, 89–90; "multicultural" empire
    of, 13; Napoleonic France, struggle
    with, 60, 63–65, 70; nonintervention
    in the Civil War, 118–19; post–
    Revolutionary War Anglo-American
    discord, 56; Seward's views regard-
    ing, 126; Seward's vision of competi-
    tion with, 106–7; Spanish control of
    East Florida, positions on, 81–82,
    85; the Suez crisis, 189–92; the U.S.,
    conflict with, 70–76; the Venezuela
    Crisis, 143–44; World War I and
    aftermath, 159, 161, 169–70
Brown, John, 115

Bryan, William Jennings, 151, 157, 159, 167–68
Buchanan, James, 116
Burgoyne, John, 52
Burr, Aaron, 66
Bush, George H. W., 19, 203–4, 212–17, 219, 222, 225
Bush, George W.: America as empire, denial of (in 1999), 1, 7, 14; empire, understanding of definition of, 11; the Global War on Terror, 233–36; liberty and freedom, rhetorical emphasis on, 236; Wolfowitz and the aggressive foreign policy of, 19, 222–28
Bush administration: the Iraq War, 224–27; September 11 attacks, response to, 3, 233–36

Cabot, George, 130
Cabot, John, 130
Calhoun, John C., 73, 82–84, 90, 95
California, 105, 107–13, 125
Cambodia, 186–87, 202
Canada, 35–36, 38, 54–56, 73–76, 123, 156
Canning, George, 89–90
Canning, Stratford, 89
Capone, Al, 171
Caracalla (emperor of Rome), 7
Carlisle, Treaty of, 30–31
Carnegie, Andrew, 151
Carnegie Endowment for International Peace, 165, 172
Caroline affair, 101
Carroll, Charles, 50
Carroll, John, 50
Carter, Jimmy, 203–5
Castillo Armas, Carlos, 195
Castlereagh, Viscount, 2nd Marquis of Londonderry (Robert Stewart), 76–79, 82, 90
Catherine II ("the Great"; Empress of Russia), 62
Cayton, Andrew, 84
Central Intelligence Agency (CIA), 180, 188, 194–95, 202–3, 212, 235
Chamberlain, Joseph, 145
Charles II (king of England), 22
Charles II (king of Spain), 21
Chase, Samuel, 50
Chatham, Lord. *See* Pitt, William

Cheney, Elizabeth, 230
Cheney, Richard B. "Dick": American use of military force, belief in, 218–19; Christmas card in 2003, 3; and the dark side, 256n.1; the Gulf War of 1991, 213, 215–16; Libby as chief of staff for, 201; Project for a New American Century, association with, 221; Rumsfeld and, 212; waterboarding, dismissal of concerns about, 235; Wolfowitz and, 19, 211
Cherokee Nation v. Georgia, 152
Cherokees, the, 94
Chile, 136, 138
China, People's Republic of, 178, 186
Chou En-lai (Zhou Enlai), 186
Church, Frank, 212
Churchill, Winston, 189
CIA. *See* Central Intelligence Agency
Civil War, U.S.: as catalyst for changing views of empire, 9; the European Powers and, 118–20; impact on Lodge of, 131
Clay, Henry, 73, 76–78, 87, 92, 102–4, 107
Clayton-Bulwer Treaty, 136
Cleveland, Grover, 140–41, 143–44, 165
Clinton, Bill, 219–22
Colby, William, 203, 212
Cold War: American Empire in opposition to the Soviets, Dulles's view of, 193–95; beginnings of, events and Dulles's thoughts regarding, 177–79; consensus underlying, Vietnam War protests as challenge to, 198; the Eisenhower-Dulles relationship and, 179–81; end of, 212–13; Guatemala and, 194–95; in Indochina, 183–89; Iran, operation in, 182; Reagan and the neoconservatives reenergize the, 204; rhetoric, anticolonialism of, 11; the Suez crisis and, 189–90
Collins, J. Lawton "Lightning Joe," 188
Collins, Perry McDonough, 124
commercial reciprocity, 80
Commission on the Reparation of Damage, 169–70
Commission to Study the Bases of a Just and Durable Peace, 176
Committee for Critical Support of the U.S. in Vietnam, 201

Committee to Maintain a Prudent Defense Policy, 201
Compromise of 1850, 107, 109
Constitutional Union Party, 117. *See also* Know-Nothing (American) Party
containment, 178–79, 181
Continental Congress, 49
Convention of 1818, 80
Coolidge, Calvin, 171
Cornell University, 198–99, 201
Cornwallis, Charles, 53
Council on Foreign Relations, 172
Crawford, William, 83–84, 92
Cromwell, Nelson, 168
Cuba, 90, 114, 147–50

Daalder, Ivo, 3
Dana, Francis, 61
Davies, John W., 167
Dawes Plan, 171
Deane, Silas, 50
Declaration of Independence, 50, 152–53
Declaratory Act, 43
Defense Planning Guidance (DPG) document, Bush's 1992, 217–20, 222
Democratic Party: doctrine of Manifest Destiny in the 1840s, 110; of New York in the 1840s, 103; as pro-slavery, 114, 116
Denmark, 126
Derrida, Jacques, 241n.27
Dewey, George, 134, 149–50
Dewey, Thomas, 177
Dickinson, Daniel, 105
Dickinson, John, 40
Diem, Ngo Dinh, 187–89, 197
Disraeli, Benjamin, 6
Dominican Republic, 118, 127
domino theory, 184
Douglas, Stephen, 107, 116
Doyle, Michael, 7
DPG. *See* Defense Planning Guidance document
Drinnon, Richard, 84
Dulles, Allen Macy, 165–67
Dulles, Allen Welsh, 166, 180, 182
Dulles, Avery, 166
Dulles, Edith Foster, 165–66

Dulles, John Foster: American empire, early vision of, 170–73; American empire, security as goal of, 173–75, 177–79, 192–95; anticolonial imperialism of, 185; bipolar lens/zero-sum calculus, perception of everything through a, 180, 182–83; childhood, education, and early career of, 165–68; choice of for this volume, 18, 232; the Cold War, beginnings of, 177–79; death of, 197; Eisenhower and, 179–81; family background of, 164–67; Geneva conference, appearance and demeanor at, 186; Guatemala, actions regarding, 193–95; Indochina, actions regarding, 183–89, 197; international affairs and government service, early involvement in, 168–70; Iran, operation in, 182; portrait of, 163; religion and, 166–67, 172–73, 176–77; as secretary of state, 167, 180–95; Soviet *vs.* American empires, focus on clash of, 168–69; the Suez crisis, actions regarding, 189–93; Sullivan & Cromwell, career at, 168, 170–71; Wolfowitz, as model for, 206, 216; World War II, analysis of and activities during, 175–77
Dulles, John Wesley, 166
Durfee, Amos, 101
Dutch Empire, 22

Eden, Anthony, 189–90
effective control, exercise of as operative principle of empire, 11–12
Eisenhower, Dwight D., 179–82, 184, 187, 189, 191, 197
Eisenhower Doctrine, 192–94
election: of 1824, 92; of 1844, 104; of 1860, 116–17
Elements of Empire in America (Seward), 106
Embargo Act of 1807, 70–71
Empire for Liberty. *See* American Empire
empire(s): American (*see* American Empire); exercise of effective control as operative principle of, 11–12; imperialism, contrasted with, 10–11;

meaning of the word for Americans, 6–12; poststructural/deconstructionalist perspective on, 241n.27; variation of, 12–13
Erben, Henry, 143
Essex Junto, 65–67, 75, 78, 130
Ethiopia, 172, 175
Europe, eighteenth-century struggle between empires for dominance in, 21–22, 26, 30–31, 33–38
European Recovery (Marshall) Program, 178
extraordinary rendition, 235

Farouk I (king of Egypt), 189
Faure, Edgar, 188
Federal Council of Churches of Christ in America, 176–77
Federalist Papers: No. 1, 1; No. 10, 37, 63
Federalists, the, 64–72, 130
Ferguson, Niall, 2–4
Field, Cyrus, 124
Fillmore, Millard, 103–5, 109, 116
Florida, 38, 72–74, 81–85
Ford, Gerald, 203–4, 212
Foreign Affairs, 172
Foreign Policy, 3
foreign policy, executive *vs.* congressional power regarding, 80
Foreign Policy Association, 172
Foster, John Watson, 18, 139, 164–68
Foucault, Michel, 241n.27
Founding Fathers, conception of the United States by, 8–9
Fourteen Points, 160
Fox, Charles James, 53
France: Britain, eighteenth-century struggle for dominance with, 21–22, 26, 30–31, 33–38; Dulles's view of, 183; Franklin's diplomatic efforts aimed at, 51–53; Franklin's view of British American expansion in opposition to, 26–27; Indochina, reclamation and loss of colony in, 183–89; Mexican intervention in response to the U.S. Civil War, 119–20; Napoleonic, acquisition and sale of Louisiana, 66–67; Napoleonic, relations between Russia and, 72–73, 75; Napoleonic, renewed conflict

between Britain and, 60, 63–65, 70; Native Americans, relations with, 30–31; Santo Domingo and Haiti, collusion with Spain regarding, 118; the Suez crisis, 190–92; World War I and aftermath, 160–61, 169–70
Franklin, Abiah Folger, 22
Franklin, Anne, 22
Franklin, Benjamin: Adamses, relations with the, 61; the Albany Plan, 32–33; American empire, initial thoughts on, 26–30; American empire, vision of, 32–33, 79; association of the colonies, meeting with the Native Americans at Carlisle and early thoughts regarding, 30–31; choice of for this volume, 15, 232; Constitutional Convention, attendance at, 58; Declaration of Independence, contribution to, 50; demographic explosion predicted by, 111; early years in the life of, 21–24; fame and accomplishments of, 21, 25; family split between patriot (father) and loyalist (son William), 49–50; French Revolution, cheering of, 60; image of, 20; Indians, views regarding, 30, 57; liberty, views on, 27, 46–47, 57; London, diplomatic mission to, 34–38; London, second diplomatic mission to, 39–49; Paris, diplomatic mission to, 50–57; Philadelphia, accomplishments in, 24–25; as postmaster, 25; public service, beginning of, 25; racial position of, 30
Franklin, Deborah Read, 24, 34, 38
Franklin, James, 23–24
Franklin, Josiah, 22
Franklin, William Temple, 24, 26, 34, 39, 49–50, 61
Franz Ferdinand, Archduke, 159
Free Soil Party, 104–5
Frémont, John C., 116
French and Indian War. *See* Great War for Empire
Fry, Joshua, 31
Fukuyama, Francis, 203, 206, 220

Gallagher, John A., 9, 11
Gallatin, Albert, 76–78, 80

Galloway, Joseph, 34, 49–50
Garfield, James, 133, 136
Garrison, William Lloyd, 95
George III (king of England), 38–39, 42
George II (king of England), 38
Germany, 159–60, 169–70, 172–73, 175
Gerson, Mark, 210
Ghent, Treaty of, 78
Gingrich, Newt, 2
Glaspie, April, 214
globalization, 2
Global War on Terror (GWOT), 224,
    233–36
Gorbachev, Mikhail, 212
Gore, Al, 222
Grant, Ulysses S., 127, 132, 165
Gray, George, 142
"great power" distinguished from
    "empire," 7
Great War for Empire (French and
    Indian War), 33–38
Greece, ancient, 7
Greek Revolution, 88, 91
Greeley, Horace, 103, 114, 116
Greenland, 156
Grenville, George, 40
Gresham, Walter Q., 144
Guadaloupe, 35–36, 38
Guadalupe Hidalgo, Treaty of, 105, 111
Guam, 150
Guatemala, 193–95
Gulf War of 1991, 213–16
GWOT. *See* Global War on Terror

Haig, Alexander, 206
Haiti, 66–67
Hamilton, Alexander, 1, 7, 62, 64–66,
    130–32
Hamilton, Richard, 30
Harding, Warren G., 162, 164, 170–71
Harrison, Benjamin, 136, 138–39,
    164–65
Harrison, William Henry, 73, 101, 103
Hawaiian Islands (Sandwich Islands),
    125–26, 136, 138–41, 149, 165
Hay, John, 122, 129, 134, 149
Hayes, Rutherford B., 133
hegemon, empire distinguished from, 7
Hendrickson, David, 13
Henry, Patrick, 41, 57
Herbert, Hillary, 143

Herring, George C., 78
Hillsborough, Earl of and 1st Marquess
    of Downshire (Wills Hill), 45, 47
Hitler, Adolf, 172–73
Hoar, George, 151
Ho Chi Minh, 183, 186, 197
Ho Chi Minh Trail, 197
Holy Alliance, 89
Holy Roman Empire, 21–22
Hoover, Herbert, 171–72
Howe, Richard, 48, 53
Huerta, Victoriano, 158
Hutchinson, Thomas, 44–48

Iklé, Fred, 202, 211, 221
immigration, Lodge's opposition to,
    154–55
imperialism: American, 10–11, 13–14,
    122, 134–54, 156, 185, 234; empire,
    contrasted with, 10; of free trade,
    10, 11; of human rights, 6; of Lodge,
    135, 137–38, 140–54, 156, 249n.27
    (*see also* Lodge, Henry Cabot)
Independent Party, 132–33, 135
Indians. *See* Native Americans
Indochina, 178, 183–89. *See also*
    Vietnam
Indonesia, 207
*Interest of Great Britain Considered
    with Regard to her Colonies and the
    Acquisitions of Canada and Guadal-
    oupe, The* (Franklin), 35–36
International Chamber of Commerce,
    172
International Monetary Fund (IMF), 12
Iran, 181–82, 204–5
Iraq, 205, 213–16, 223–27, 229, 234
Iraq War, 224–27
Iroquois Nation, 30–32
"Irrepressible Conflict" speech
    (Seward), 116
Israel, 190–91
Italy, 172, 175

Jackson, Andrew, 16, 75, 81–85, 92–94,
    111
Jackson, Henry "Scoop," 201–2
James, William, 151
Japan, 172, 175, 178, 183–84, 215
Jaruzelski, Wojciech Witold, 210
Jay, John, 53, 55–56

Jay's Treaty, 64
Jefferson, Thomas: Canada, optimism about ease of acquiring, 75; Canning's proposal for European powers to withdraw from America, approval of, 90; Declaration of Independence, drafting of, 50; "Empire" and America, proud association of, 7; Empire "of" to Empire "for" Liberty, distinction between, 5; expansionist policies as president, 65–73; French Revolution, recoil at the carnage of, 64; John Quincy Adams and, 62; Lodge's citation of the Louisiana Purchase as precedent, 152; Lodge's view of, 131
Johns Hopkins University, Paul H. Nitze School of Advanced International Study (SAIS), 219–20
Johnson, Andrew, 122–23, 127
Johnson, Lyndon Baines, 197
Juárez, Benito, 120
Junto, the, 24

Kagan, Robert, 220
Kamehameha V (king of Hawaii), 125
Kames, Lord Henry Home, 37, 42
Keith, Sir William, 24
Kennan, George, 210
Kennedy, Paul, 208
Khalilzad, Zalmay, 206, 217–18, 221
Khrushchev, Nikita, 197
King, Martin Luther, 201
Kirkpatrick, Jeane, 210–11
Kirkpatrick Doctrine, 210–11
Kissinger, Henry, 202–4, 208–10
Know-Nothing (American) Party, 116–17
Korean War, 178–79
Krauthammer, Charles, 211
Kristol, Irving, 208–9
Kristol, William, 209, 220
Kubrick, Stanley, 200
Kuwait, 213–16

LaFeber, Walter, 17, 60
Langer, William, 11
Lansing, Eleanor Foster, 167
Lansing, Robert, 167–68
Laos, 186–87
Latin America, 87–92

Laurens, Henry, 56
League of Armed Neutrality, 62
League of Nations, 161–62, 164, 176
Lee, Arthur, 50
Lee, Robert E., 120
Libby, Lewis "Scooter," 201, 206, 217, 219, 221
Liberal Party, 104
liberty: the Alien and Sedition Acts, 65; the American Empire and, contemporary challenges to the narrative of, 233–37; American empire-building and the promotion of, 5, 13–14; American exceptionalism and, 233; American foreign policy actions undermining, 195; Americans' belief in America as the land of, 232–33; Anglo-Saxonism and, 111–12; democracy and, neoconservatives' belief in, 209–10; democratization and, Wolfowitz's belief in, 207; Dulles's view of, security concerns and, 173–75, 178–79, 183, 195; European colonization, abolishment of, 91; Federalist opposition to the embargo as threat to, 71; the Federalists' conception of, 67; Foster's minimal concern regarding, 165; Franklin's views on, 27, 46–47, 57; imperialism and, 10, 135, 141; liberation as the goal of empire-building, 179–80; Lodge's minimal concern regarding, 137, 147–48; meaning of the term for Americans, 5–6; non-Americans as the enemy of, Jackson's belief in, 93; the public imagination of the 1920s regarding, 172; Seward's empire of, 106–7, 109–13; the slaveholder's view of, 95; slavery (*see* slavery); territorial expansion and, 67, 69; territorial expansion/slavery and, 86–88, 94–96, 102–4; Wolfowitz's incorporation into his vision of American Empire, 218–19; the World Bank and the enhancement of, 228
Library Company of Philadelphia, 24
Liliuokalani (queen of Hawaii), 139–40
Lincoln, Abraham, 107, 116–18
Lindsay, James, 3
Livingston, Edward, 67

Livingston, Robert R., 50–51
Lloyd, James, 72
Lodge, Anna "Nanny" Cabot Mills (née Davis), 131, 134, 143
Lodge, Giles, 130
Lodge, Henry Cabot: appearance and manner of, 129–30; Blaine, support for, 133, 136–37; choice of for this volume, 17–18, 232; as congressman, 134–38; Hawaiian annexation, support for, 139–41, 165; as historian, 131–32; immigration, opposition to, 154–55; imperialism of, 135, 137–38, 140–54, 156, 249n.27; Khalilzad's draft DPG inspired by, 218; League of Nations, opposition to, 161–62, 164; liberty, minimal concern regarding, 137, 147–48; Mahan, impact of, 142–43; pedigree and basic beliefs of, 130–31; the Philippines, advocacy of taking, 148–54, 156; political beginnings of, 132–34; portrait of, 128; racial views of, 153–56; Roosevelt and, 133–34, 137; as senator, 138–62; Seward's legacy and, 127, 129–30; shift away from interventionist perspective, 156; Spanish possessions, responsibility to take, 147–48; Venezuela Crisis, impact of, 143–46; Wilson, hatred of and opposition to, 157–62
Long, John D., 149
Louisiana territory: American purchase of, 67–70, 152; French retention of following the Great War for Empire, 38; governance of, Adams's concerns regarding liberty and, 69; Napoleon's acquisition of, 66–67; slavery question and the admission of new states out of, 86–87
Louis XV (king of France), 26
Luce, Stephen, 134, 142–43

Macchiavelli, Niccolo, 27
MacKenzie, William, 101
Madison, James, 36, 58, 63–64, 66, 70, 72–78, 81, 90
Mahan, Alfred Thayer, 134, 142–43, 145
Maine, 87
Maliki, Nouri al-, 227

Malthus, Thomas, 27
Manifest Destiny: the Franklin/Adams version of, 54, 56, 68, 71, 85, 91, 93; the Jackson version of, 93–94; Polk and the period of rabid, 105; Seward's version of, 114; slavery and, American empire and the juxtaposition of, 103. *See also* American Empire
Mann, James, 202, 223
Marcos, Ferdinand, 207, 210
Marcy, William L., 101, 103
Marshall, John, 86, 152
Mason, James, 119
Mather, Cotton, 23
Mather, Increase, 23
Maximilian I (emperor of Mexico), 120
May, Ernest, 146
McCarthy, Joseph, 194
McCormick, Vance, 168
McCulloch v. Maryland, 86
McGovern, George, 208
McKinley, William, 7, 17–18, 147–48, 150
McKinley Tariff, 139
McLeod, Alexander, 101–3
Mead, Russell, 249n.27
melting pot, metaphor of the, 13
mercantilism, Franklin's challenge to conventional, 29–30
Metropolitan Club, 134
Mexico: the All-Mexico movement, Seward's opposition to, 111; conflict with, plans to annex Texas and, 95–97; French intervention in, 119–20; opposition to the Mexican War, 97, 99, 104–5; Seward's optimism regarding future statehood of, 122–23; Wilson's interventions in, 158
Meyer, Eugene, 228
Middle East Resolution (Eisenhower Doctrine), 192–93
Midway Island, 125
Miller, Elijah, 100
Missouri, 86–87
Missouri Compromise, 87, 91–92
Monet, Jean, 171
Monroe, James, 67, 76, 79, 82–85, 88, 90–92, 94
Monroe Doctrine, 16, 90–92, 144, 156, 161, 194
Morgan, J. P., 170

Morris, Gouverneur, 132–33
Mortefontaine, Treaty of, 65
Mossadegh, Mohammad, 182

Napoleon Bonaparte (emperor of France), 60, 63, 66–68, 72, 76, 79
Napoleon III (emperor of France), 6, 119–20
Nasser, Gamal Abdul, 189–91
National Origins Act of 1924, 155
National Security Agency, 236
Native Americans: assimilation, Adams's hope for, 93; British incitement of, 73, 75; Carlisle, meeting at and treaty of, 30–31; colonial migration, impact of, 26–27; Franklin's views regarding, 30, 57; the French, relations with, 30–31; Jackson's belief in removal or annihilation of, 93–94, 111; Jackson's Florida campaign against, 81–82; Seward's view of the future of, 111; war-making against, Americans' understanding of, 9
NATO. *See* North Atlantic Treaty Organization
neoconservatives/neoconservatism: Bush the elder and, 219; departure from America's nonimperial traditions, blame for, 3; origins and beliefs of, 208–10; Project for a New American State and, 220–22; Reagan, concerns about, 210; Republican foreign policy officials, increasing presence among, 202–4; Straussianism and, 200; Wolfowitz and, 200, 208, 211, 223
New England Courant, 23–24
Niebuhr, Reinhold, 209, 216
Ninkovich, Frank, 146
Nitze, Paul, 201–3, 206, 211
Nixon, Richard M., 201–2, 204
North, Lord Frederick, 46, 52
North Atlantic Treaty Organization (NATO), 12, 178–79
Notes on Virginia (Jefferson), 67

Obama, Barack, 4, 236–37
Observations Concerning the Increase of Mankind, People of Countries, etc. (Franklin), 27–30

Olney, Richard, 144–45
Onís, Juan de, 83–86
Open Door concept, 123
Operation AJAX, 182–83
Operation Musketeer, 191
Operation PBSUCCESS, 194–95
Operation Solarium, 181
Ordinance of 1787, 58
Oregon Territory, 80, 85–86, 89, 92, 94, 104, 107
Organization of American States (OAS), 12
O'Sullivan, John L., 93
Oswald, Richard, 54–56
Otis, James, 40, 57

Paine, Thomas, 51
Palestine Liberation Organization, 213
Palmerston, 3rd Viscount (Henry John Temple), 101
Panama Canal, 156, 168
Pan American Conference, 136
Panic of 1819, 86
Paris, Treaty of (1763), 38
Paris, Treaty of (1783), 56
Peace of Aix-la-Chappelle, 26
Penn, William, 30
Pennsylvania, 26, 30–31
Perle, Richard, 201, 203, 211, 217, 230
Perry, Matthew, 114
Pershing, John J. "Black Jack," 158
Persian Gulf region, 205
Petraeus, David, 227
Philadelphia, Franklin's accomplishments in, 24–25
Philadelphia Gazette, 24–25
Philippines, the, 148–54, 156, 207
Pickering, Timothy, 71
Pinckney, Charles C., 72
Pinckney's Treaty, 64
Pipes, Richard, 203
Pitt, William, 34, 39, 45, 48, 53
Platt Amendment, 149
PNAC. *See* Project for a New American Century
Podhoretz, Norman, 225
Polish Stabilization Plan, 171
"political gravitation, process of," 122, 171
Polk, James K., 94, 96–97, 104–6, 111
Pontiac's War, 39

Poor Richard's Almanack, 24–25
population growth, predictions
  regarding, 111–12
Portuguese Empire, 22
Powell, Colin, 213, 239n.3
Pratt, Julius, 140
Proclamation of Emancipation
  (Lincoln), 118
Progressive Party, 157
Project for a New American Century
  (PNAC), 220–22
Puerto Rico, 149–50

Quebec Act, 54–55

race: Adams's views on, 111; Frank-
  lin's views on, 30; Lodge's views on,
  153–56; Seward's views on, 111–12,
  121
railroads, transcontinental, 115, 125
Ravelstein (Bellow), 199
Reagan, Ronald, 19, 203–8, 210–11, 219
Reagan doctrine, 210
Reciprocity Treaty, 125, 138–39
Red Stick Creek Indians, 81–82, 93
Reed, Thomas, 147
religion: Adams and, 62, 68; Dulles and,
  166–67, 172–73, 176–77; Franklin's
  views and, 27; Manifest Destiny (*see*
  Manifest Destiny)
Republican Party: Dulles and, 176–77;
  Lodge's view of the Federalists and,
  130; Radical Republicans of the
  Reconstruction era, 121–22; Rea-
  gan's impact on, 208; of the 1860s,
  116–17
Reza Pahlavi, Mohammad (shah of
  Iran), 181–82, 205
Rhodes, James Ford, 129
Rice, Condoleeza, 223
Riza, Shaha, 230
Robinson, Ronald A., 9, 11
Rockingham, Marquis and 6th Baron of
  (Charles Watson-Wentworth), 42, 53
Roman Empire, 7–8
Roosevelt, Franklin D., 11, 173, 176–77,
  197
Roosevelt, Theodore, 7, 17–18, 133–34,
  142–43, 147–50, 156–57
Root, Elihu, 134
Rosenberg, Emily, 172

Ross, Dennis, 206
"Rules for Reducing a Great Empire to
  a Small One" (Franklin), 47
Rumsfeld, Donald, 211–12, 214,
  221–23, 225
Rush, Richard, 79–80
Rush-Bagot pact of 1817, 79
Russell, Jonathan, 76
Russia: Alaska, sale of, 124; interest in
  the Americas, 89; mediation to end
  Anglo-American hostilities, 75–76;
  Napoleonic France, agreement with,
  72; Napoleonic France, invasion by,
  75; trade with the U.S., edict pro-
  moting, 73. *See also* Union of Soviet
  Socialist Republics
Russian Bureau, Inc., 168–69
Russian Empire, 22
Ruth, Babe, 171

Sadat, Anwar, 204
Saddam Hussein Abd al-Majid al-Tikriti,
  205, 211, 213–16, 221–22, 224–26,
  234
SAIS. *See* Johns Hopkins University,
  Paul H. Nitze School of Advanced
  International Study
Salisbury, 3rd Marquess of (Robert
  Cecil), 144–45
SALT I agreement, 202
Samoa, 136
Santa Anna, Antonio López de, 95
Santo Domingo. *See* Dominican
  Republic
Sargent, John Singer, 129
Schlesinger, Arthur M., Jr., 8, 12
Schlesinger, James, 212
Schultz, George, 206–7, 211
Schurz, Carl, 132
Schwartzkopf, H. Norman, 213, 215
SEATO. *See* Southeast Asia Treaty
  Organization
security, Dulles's emphasis on, 173–75,
  177–79
Seminoles, the, 81–82, 93
September 11 terrorist attacks, 3,
  223–24
Seward, Frances "Fan" Adelaide (née
  Miller), 100
Seward, Frederick, 127, 129
Seward, Samuel, 100

Seward, William Henry: Adams and, 99–100, 102, 104, 127; Alaska, purchase of, 124–25; American empire, strategy for realizing, 113–15, 121–23; American empire, vision of, 99, 103–9, 113–14, 120–21; assassination attempt against, 120; Blaine as parallel to, 135–36; choice of for this volume, 16–17, 232; Civil War diplomatic efforts, 118; early life of, 99–100; *Elements of Empire in America* (address to the Phi Beta Kappa Society), 106; empire and liberty, nexus of, 110–13; European powers, recommendation to seek war against, 117–18; experience of as object lesson about the national temper, 135; as governor, 100–3; Hay and, 129; the "Irrepressible Conflict" speech, 116; Jackson's Indian policy, opinion of, 111; and political gravitation, 122–23, 171; portrait of, 98; racial views of, 111–12, 121; Republican nomination for president, campaigns for, 116–17; as secretary of state, 117–27; as senator, 105; slavery, position on, 102–4, 109–13, 115–17; territorial acquisitions, efforts regarding, 124–27
Seward Doctrine, 114–15
Shays, Daniel, 56
Shelburne, Earl of (William Petty-FitzMaurice), 53, 55
Sherman, Roger, 50
"Short Hints towards a Scheme for Uniting the Northern Colonies" (Franklin), 32
"Six Pillars of Peace" (Commission to Study the Bases of a Just and Durable Peace), 176–77
slavery: Adams's position on, 80, 87, 91–92; Constitutional abolishment of, 121; empire as commerce and, 109–13; empire as territorial expansion and, 86–88, 94–96, 102–4; Franklin's acceptance of, 57; the "gag rule," 95–97; "Irrepressible Conflict" speech, 116; "popular sovereignty" and the Compromise of 1850, 107; Seward's position on, 16, 102–4, 109–13, 115–17

Slidell, John, 119
Southeast Asia Treaty Organization (SEATO), 187
Soviet Union. *See* Union of Soviet Socialist Republics
Spanish Empire, 21–22, 56, 81–87, 118
Spring Rice, Cecil, 134
Stalin, Joseph, 186
Stamp Act, 40–44
Stanford, Leland, 125
"state" and "empire," comparison of conceptions of, 8–9
Stephanson, Anders, 94
Stevens, John L., 139
Stevenson, Margaret, 34
Stoeckl, Edouard de, 124–25
Strauss, Leo, 19, 199–200
Students for a Democratic Society, 198
Suez Canal Company, 190
Suez Canal User's Association (SCUA), 190
Suez crisis, 189–93
Sugar Act, 40
Suharto, 207
Sullivan & Cromwell, 168, 170–71
Sumner, Charles, 99, 126–27

Taft, William Howard, 156–57, 167
Taliban, the, 234–35
Talleyrand Périgord, Charles Maurice de, 67
Tanenhaus, Sam, 223
Taylor, Zachary, 104–5, 109
Tecumseh, 73
Teller Amendment, 149
Telluride Association, 199
Tenskwatawa the Prophet, 73
terrorism, war on, 224, 233–37
Texas, 72, 85–87, 92, 94–97, 103–4, 109
Thurston, Lorrin, 139
Tilden, Samuel, 133
Tippecanoe, battle of, 73
Townshend, Charles, 40
Townshend Acts, 43–44
Transcontinental Treaty, 16, 85–86, 94
Treaty of Alliance (France and America), 52–53
Treaty of Amity and Commerce, 52
Treaty of Carlisle, 30–31
Treaty of Ghent, 78
Treaty of Guadalupe Hidalgo, 105, 111

Treaty of Mortefontaine, 65
Treaty of Paris (1763), 38
Treaty of Paris (1783), 56, 149, 151–52
Treaty of Utrecht, 21
Treaty of Versailles, 18
Triple Entente, 159–60
Truman, Harry S., 177, 182, 197
Turner, Frederick Jackson, 13, 155
Twain, Mark (Samuel Clemens), 151
"Two Million Act," 72
Tyler, John, 96, 102, 138
Tyler Doctrine, 138

Ubico Castañeda, Jorge y, 194
UFCO. *See* United Fruit Company
Union of Soviet Socialist Republics
    (Soviet Union): Afghanistan, invasion
    of, 204; the Cold War (*see* Cold War);
    Dulles's view of, 177; Evil Empire,
    as Reagan's, 204; Geneva confer-
    ence on Indochina, position at, 186;
    Hungary, actions in, 191; Iran, loss
    of, 181–82; military threat posed by,
    controversy over estimates of, 203.
    See also Russia
United Fruit Company (UFCO), 193–95
United Nations, Dulles's Suez crisis
    remarks at, 191–92
Universal Christian Council for Life and
    Work, 176
U.S. Arms Control and Disarmament
    Agency (ACDA), 202
USS *Baltimore,* 136

Van Alstyne, Richard, 2
Van Buren, Martin, 100–1, 103–5
Vandenberg, Arthur, 176
Venezuela Crisis, 143–44
Vergennes, Count de (Charles Gravier),
    51–55
Versailles Treaty, 18
Victoria (queen of England), 2
Vietminh, 183–86
Vietnam: atrocities committed in, 235;
    college student protests against
    America's involvement in, 198, 201;
    insurgency against Diem regime
    and American military action,
    beginning of, 197–98; U.S. exit from,
    202. *See also* Indochina

Villa, Pancho, 158
Virginia, 26, 31
Virginia Resolves, 41
Virgin Islands (Danish West Indies),
    126–27
Vulcans, the, 222–23

Wahid, Abdurrahman, 207
War, Peace, and Change (Dulles),
    173–75, 177–78, 193
War of the Austrian Succession (King
    George's War), 21–22, 26
War of the League of Augsburg (King
    William's War), 21
War of the Pacific, 138
War of the Spanish Succession (Queen
    Anne's War), 21
Washington, George: Adams (John
    Quincy), diplomatic appointments of,
    62; on America as empire, 1, 7; con-
    flict with the French and Indians,
    33; "empire," meaning of the word
    for, 8; Giles Lodge, friend of, 130;
    Henry Cabot Lodge as biographer
    of, 132; international entangle-
    ments, warning against, 88; as land
    speculator, 26; Proclamation of Neu-
    trality and Farewell Address of, 64;
    surrender at Fort Necessity, 31
Weapons of Mass Destruction (WMD),
    224–25
Webster, Daniel, 17, 101–2, 108–9, 132,
    138
Wedderburn, Alexander, 48
Weed, Thurlow, 100, 103, 107
Wellington, Duke of (Arthur Wellesley),
    78–79
West Indies, Danish (Virgin Islands),
    126–27
Whig Party, 100–5
Williams, William Appleman, 2, 6, 12, 16
Wilmot Proviso, 109
Wilson, Valerie Plame, 201
Wilson, Woodrow: anticolonialism of,
    11; Dulles and, 167–70; "empire,"
    baggage associated with the term, 7;
    literacy requirement for immigrants,
    veto of, 155; Lodge's opposition to,
    17–18, 134, 157–62, 164; Seward's
    anticipation of the strategies of, 122

Wohlstetter, Albert, 19, 200–3, 211, 215, 217

Wolfowitz, Clare Selgin, 199, 207

Wolfowitz, Jacob "Jack," 198, 200, 252n.8

Wolfowitz, Paul: American Empire, vision of the post–Cold War, 216–20; choice of for this volume, 18–19, 232; as dean of SAIS at Johns Hopkins, 219–20; as deputy secretary of defense, 223–27; family background, education, and political beginnings of, 198–201; governmental foreign policy positions and the neoconservative Right, climbing the ladders of, 201–8; in Indonesia, 207; Iraq and the Persian Gulf, identification of danger in, 205, 213; the Iraq War, 224–27; Kissinger, opposition to, 202–3; as neoconservative, 200, 208, 211, 223; Persian Gulf War ground operations, disagreement with halting, 215–16; photo of, 196; preemptive military action against despots, belief in, 216; Project for a New American Century, association with, 220–22; Reagan administration, experiences in and with, 210–11; Republican foreign policy realists helping to promote, 211–12; as undersecretary of defense for policy, 212–19; at the World Bank, 227–31

Woolsey, James, 222

World Bank, 12, 227–31

World Trade Organization (WTO), 12

World War I, 158–61

World War II, 175–77

Young, Owen, 170

Young Plan, 170–71

Zahedi, Fazlollah, 182